Fun With Phonics and Spelling

Level 3

Julie Crimmins-Crocker

Collins

Fun With Phonics and Spelling

Level 3

Julie Crimmins-Crocker

Published by Collins India
A division of HarperCollins *Publishers* India Private Limited
A-75, Sector 57, Noida, Uttar Pradesh 201301, India
1 London Bridge Street, London SE1 9GF, United Kingdom
2 Bloor Street East, Toronto, Ontario M4W 1A8, Canada
Lvl 13, 201 Elizabeth Street (PO Box A565, NSW, 1235),
Sydney NSW 2000, Australia
195 Broadway, New York, NY 10007, USA

Reprint edition 2014
Latest Indian edition 2018

Reprint: Ninth
ISBN-13: 978-9-35-136004-9

Typeset by Planman Technologies

Artwork and layout by Planman Technologies

Printed and bound by Shiv Shakti Printing & Trading Co.

MRP: ₹ 218

Contents

This contents list provides an overview of the learning objectives of each puzzle page.

Tips for parents and teachers

1. Read through the title, introduction and instructions for each puzzle to ensure that the child knows what to do.
2. Point to the phonemes and words covered in the puzzle.
3. Demonstrate what the phonemes and words look like and sound like.
4. Let the child practise saying the phonemes, blending the phonemes and saying the words in each puzzle.
5. Relate the phonemes to other words they know, for example, items in the classroom and at home that also have the same phoneme, rhyme, first phoneme, last phoneme and so on.
6. Give the child practice writing the phonemes using a range of materials, for example, sand, whiteboards, crayons, paints and Plasticine.
7. Let the child practise writing the phonemes 'in the air' and with pencil and paper, ensuring correct pencil grip and sitting posture.
8. Provide additional support if the child needs it, by filling in letters and/or more challenging words/answers.
9. After each puzzle ask the child to go to 'What's next?' (see page 4) and cross off the completed activity. Let the child choose the next one.
10. This book supports learning at schools and the requirements of National Curriculum Framework (NCF).

Synonym: the same or similar meaning, for example, ***big*** – ***large***.

Antonym: the opposite meaning, for example, ***big*** – ***small***.

Anagram: the word is muddled up, for example, **GREAL** – **LARGE**.

Informal: the word is simple or slang, for example, ***rabbit*** – ***bunny***.

Verbs are action and 'doing' words, for example, ***run***, ***talk*** and ***think***.

Nouns are naming words, for example, ***pen***, ***hat***, ***apple*** and ***school***.

Adjectives are describing words, for example, ***small*** bird.

Adverbs add more information to verbs, for example, He ran ***quickly***.

Phoneme: a letter or letters that create a single sound when said aloud, for example, **TH** and **OO**.

Letter string: a collection of phonemes, for example, **ELL**.

Vowels are the letters **a**, **e**, **i**, **o** and **u**.

Consonants are the letters of the alphabet which are <u>not</u> vowels.

What's next?

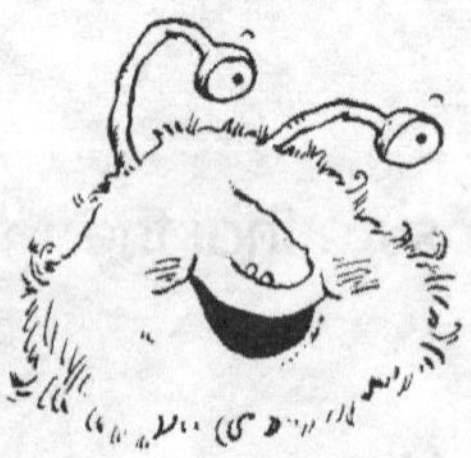

Use the words in the puzzles you have done to complete these activities.

Activity	Puzzle title	Date
Practise your handwriting. Write each phoneme or word five times in your book.		
Practise writing the words and then draw a picture for each one.		
Find three more words that begin with the same phoneme. For example, *cap, cat, cut,* all begin with **c**.		
Find three more words that begin with the same blend of phonemes. For example, *flag, flip, flop,* all begin with **fl**.		
Find five more words that end with the same phoneme. For example, *cat, hit, but, wet, net,* all end with **t**.		
Find three more words that end with the same blend of phonemes. For example, *fast, fist, post,* all end with **st**.		
Find three more words that rhyme.		
Sort the words into alphabetical order and put them in a list.		
Put the words into sentences. Remember to start with a capital letter and end with a full stop.		
Put the words into sentences that are questions. Remember to start with a capital letter and end with a question mark. For example, *Where is my cat?*		
Find opposites (called **antonyms**) for the words and write them in pairs or groups. For example, *big – small.*		
Sort the words into groups with the same number of syllables.		

Know your phonemes

Blend the phonemes to read the words. Circle the phoneme in each word that is the same as the phoneme in the star. One has been done for you.

Star	Words		
b	bed	rub	black
c	cat	cut	club
d	dog	bed	drum
f	fox	fat	flag
g	go	bug	green

Star	Words		
h	hen	hat	hop
j	jam	jog	jet
l	leg	ball	clap
m	mop	jam	plum
n	nut	hen	run

Know your phonemes

Blend the phonemes to read the words. Circle the phoneme in each word that is the same as the phoneme in the star.

Star	Words		
p	peg	cup	pit
qu	queen	quick	quack
r	rat	rain	tree
s	sun	bus	sail
t	tap	pet	trip

Star	Words		
v	vet	vest	have
w	wet	we	went
x	box	fix	fox
y	yes	yelp	you
z	zip	zoo	zebra

Know your phonemes

Blend the phonemes to read the words in each rocket. Circle the phoneme in each word that is the same as the phoneme in the star. One has been done for you.

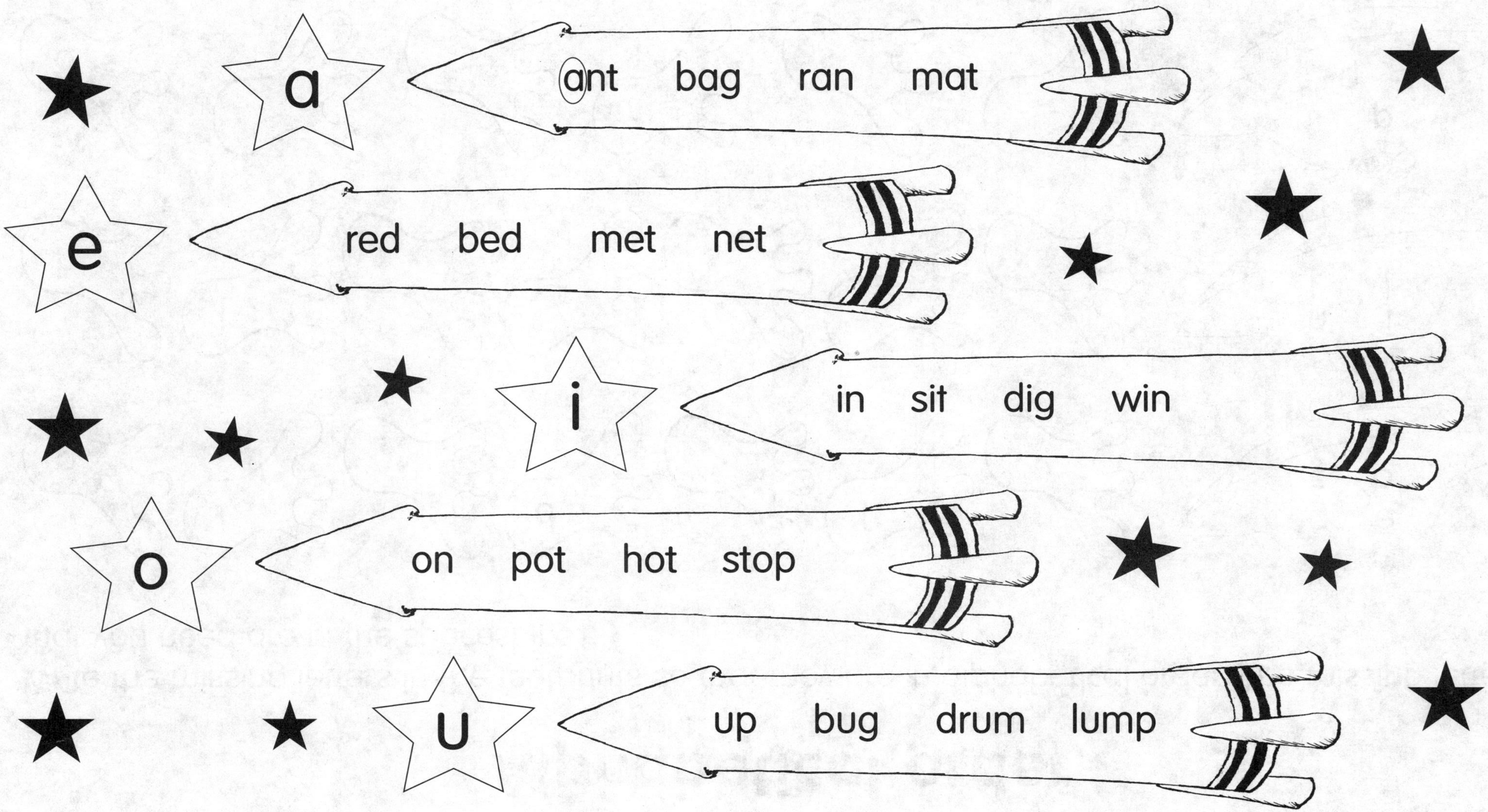

Alphabetical order

Write the missing letters in the footprints so that they are in alphabetical order. The missing letters that you need are in the spaceships.

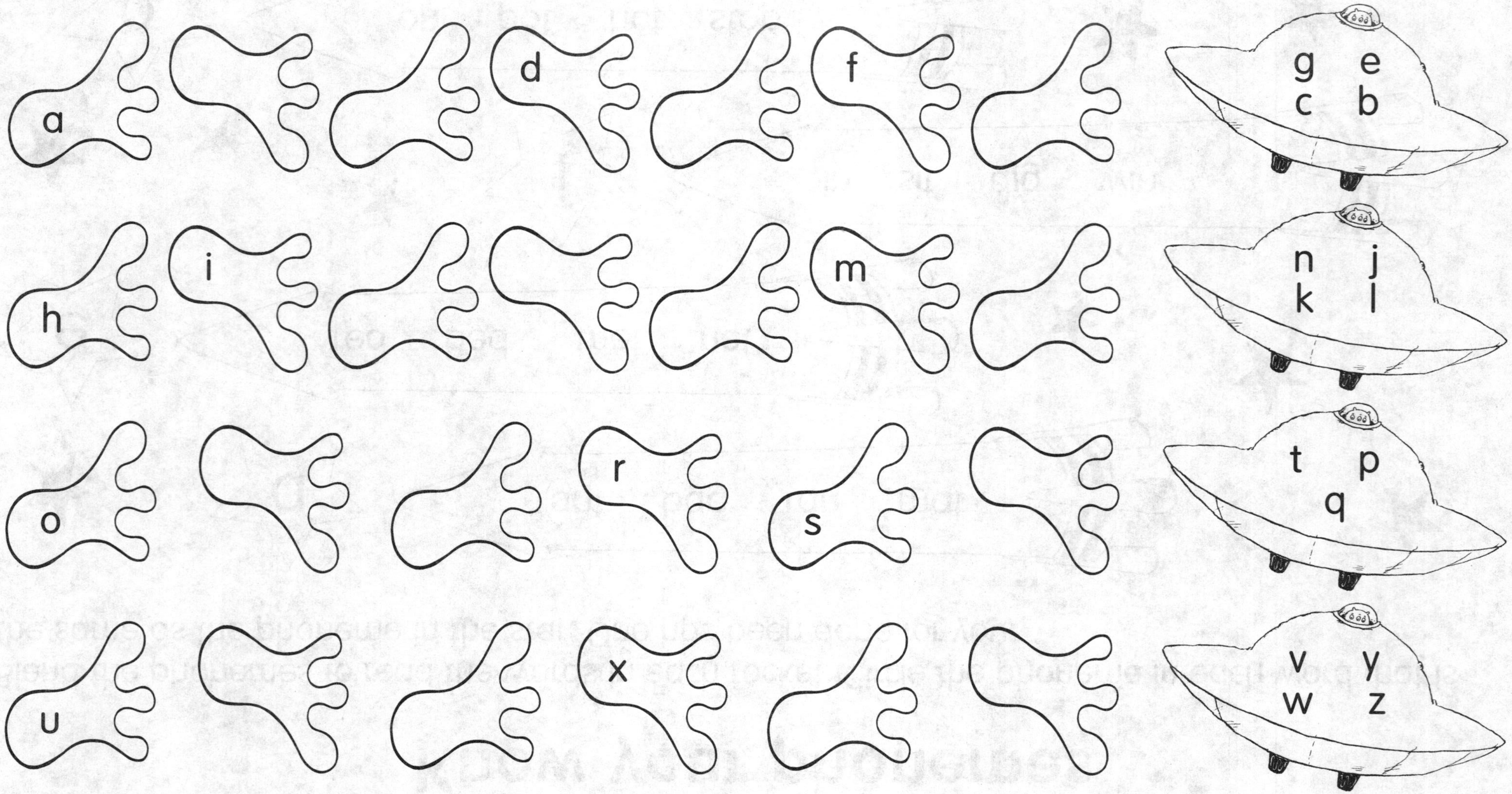

Alphabetical order

Put these letters into alphabetical order and write them in the stars.

f c b d ~~a~~ e g

a

j i k ~~h~~ o l m n

h

s ~~p~~ t q r

p

w z ~~u~~ y v x

u

Fill in the gaps in the alphabet alien snake. The missing letters are in the stars.

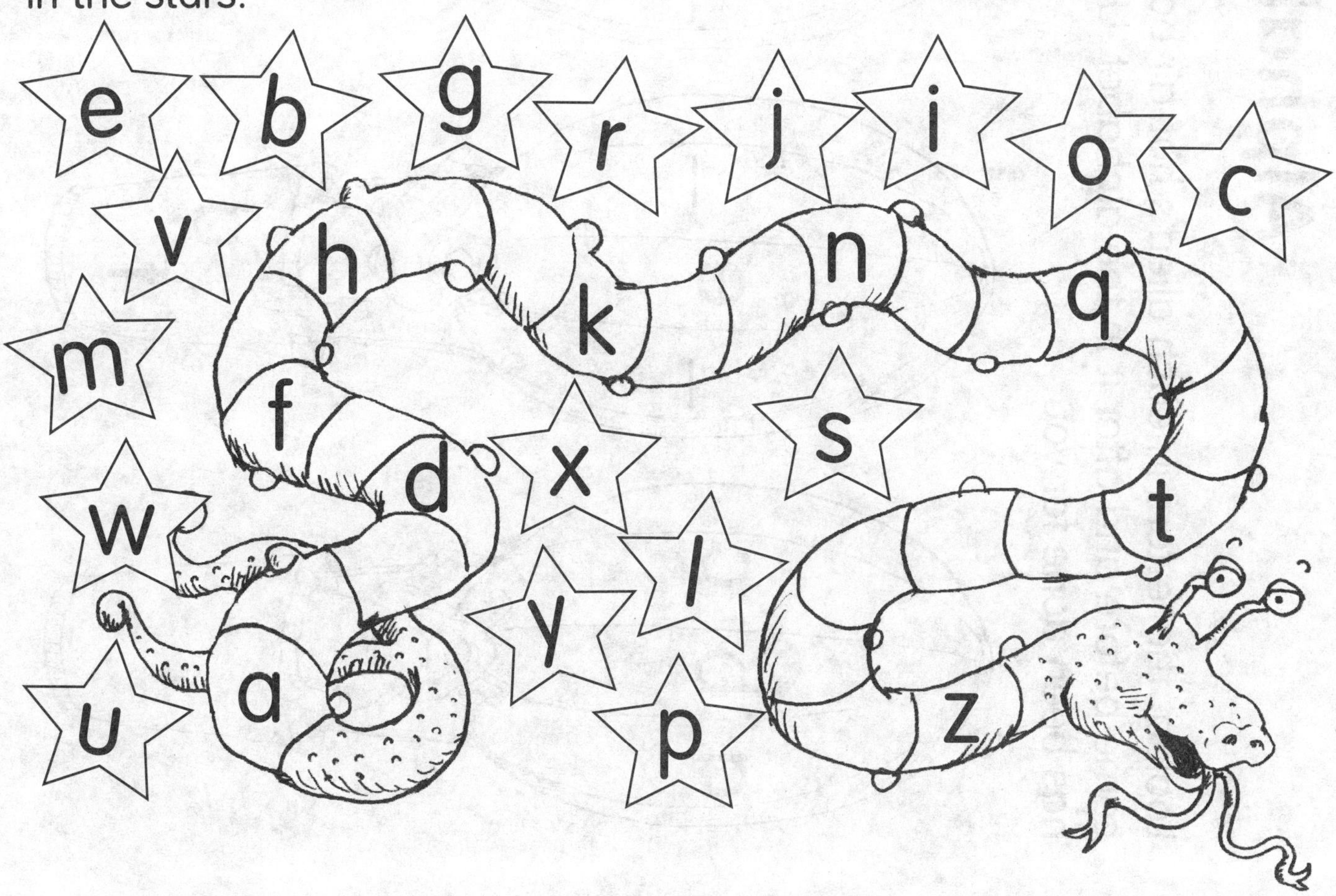

Alphabetical order

Look at the letters in each alien's hot-air balloon. Can you say each letter? Add the letters that come before and after it in the alphabet. Use the letters in the basket to help you. The first one has been done for you.

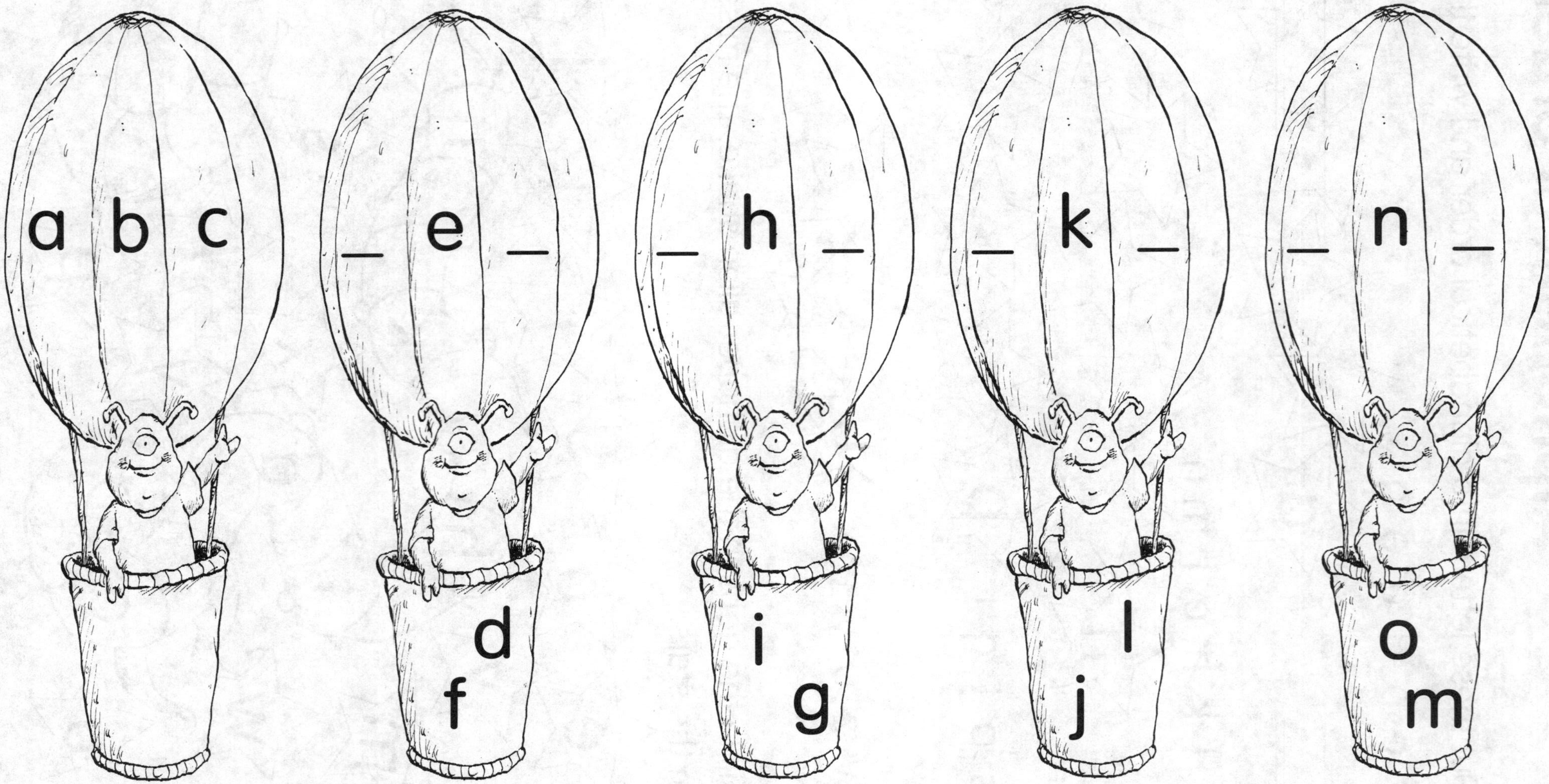

Alphabetical order

Look at the letters in each alien's hot-air balloon. Can you say each letter? Add the letters that come before and after it in the alphabet. Use the letters in the basket to help you.

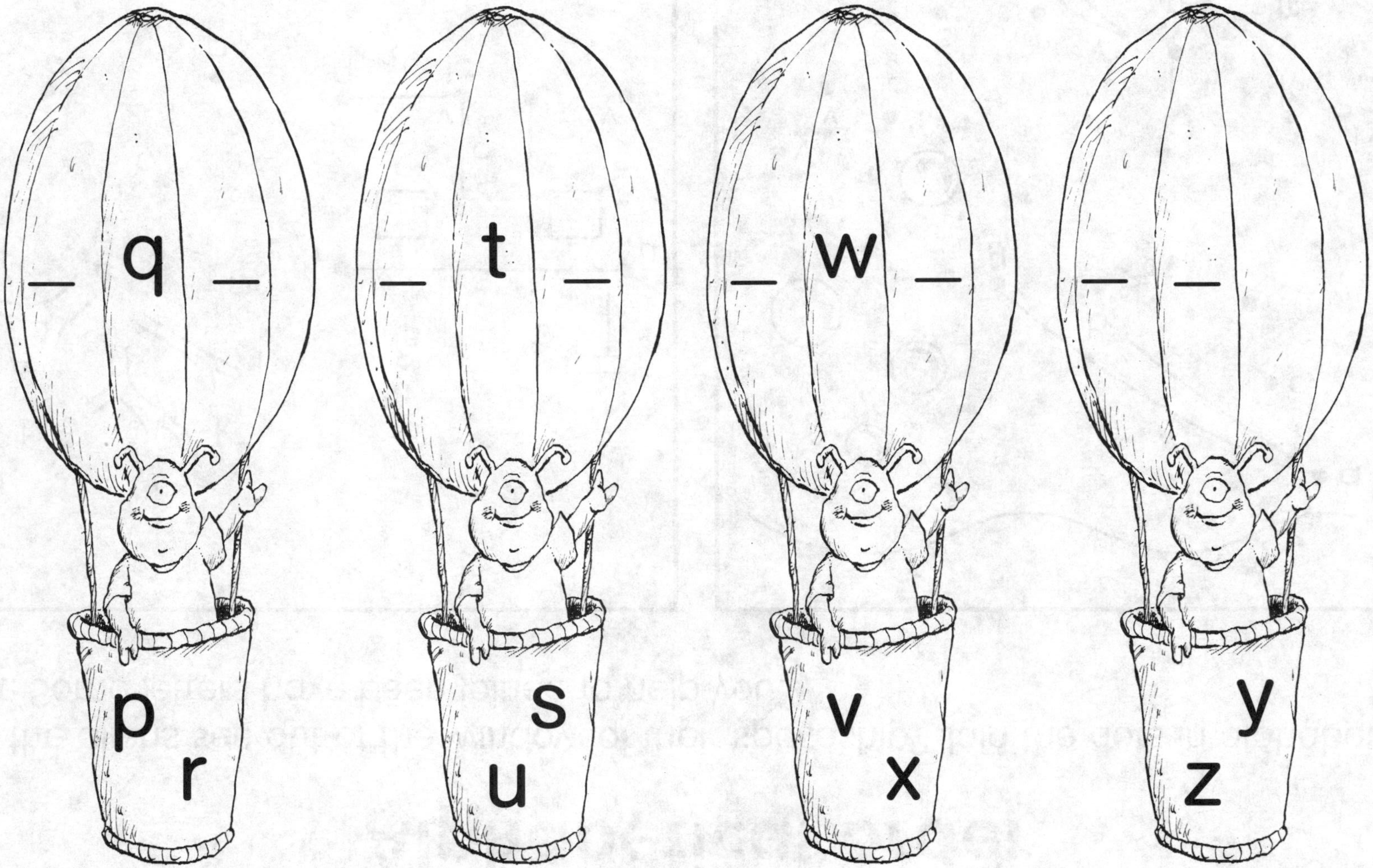

Alphabetical order

What can the aliens see out of the window of their spaceship? Join the dots in alphabetical order to find out. Some letters have been joined to help you.

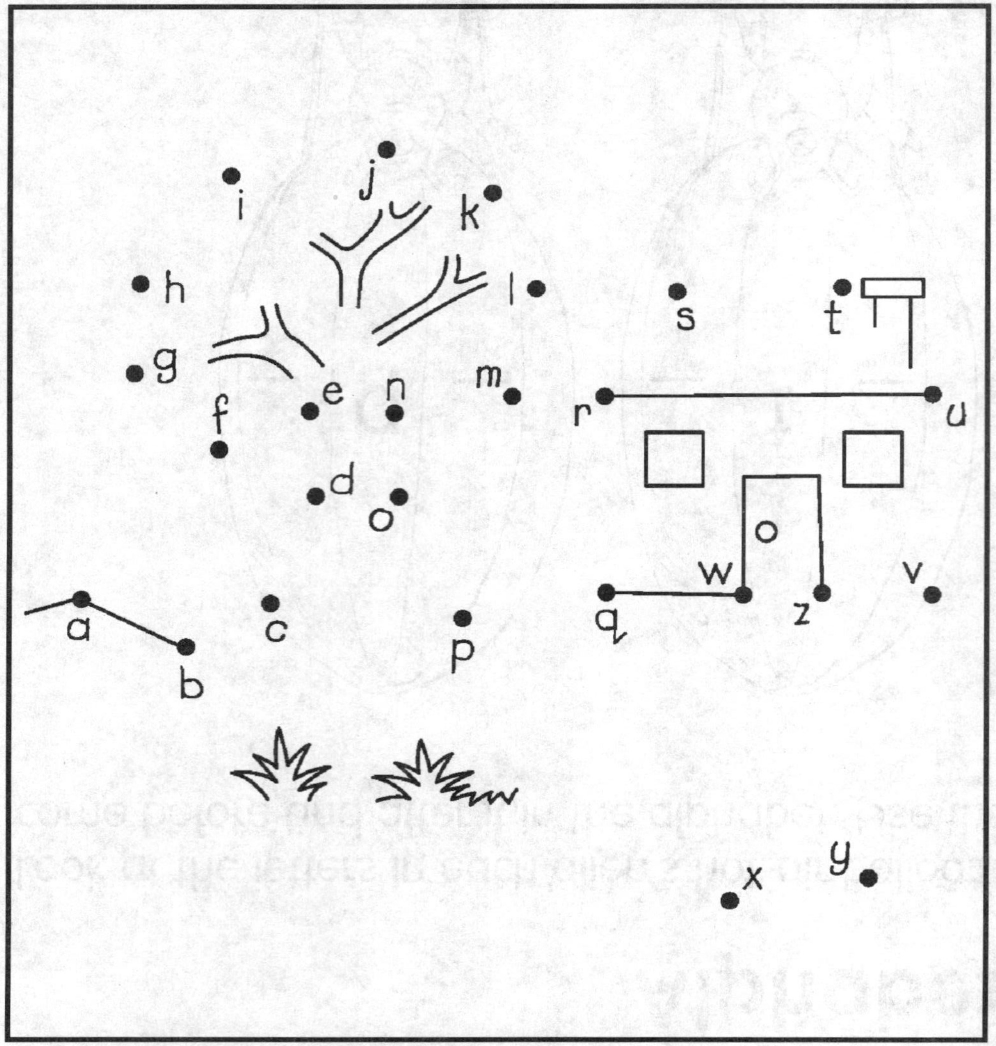

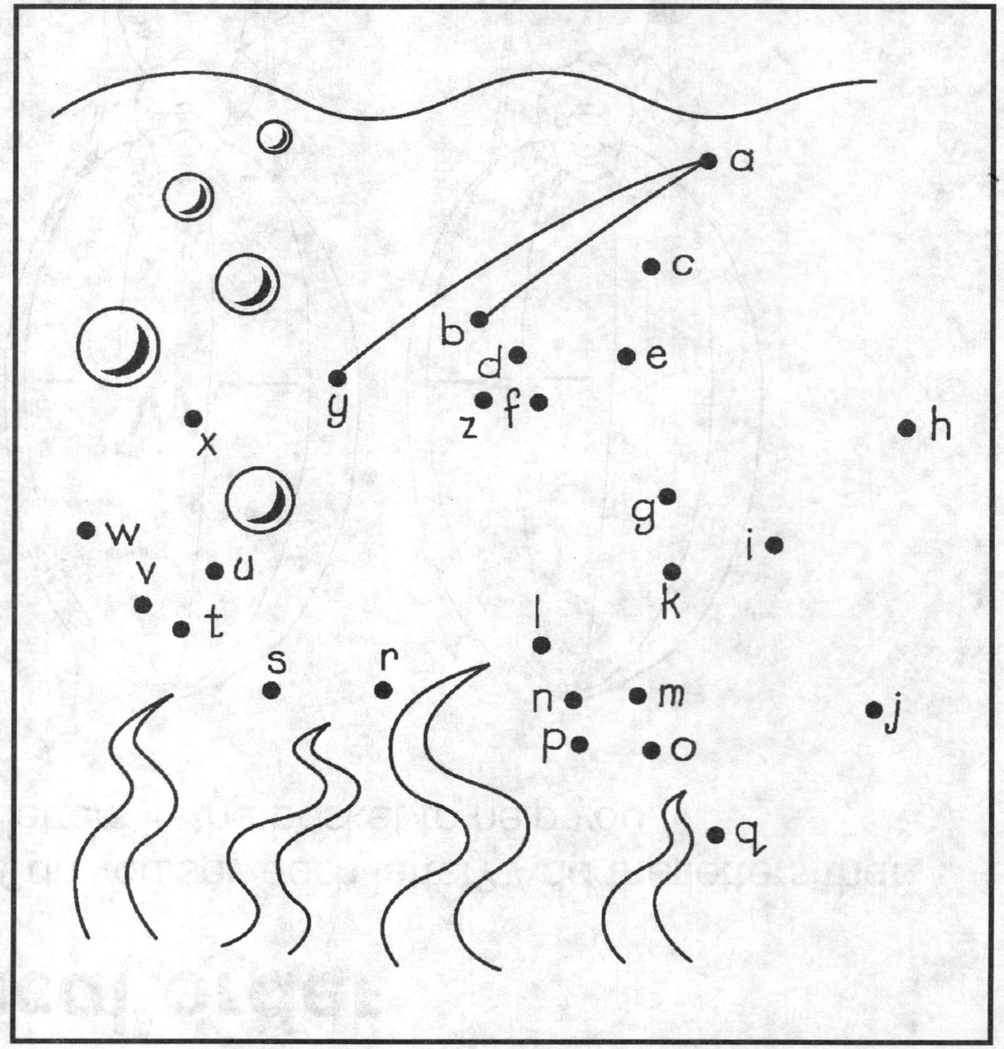

Alphabetical order

What can the aliens see out of the window of their spaceship? Join the dots in alphabetical order to find out. Some letters have been joined to help you.

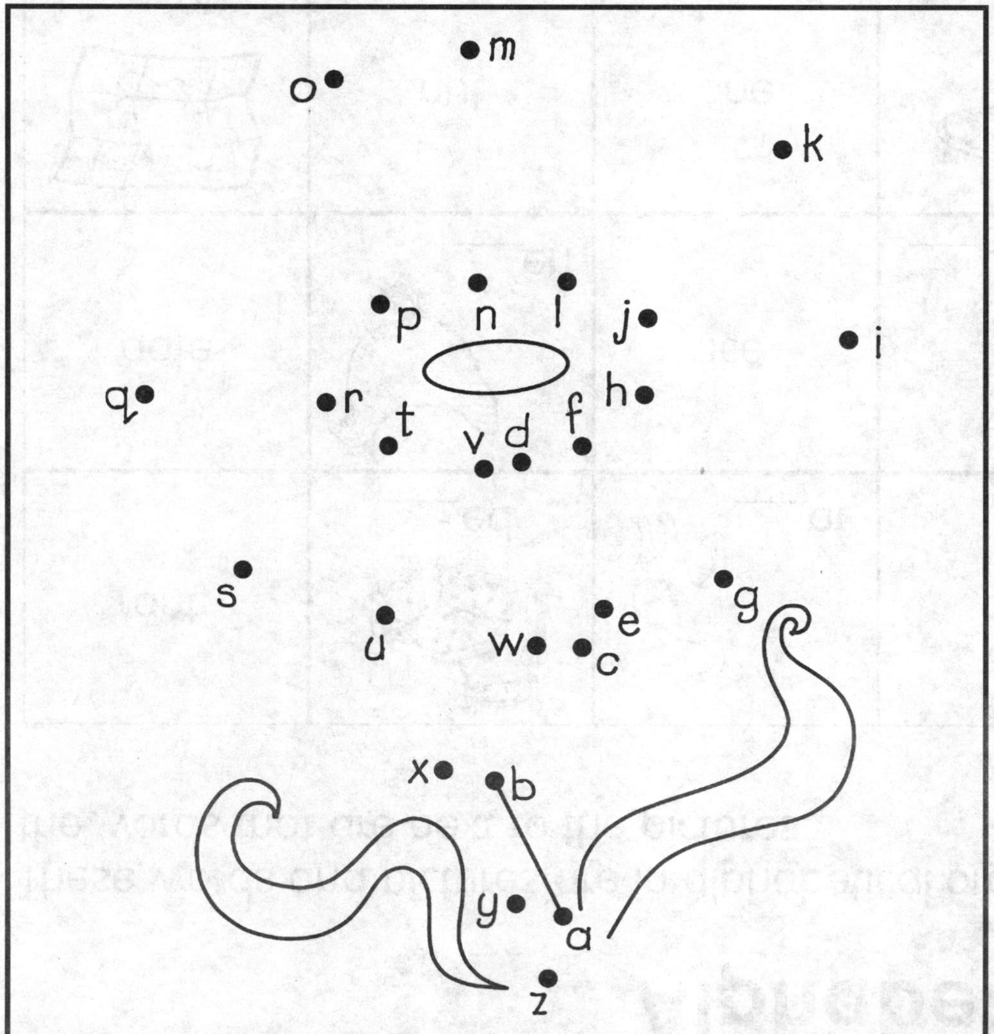

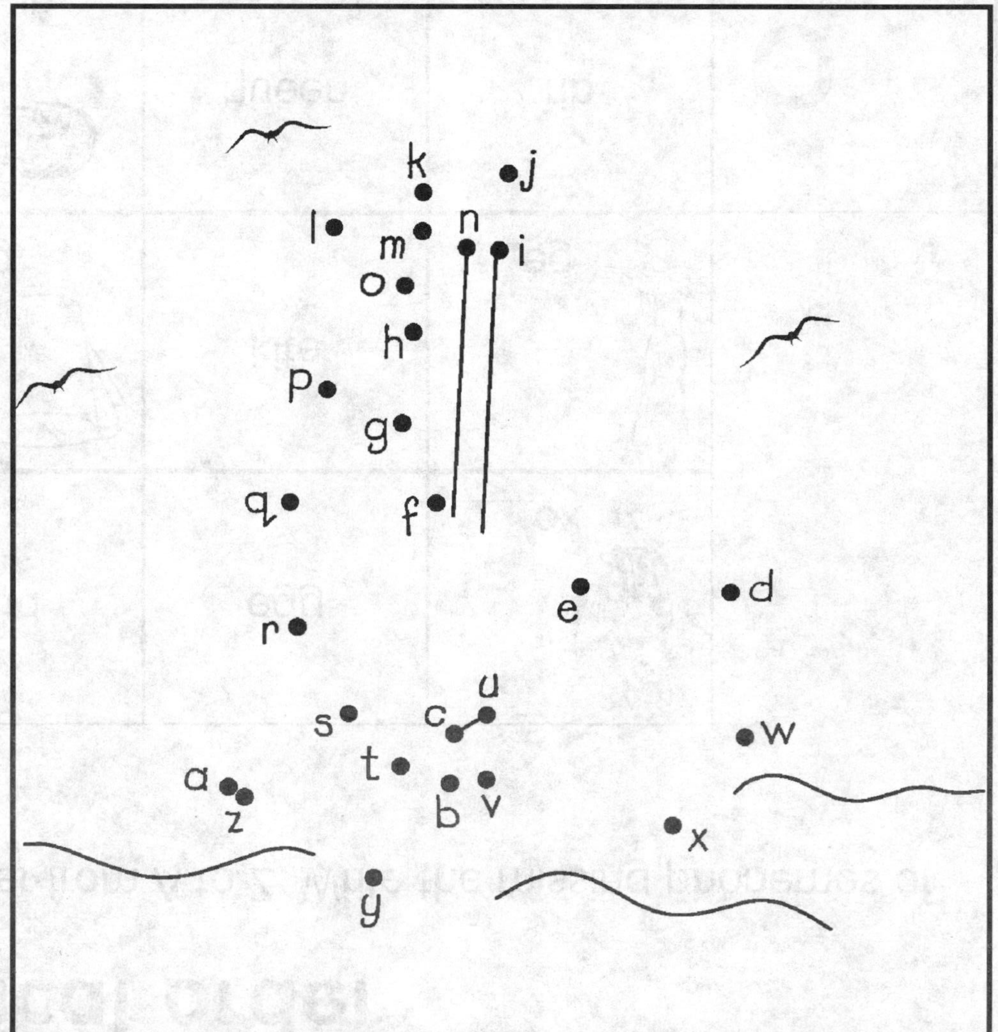

Alphabetical order

These words and pictures are in alphabetical order from A to Z. Write the missing phonemes of the words that are next to the pictures.

ant	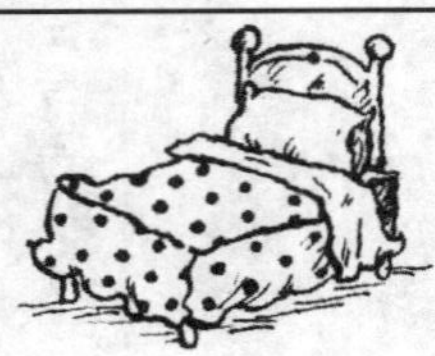 ___ed	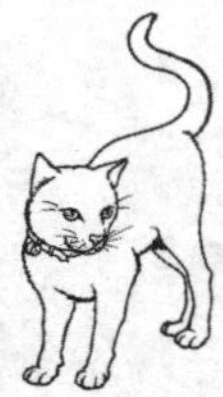 ___at	dad	egg	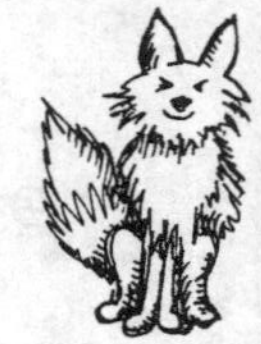 ___ox	
gate	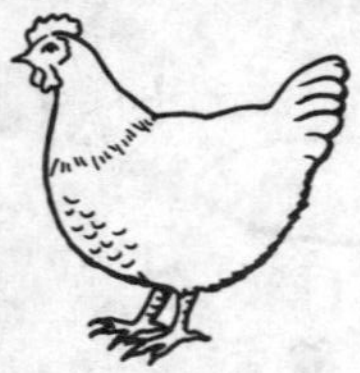 ___en	ice	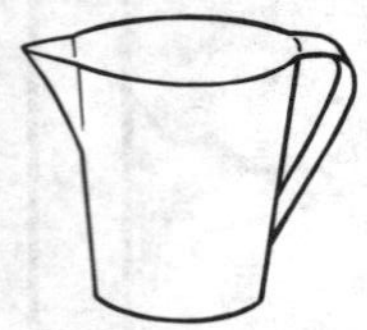 ___ug	kite	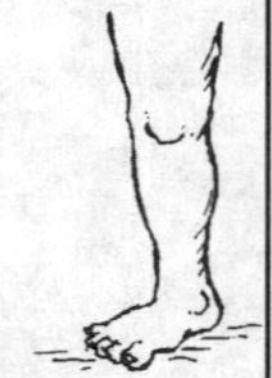 ___eg	
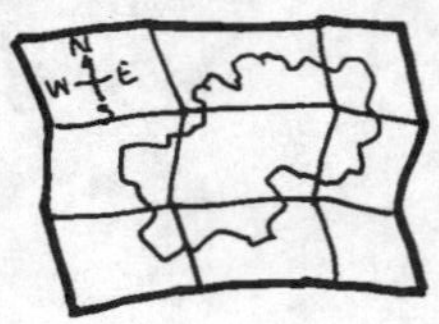 ___ap	nut	one	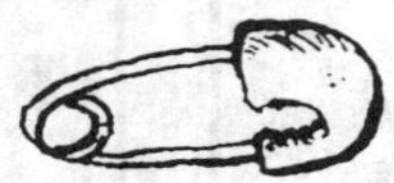 ___in	queen	rib	6 ___ix
10 ___en	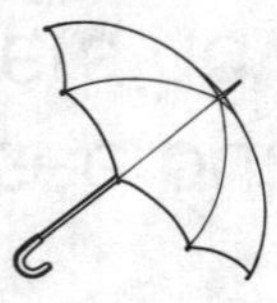 ___ mbrella	vest	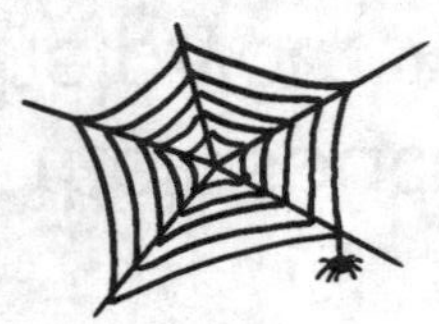 ___eb	x-ray	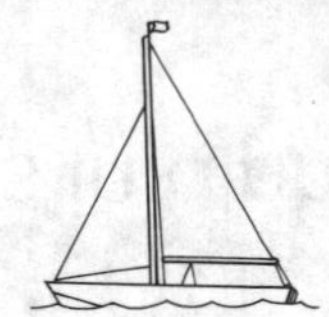 ___acht	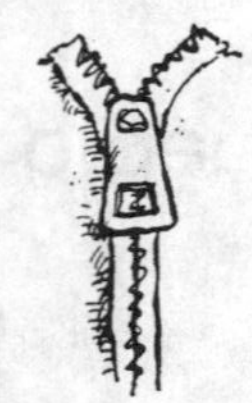 ___ip

Alphabetical order

These words and pictures are in alphabetical order, but the letters are jumbled up. Unjumble the letters and write the words on the lines.

apple	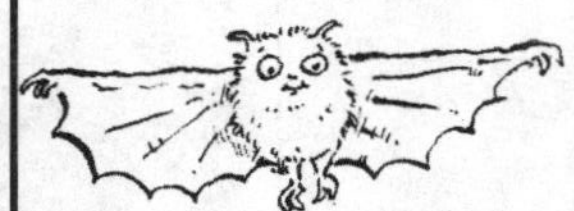 tba ___ ___ ___	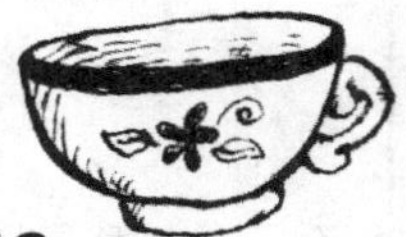 puc ___ ___ ___	dad	egg	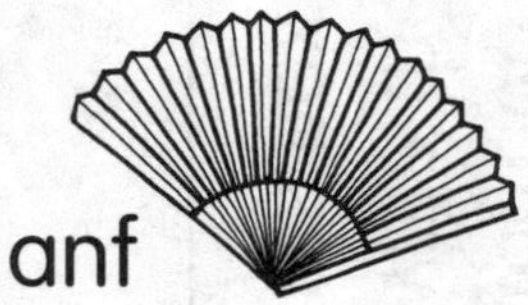 anf ___ ___ ___	
girl	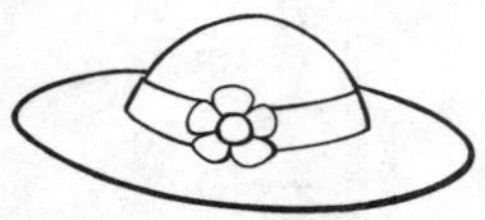 ath ___	ice	jam	king	leaf	
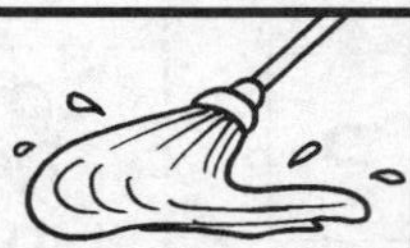 omp ___ ___ ___	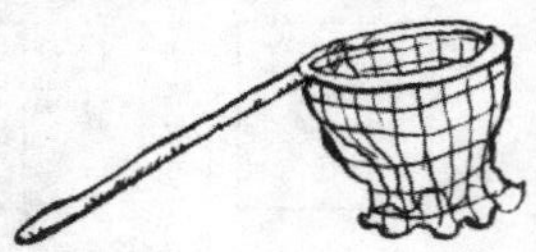 ten ___ ___ ___	oil	peg	queen	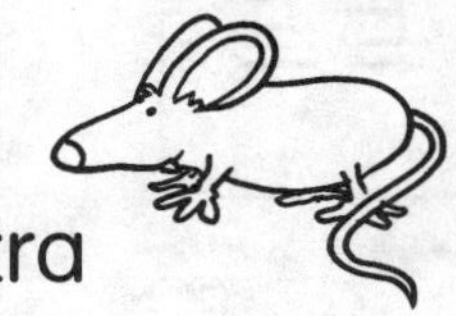 tra ___ ___ ___	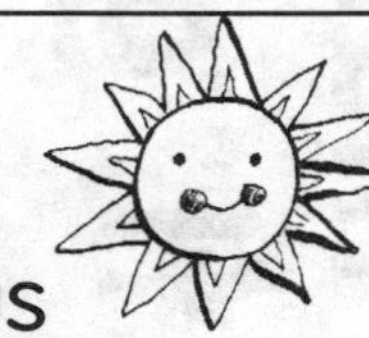 nus ___ ___ ___
three	ugly	stev 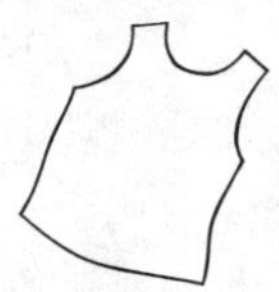 ___ ___ ___ ___	lawa 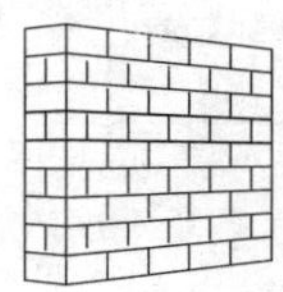 ___ ___ ___ ___	x-ray	yacht	zoo

Words that begin with bl, cl, fl, gl, pl and sl

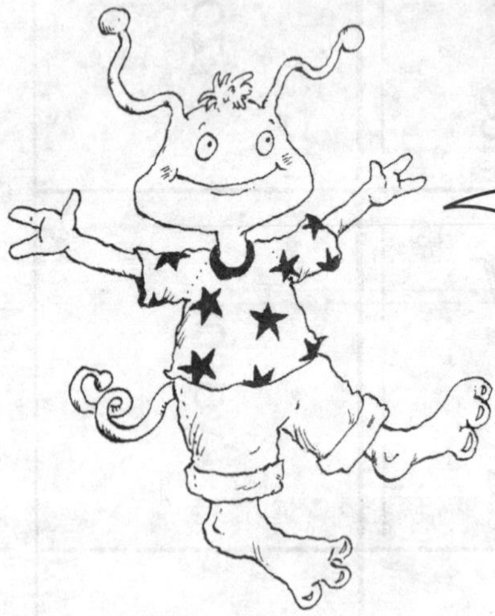

Blend the phonemes to read the words. Join the phonemes and write the words on the lines. Draw the pictures next to the words.

b + l + ow = ____________

c + l + aw = ____________

f + l + a + g = ____________

g + l + ue = ____________

p + l + u + g = ____________

s + l + u + g = ____________

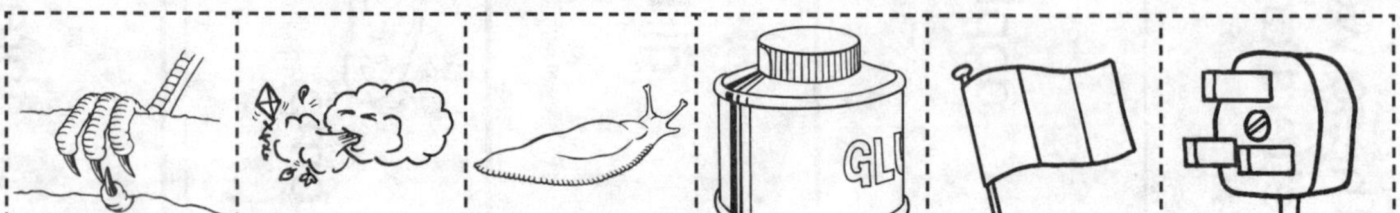

Words that begin with cr, dr, fr, gr, pr and tr

Look at the pictures and say what they show. Can you hear the phonemes in the words? Choose from the phonemes in the planets and write them underneath the pictures to spell the words. You must use phonemes from each planet to make a word. Blend the phonemes to read the words.

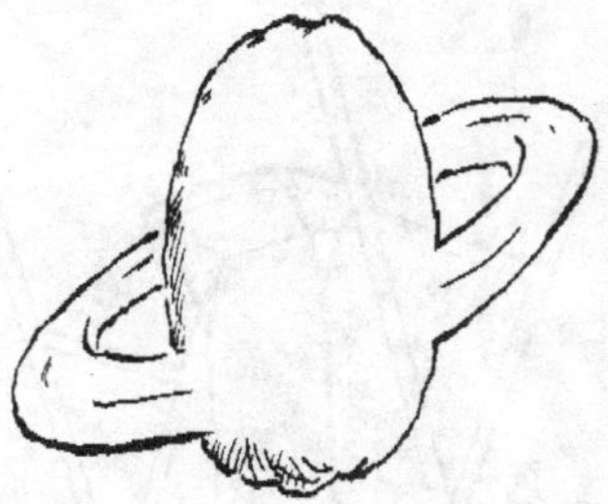
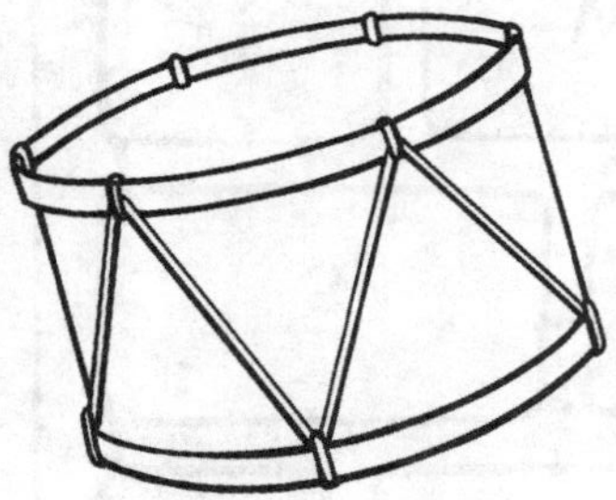
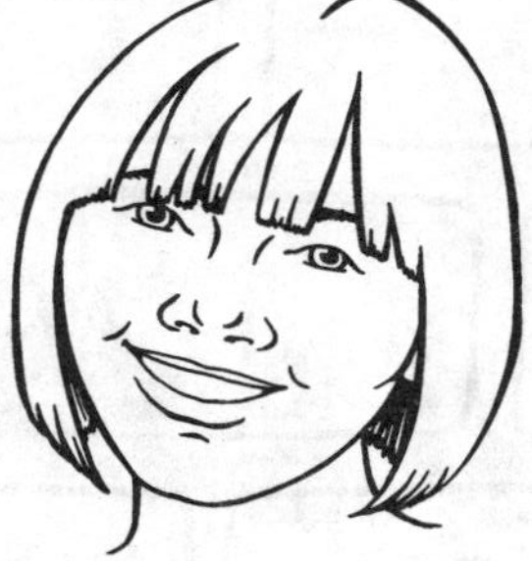
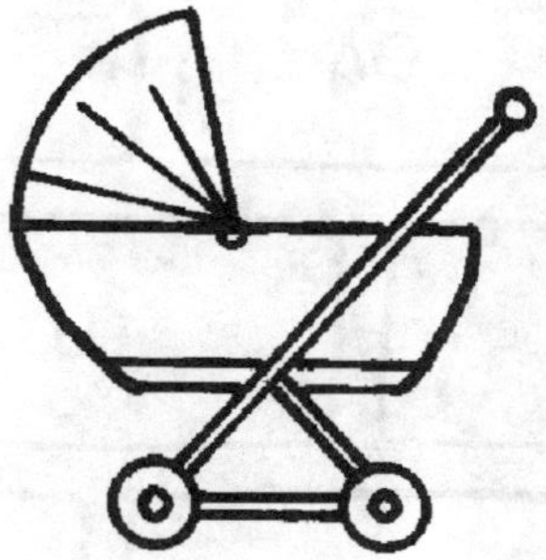
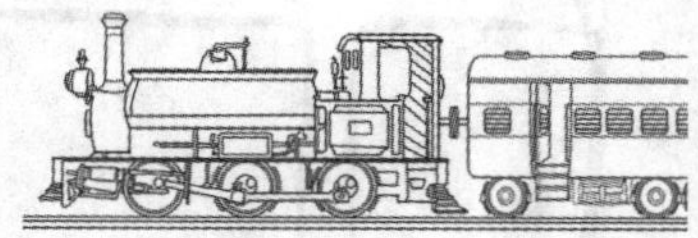
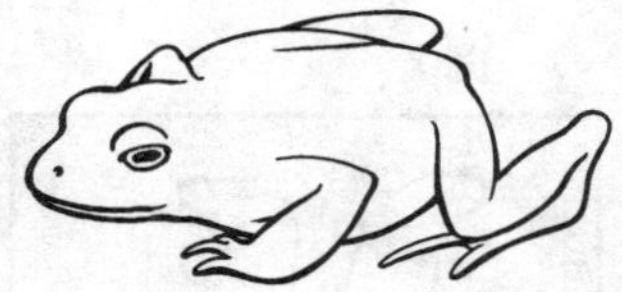

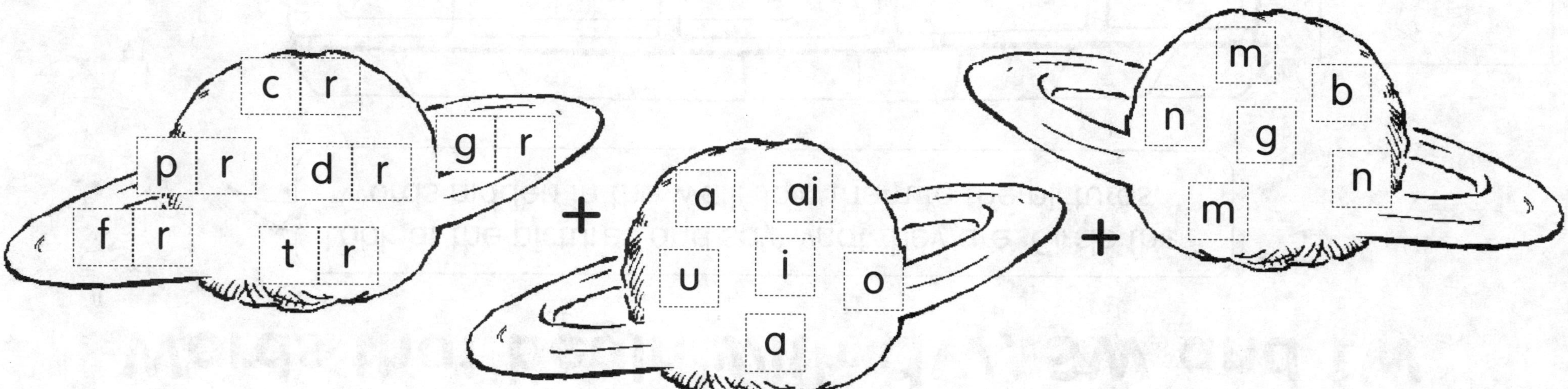

Words that begin with dw, sw and tw

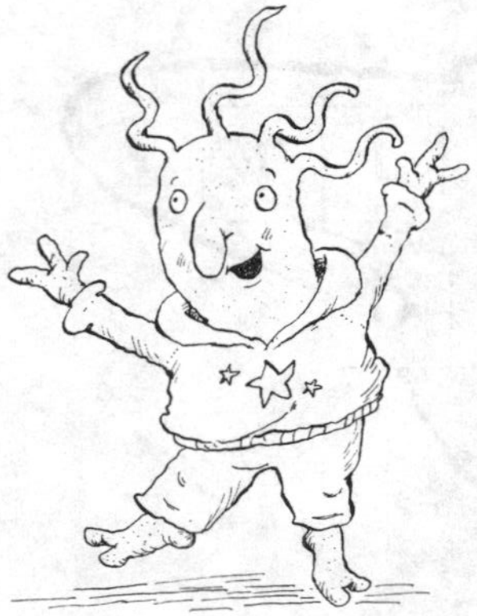

Look at the pictures and say what they are. Circle the words hidden in the wall. Join them to the pictures.

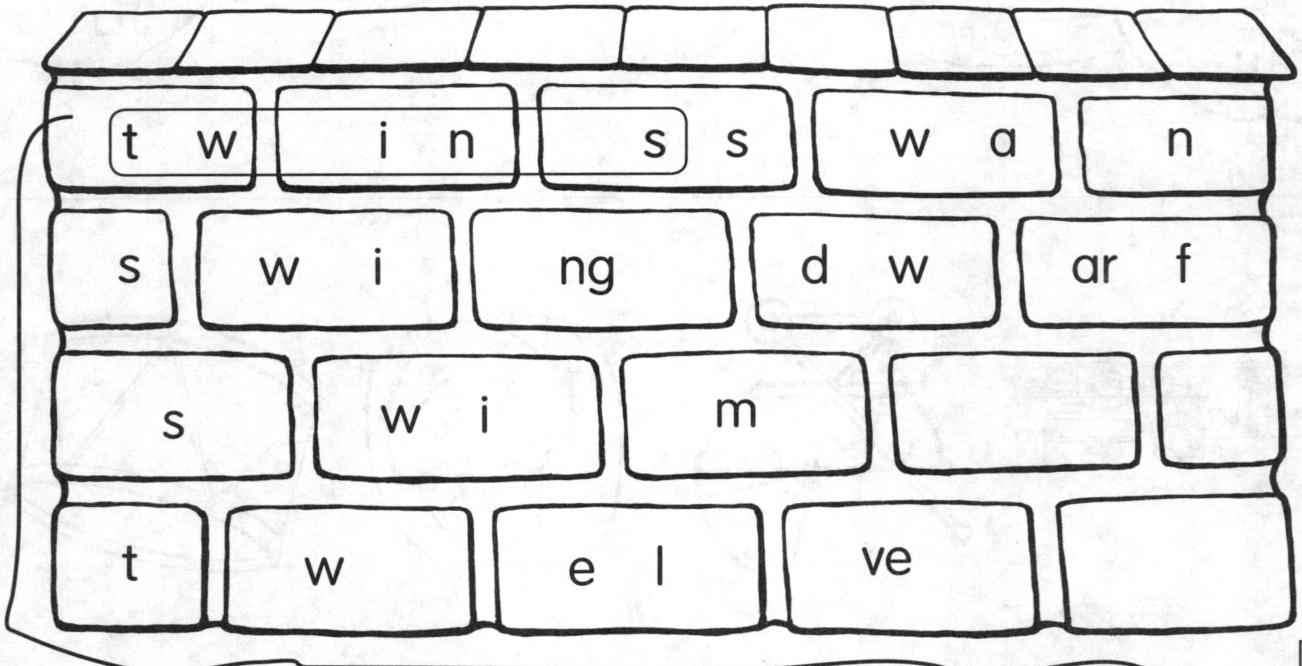

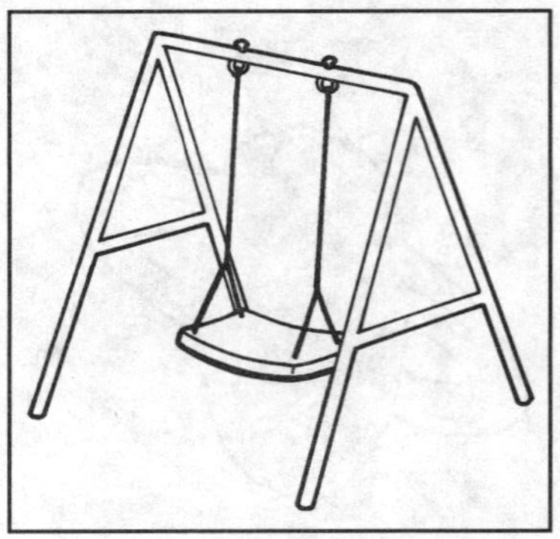

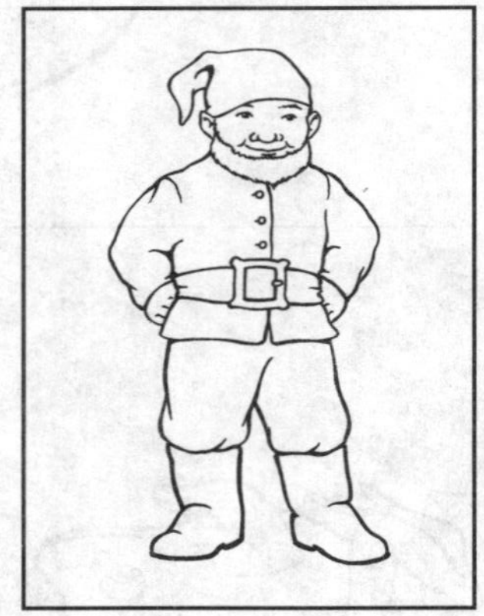

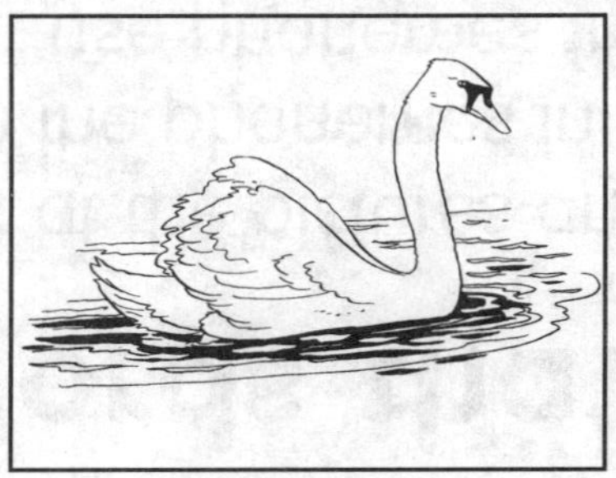

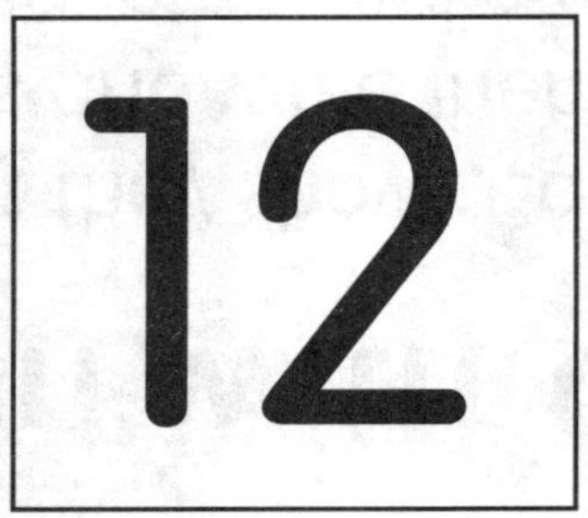

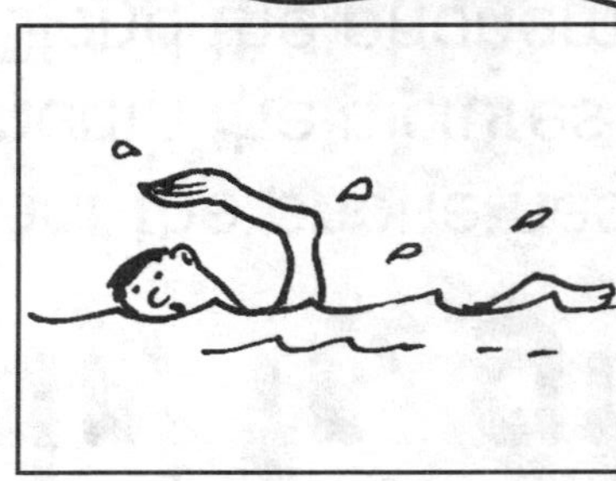

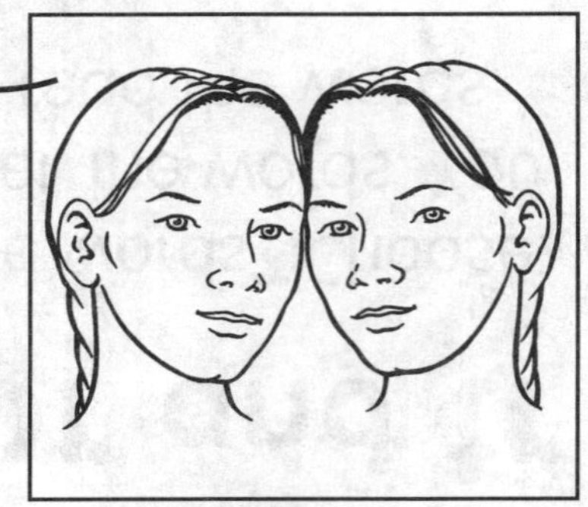

Words that begin with sc, sk, sm, sn, sp and st

Read the sentences. Circle the words that begin with **sc**, **sk**, **sm**, **sn**, **sp** and **st**.

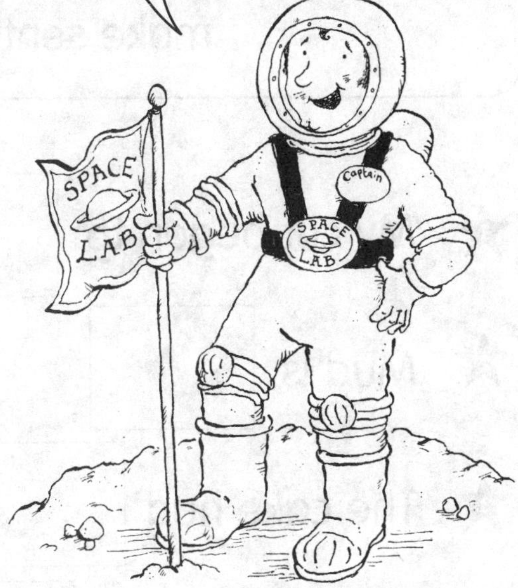

1. The cut on my leg left a bad scar.
2. I like to skip to keep fit.
3. Some flowers smell nice.
4. Snap is a good card game.
5. It is very rude to spit.
6. The bus stop is next to the shop.

Look at the blends in the helmets. Write the words that you circled above on the lines next to the correct blends. One has been done for you.

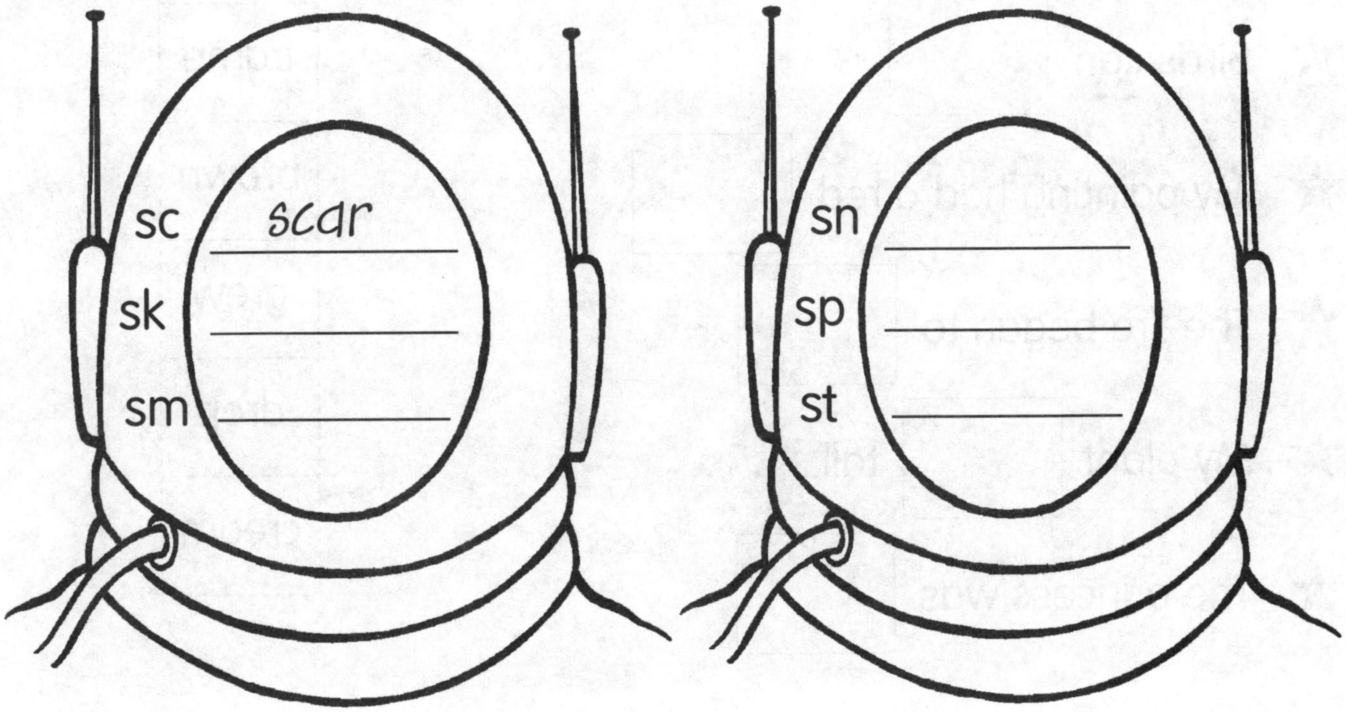

Words that begin with two phonemes blended together

Read the sentences. There is a word missing from each sentence. Blend the phonemes to read the words in the boxes. Write the words in the correct boxes to make sentences.

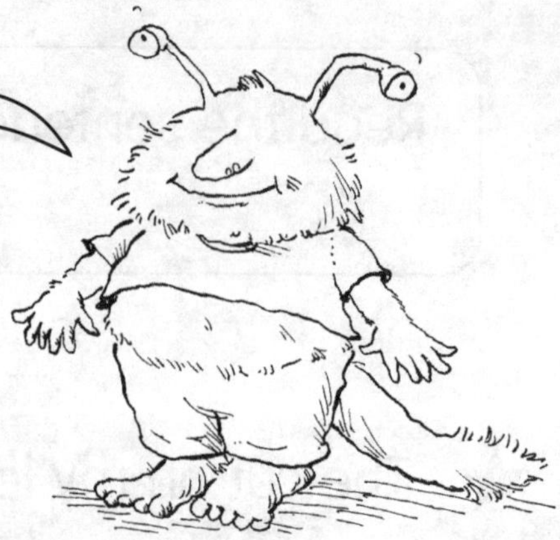

1. My cut began to ☐.
2. Mud is ☐.
3. The cake had ☐ on it.
4. He was a funny ☐.
5. Catch the ball, don't ☐ it.
6. Birds can ☐.
7. My painting had a red ☐.
8. The fire began to ☐.
9. My plant ☐ tall.
10. The princess was ☐.

bleed
pretty
glow
fly
clown
frame
brown
grew
drop
cream

Words that begin with two phonemes blended together

Blend the phonemes to read the words in the word bank. Can you hear the first two phonemes?

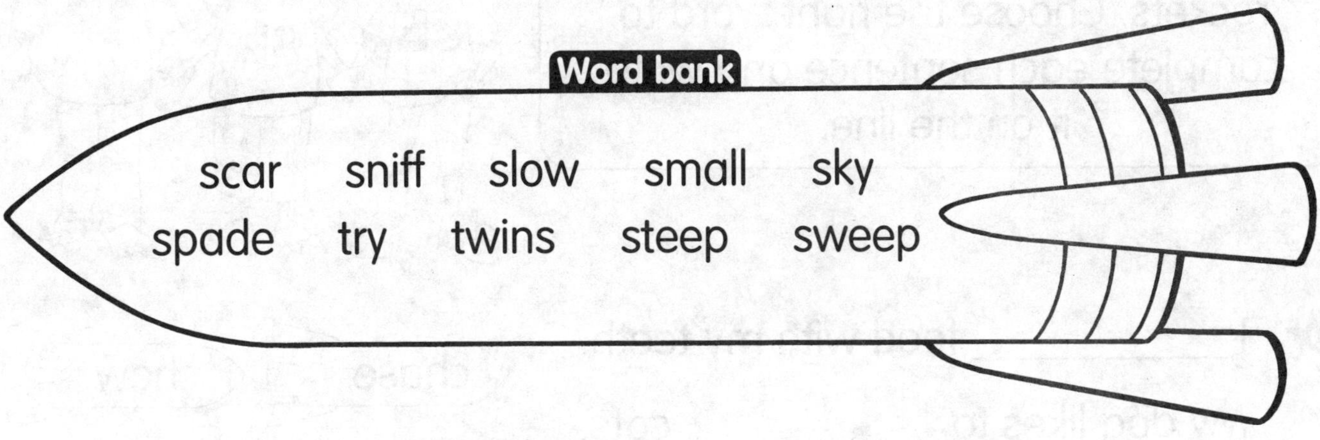

Highlight the words from the word bank in the word search. The words can be read across and down.

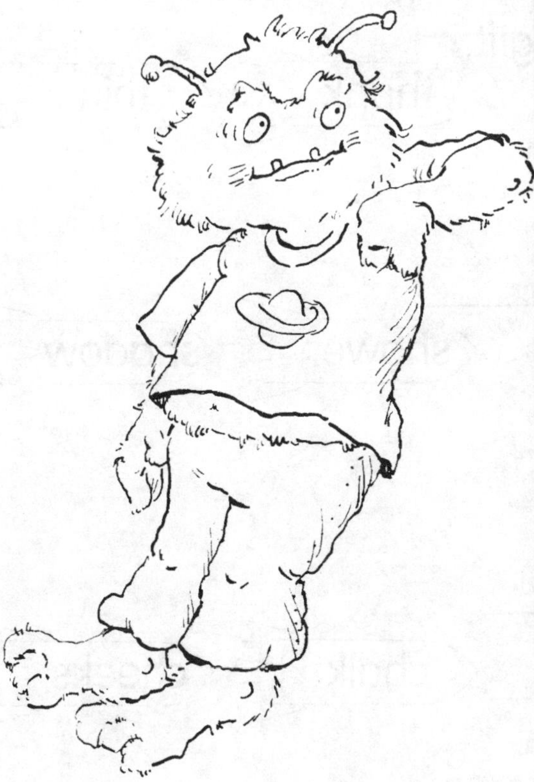

t	s	n	i	f	f	m	l
w	z	s	t	e	e	p	l
i	l	s	m	p	t	l	s
n	s	p	v	j	m	d	k
s	m	a	s	l	o	w	y
k	a	d	q	t	r	y	x
h	l	e	s	w	e	e	p
r	l	n	s	c	a	r	c

Words that begin with ch, sh and th

Blend the phonemes to read the sentences and the words in the rockets. Choose the right word to complete each sentence and write it on the line.

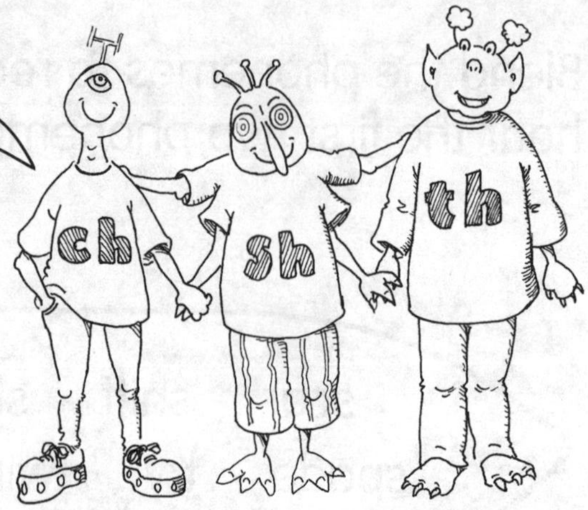

1. I ___________ food with my teeth.
   My dog likes to ___________ cats.

   chase | chew

2. I put the tins on the ___________.
   The ___________ sells ice creams.

   shelf | shop

3. You must ___________ her for the gift.
   The old dog was very ___________.

   thank | thin

4. After my swim, I had a hot ___________.
   The sun made a big ___________ under the tree.

   shower | shadow

5. My doll has bright red ___________.
   Our teacher writes with ___________.

   chalk | cheeks

Words that begin with
scr and spl

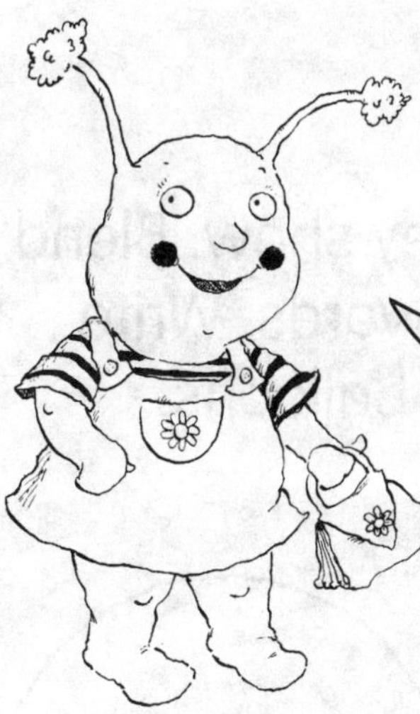

Blend the phonemes to read the letter strings in the rockets. Join the parts together and write them on the lines. The first one has been done for you.

screen

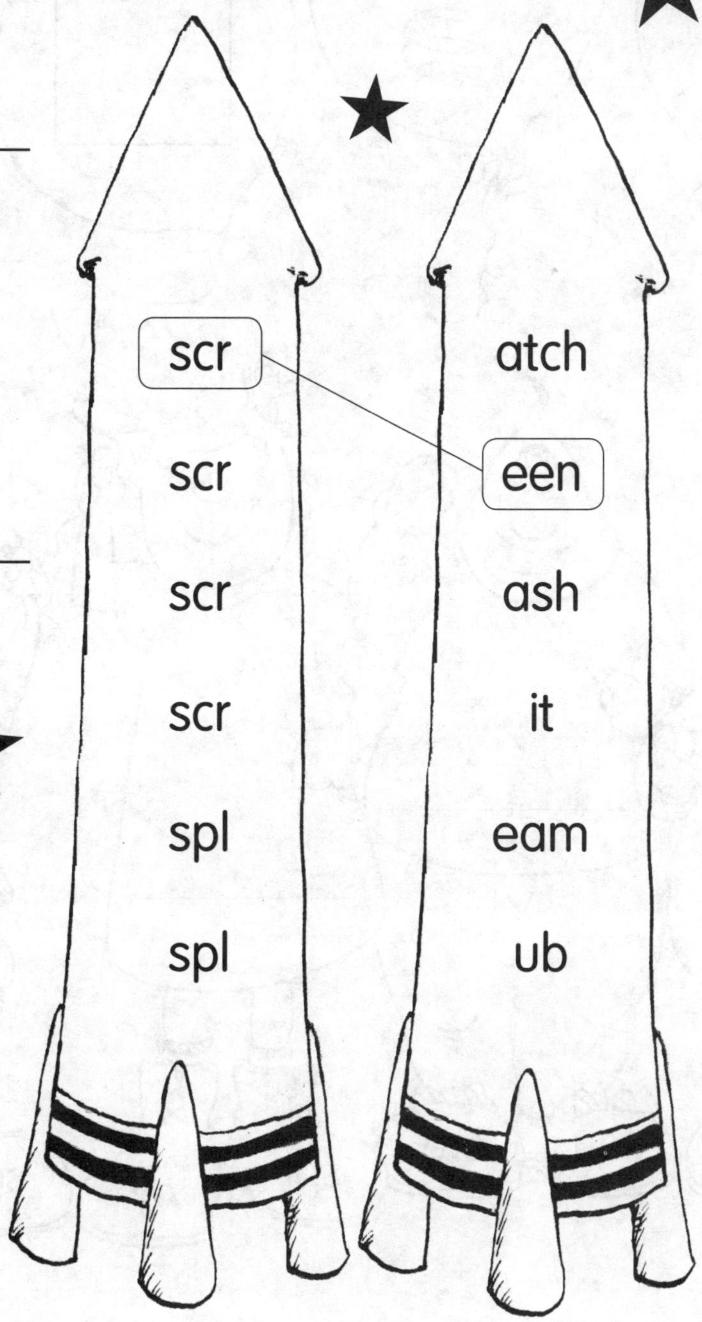

Words that begin with spr and squ

Look at the pictures in the balloons and say what they show. Blend the letter strings in the feet of the aliens to read the words. Write the words in the aliens. Join the aliens to the correct balloons.

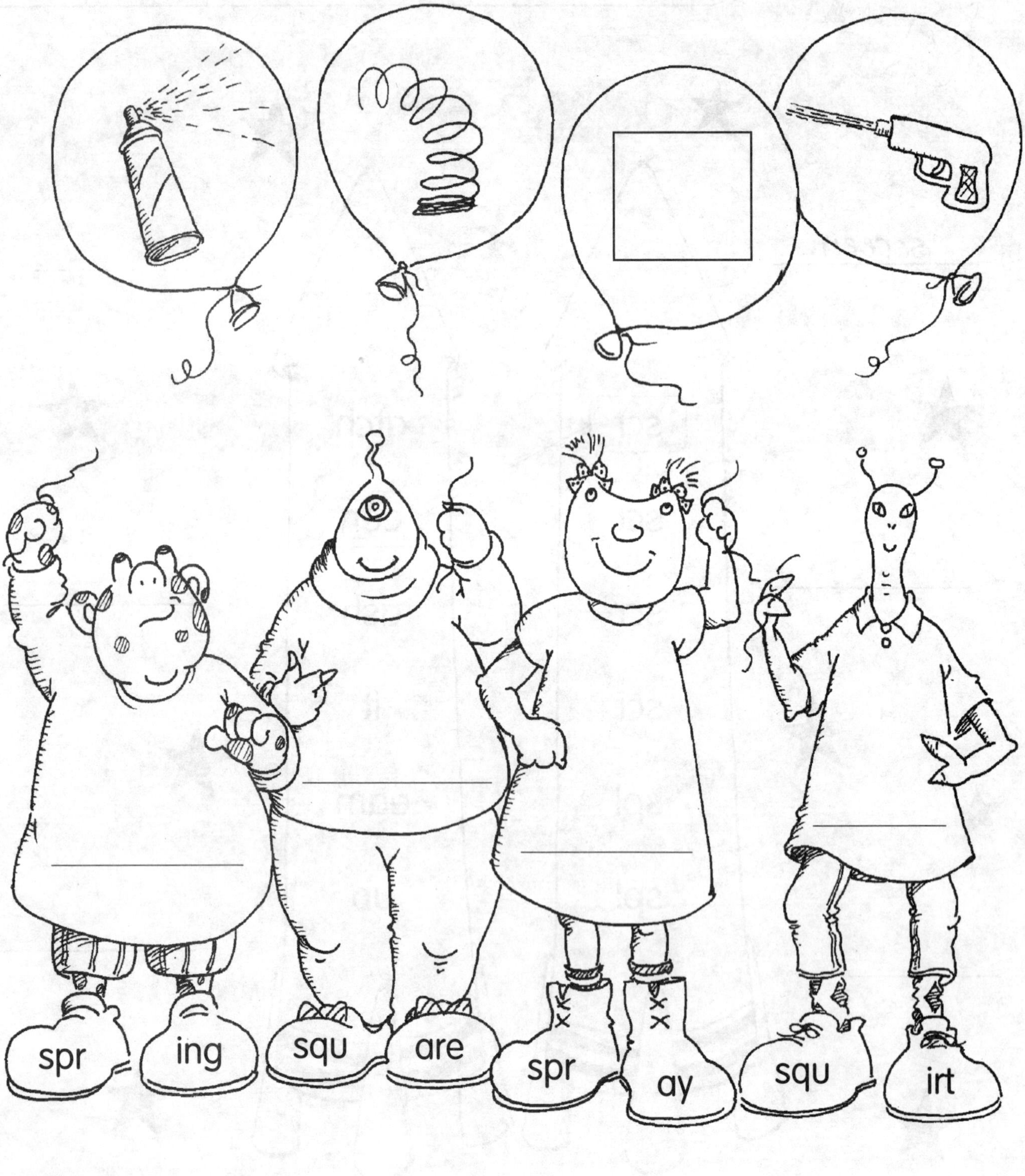

Words that begin with str

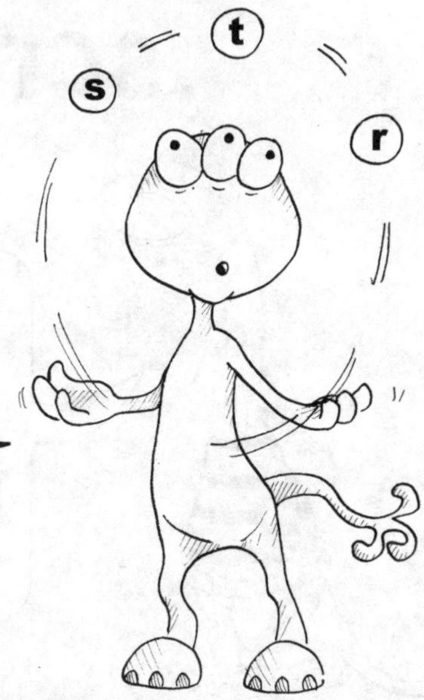

Look at the pictures and say what they show. The phonemes in the words are jumbled up. Sort them out and write them in the boxes. Each word begins with **str**.

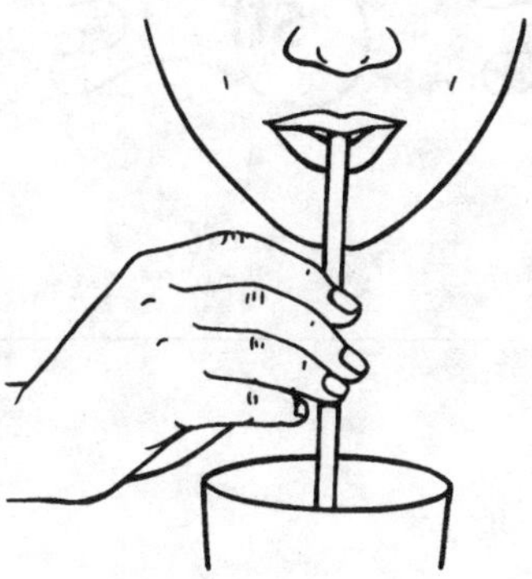

t s r aw

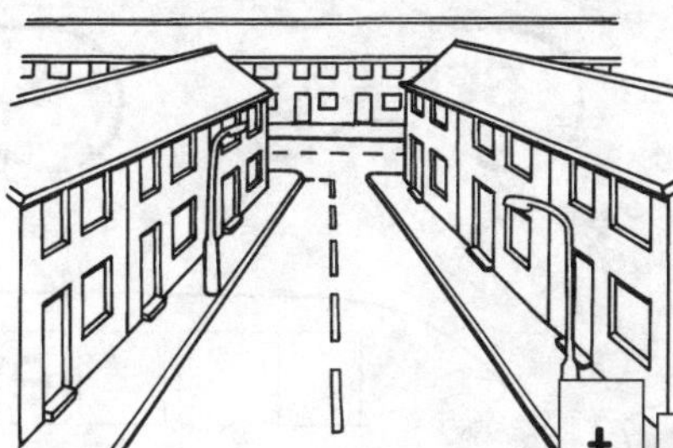

t r ee t s

i r t ng s

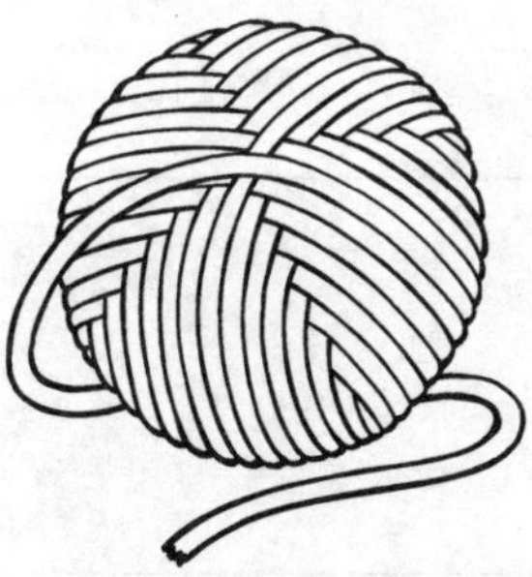

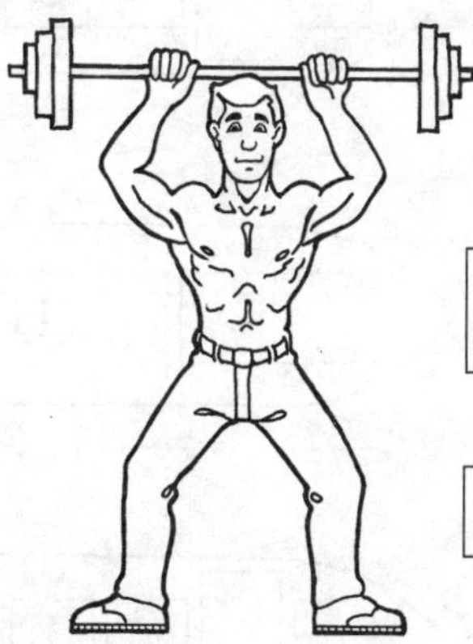

t r ng s o

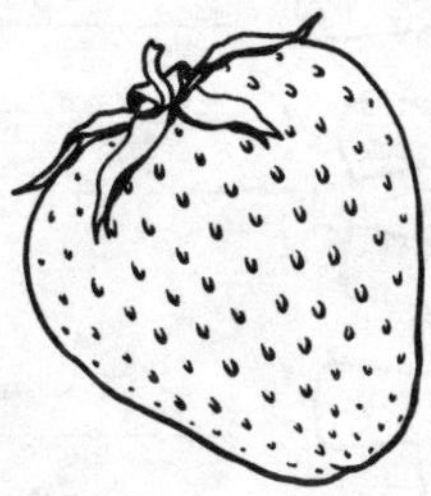

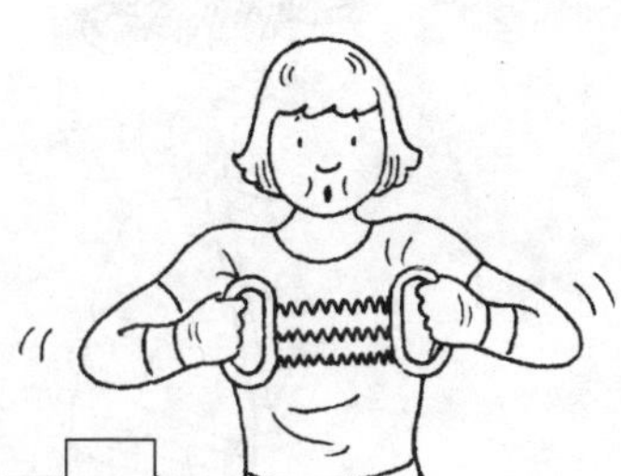

r s aw t e b y rr

s e t r tch

Words that begin with scr, spl, spr and str

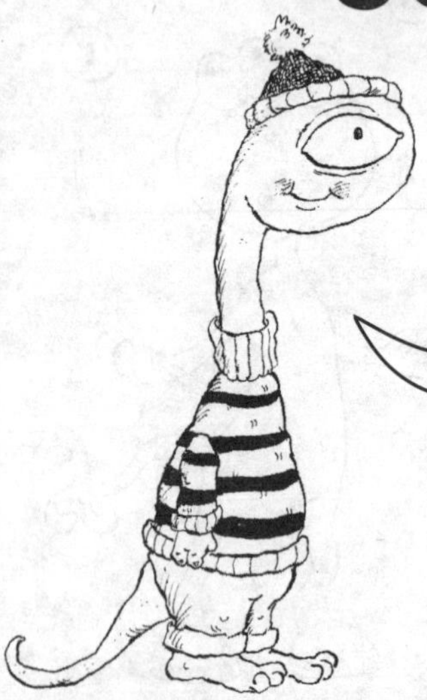

Look at the pictures and say what they are or what action they show. Can you hear the blend at the start of the word? Choose the missing blend from the footprints and write it in the boxes in the rockets. Write the words on the lines.

scr | spl | spr | str

1. 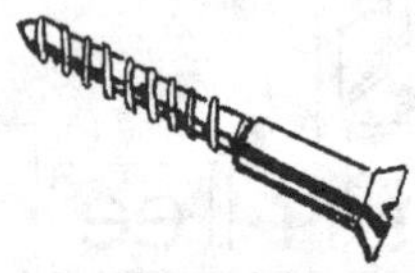 ☐☐☐ew ____________________

2. 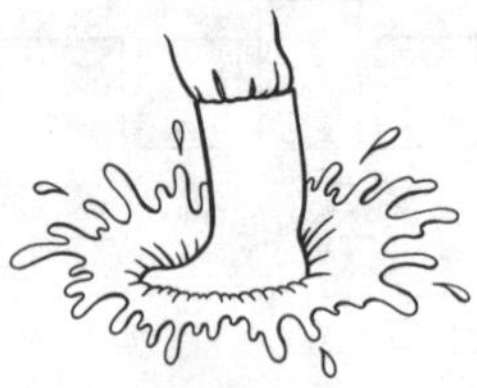 ☐☐☐a sh ____________________

3. 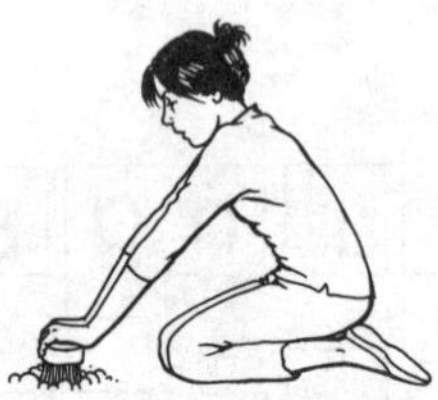 ☐☐☐u b ____________________

4. 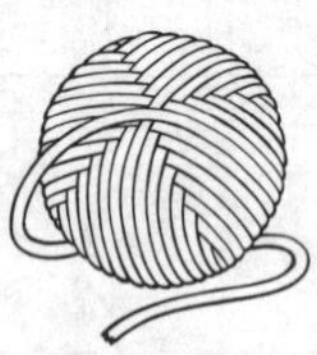 ☐☐☐i n g ____________________

5. 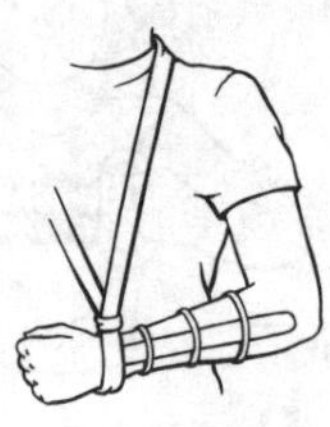 ☐☐☐i n t ____________________

6. 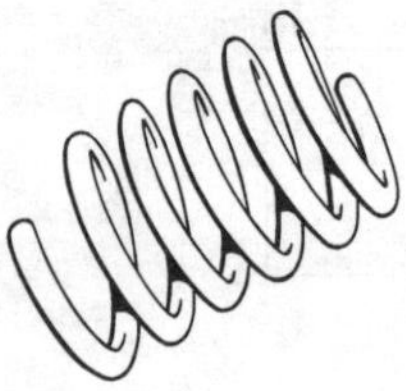 ☐☐☐i n g ____________________

Words that begin with thr

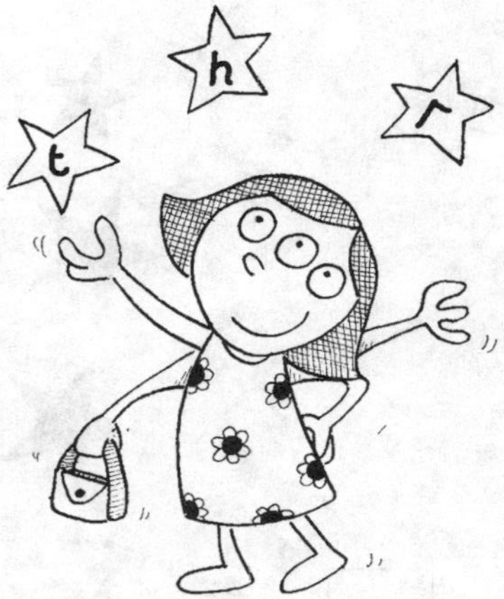

Look at the pictures in the leaves and say what they show. The phonemes in each snails' shells spell the words. Write them on the lines and join each snail to the right picture.

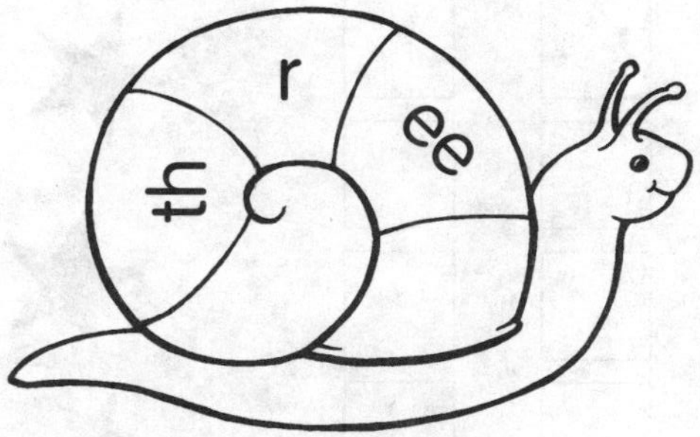

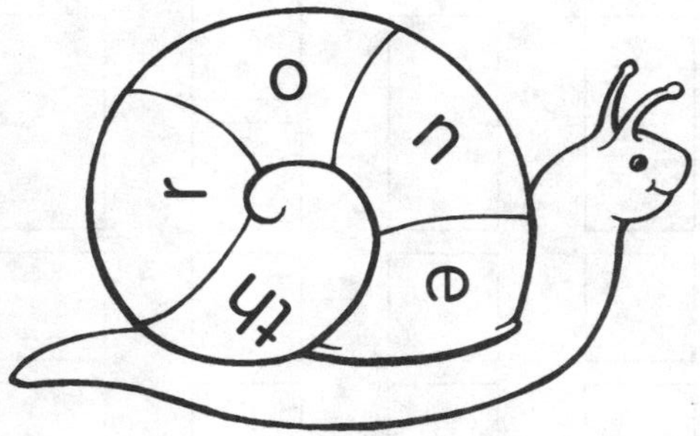

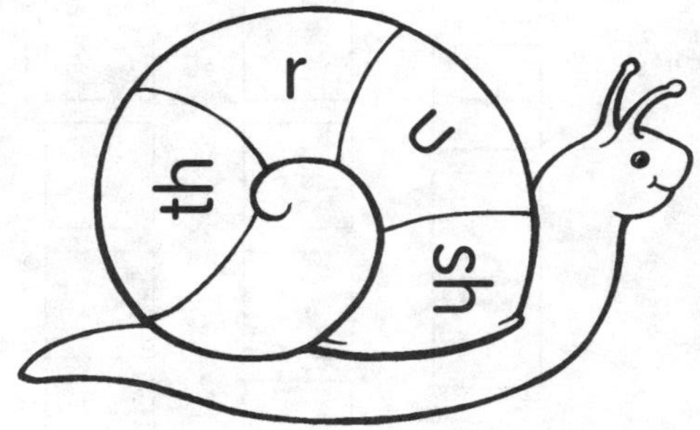

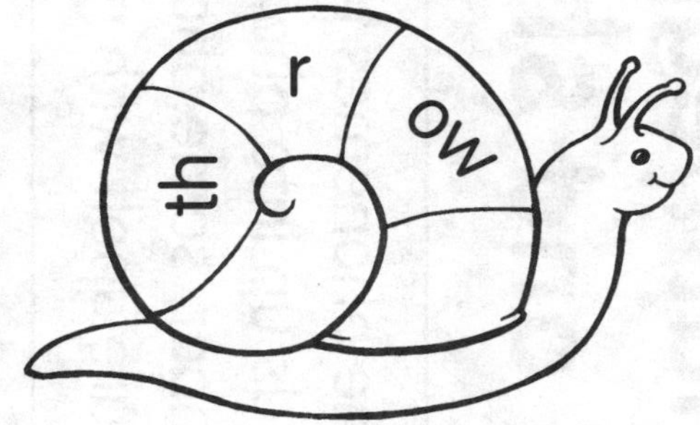

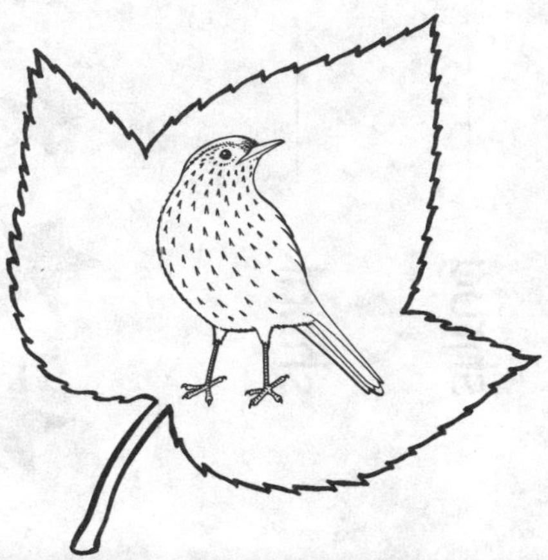

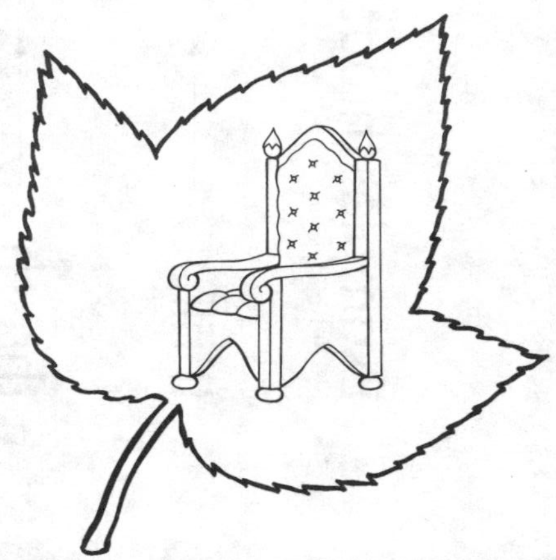

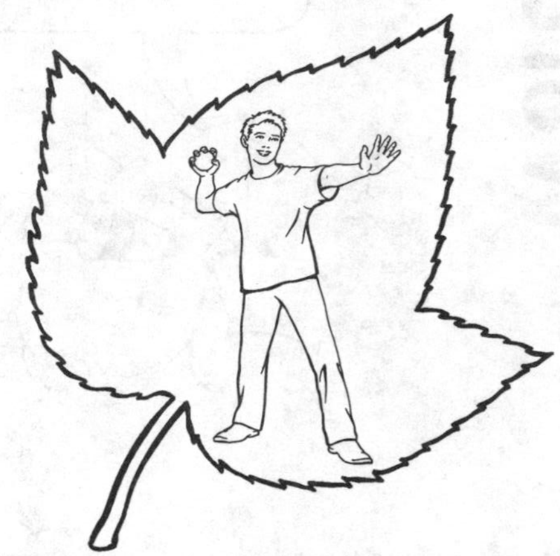

Words that begin with thr and shr

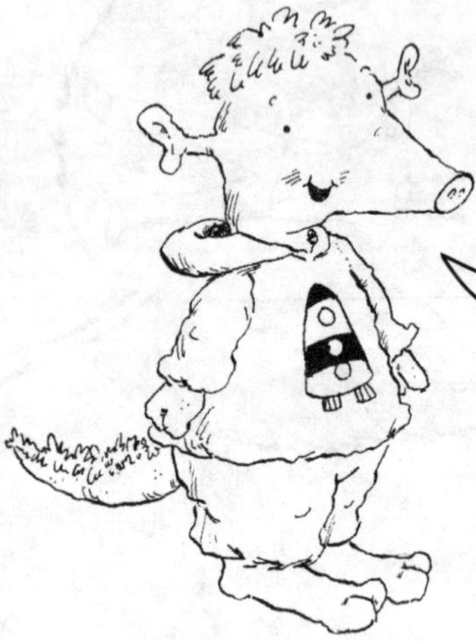

Blend the phonemes to read the words. Break the words up into phonemes like the example. Remember, some phonemes, such as **th** and **sh**, are spelt with more than one letter.

Example: throat → | th | r | oa | t |

3

thrill →

thrush →

throw →

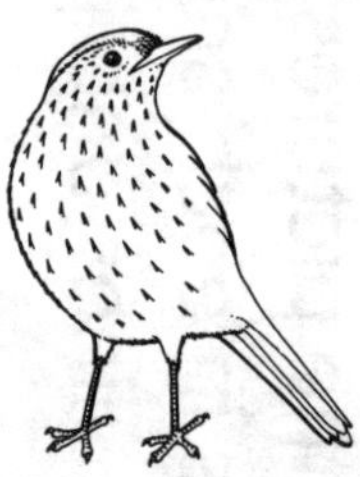

three →

shrub →

shriek →

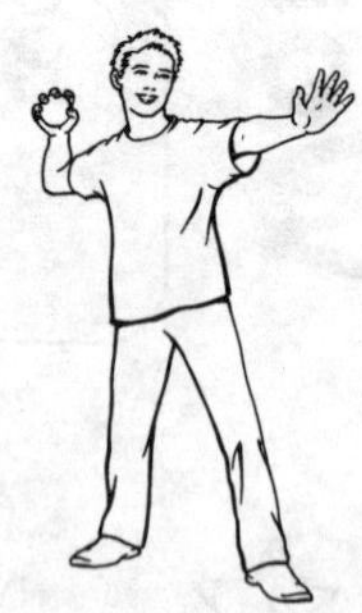

shrug →

shrink →

Words that begin with scr, spl, spr, squ, str and thr

Blend the phonemes to read the letter strings in the planets. Now read the sentences below. Add a letter string from the planets to complete the missing word in each sentence. The first one has been done for you.

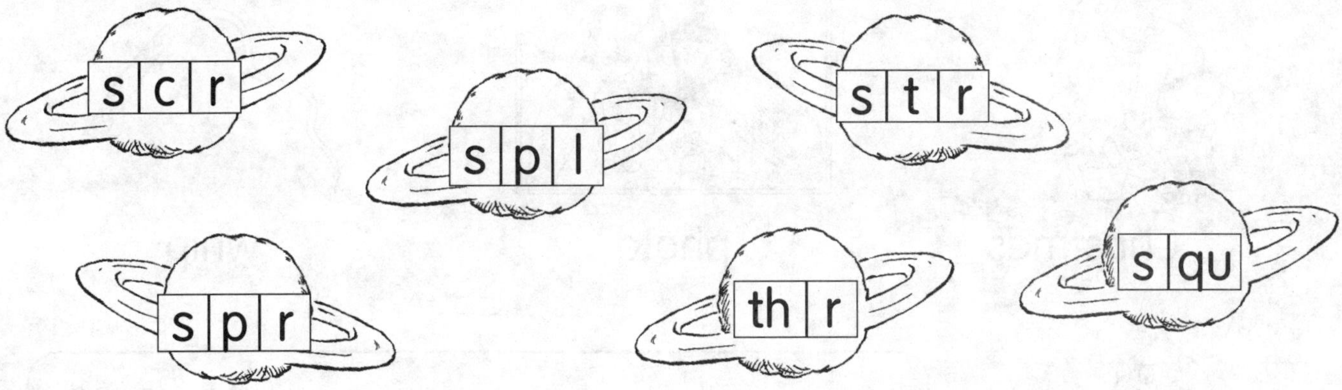

1. I had a small s c r a p of paper to write my name on.
2. The _ _ _ a y dog had no home.
3. We had to _ _ _ a s h the clothes into the small case.
4. The fish were in the _ _ _ ea m.
5. I had to _ _ ea d the needle to sew.
6. I _ _ ew the ball into the net.
7. He had a _ _ _ i n t er of wood in his finger.
8. She jumps up and down as if she is on _ _ _ i n g s.
9. I _ _ _ ea d the jam on my toast.
10. The mouse made my mum _ _ _ ea m.

The blends **ch**, **ph** and **wh**

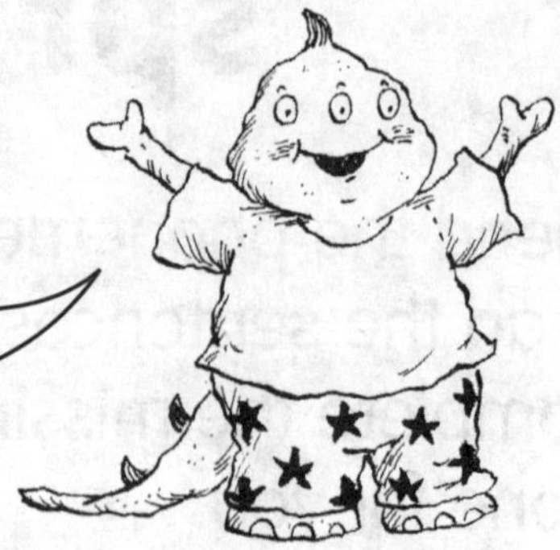

Look at the pictures and read the words to say what they are.

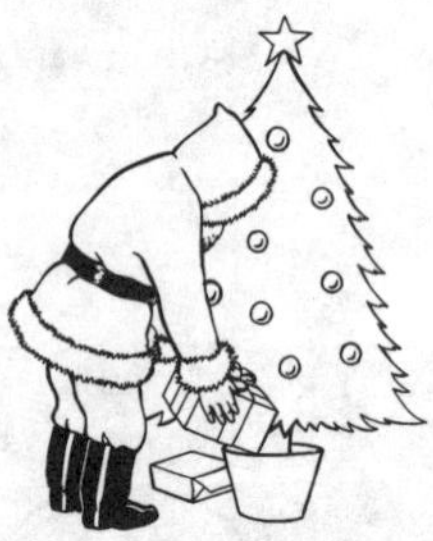

Christmas

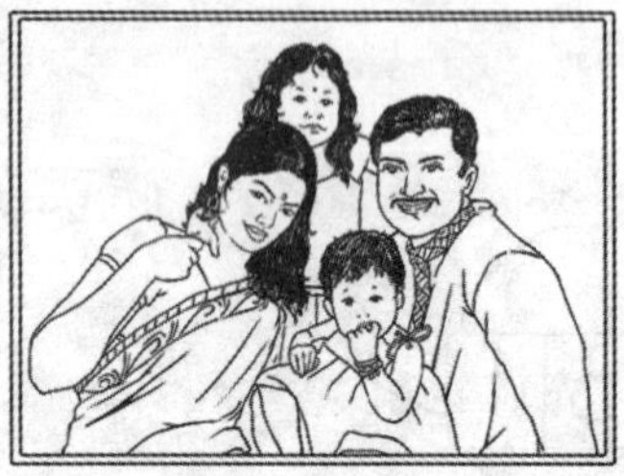

photo

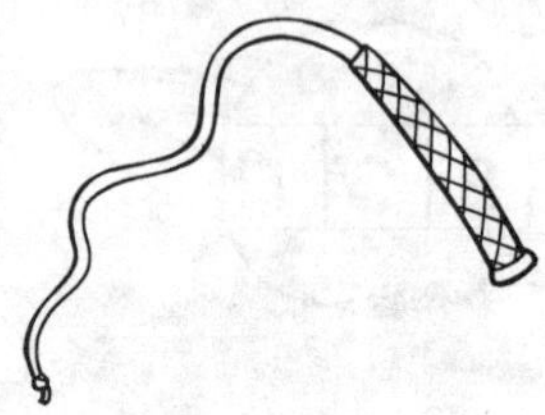

whip

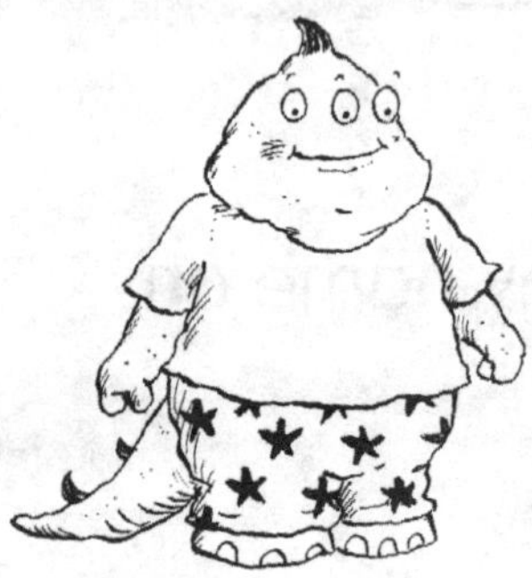

Can you hear the phonemes at the start? Look at the way they are spelt.

ch says **c** or **k**   **ph** says **f**

wh says **w**

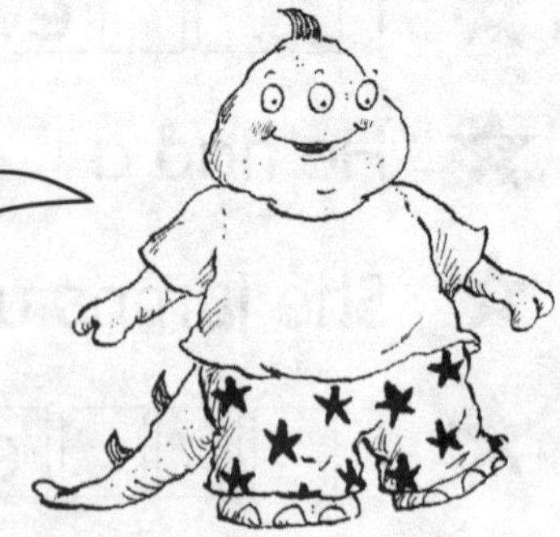

Blend the phonemes to read the words below. Find and circle the **ch**, **ph** or **wh** in these words.

white	elephant	when
chorus	whip	wheel
whale	photo	telephone

Words that rhyme

Blend the phonemes to read the words on the planets. Some of these words rhyme. Help the aliens get back to their spaceships. Colour the words that rhyme with the shaded word to show them the way.

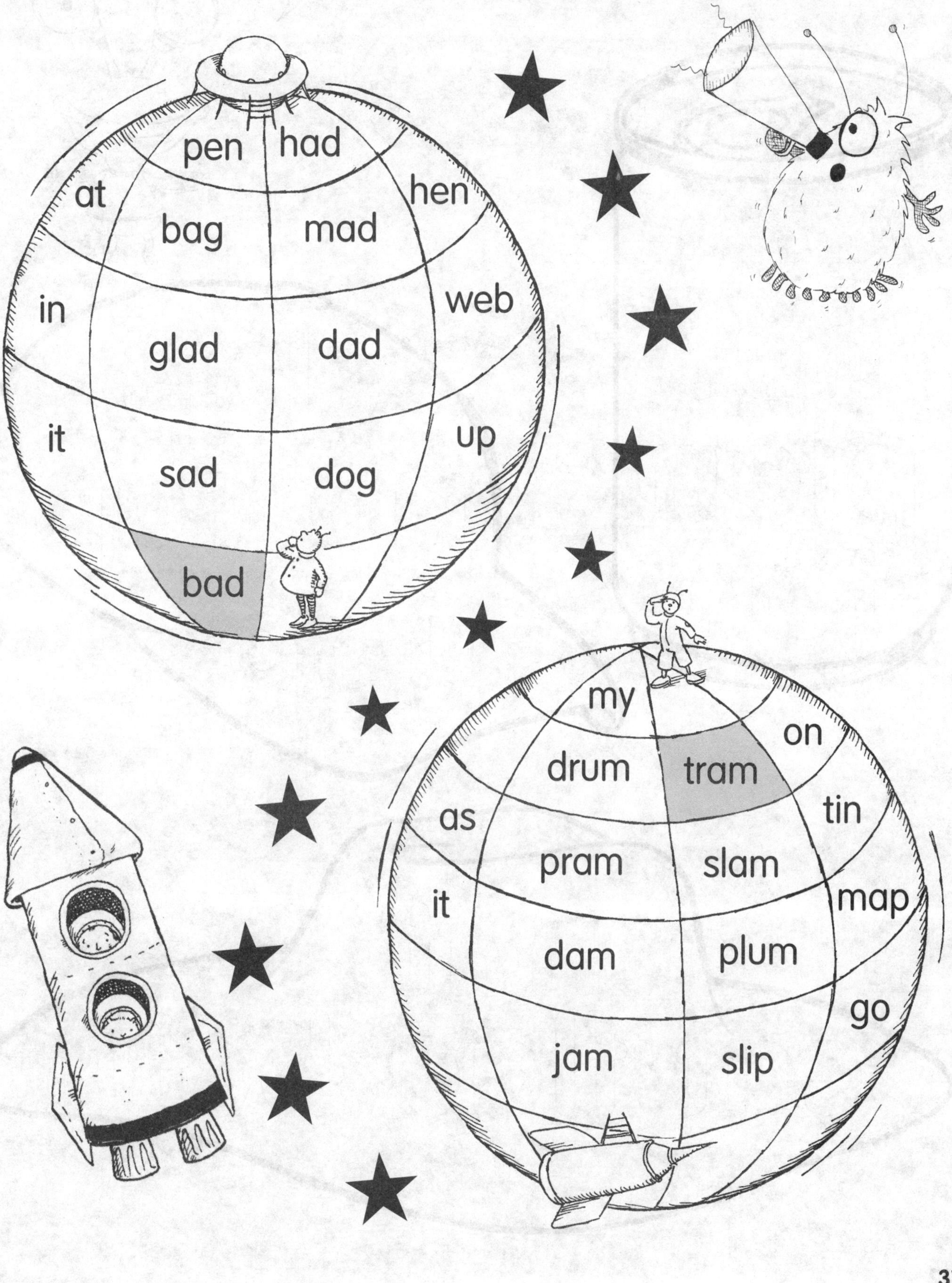

Words that rhyme

Blend the phonemes to read the words. Can you hear the words with the same middle and end phonemes? These words rhyme. Colour the words that rhyme in each group.

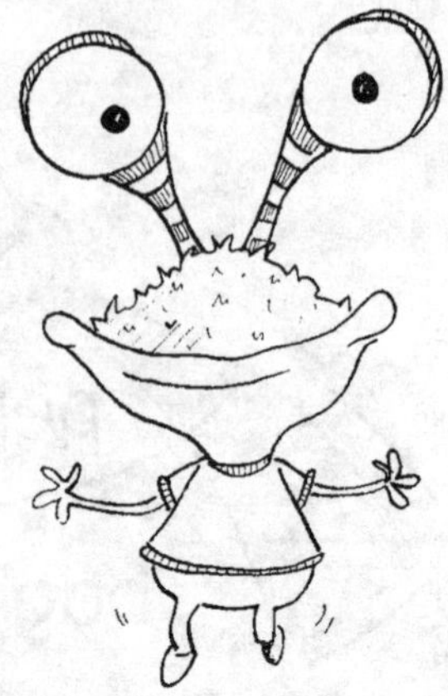

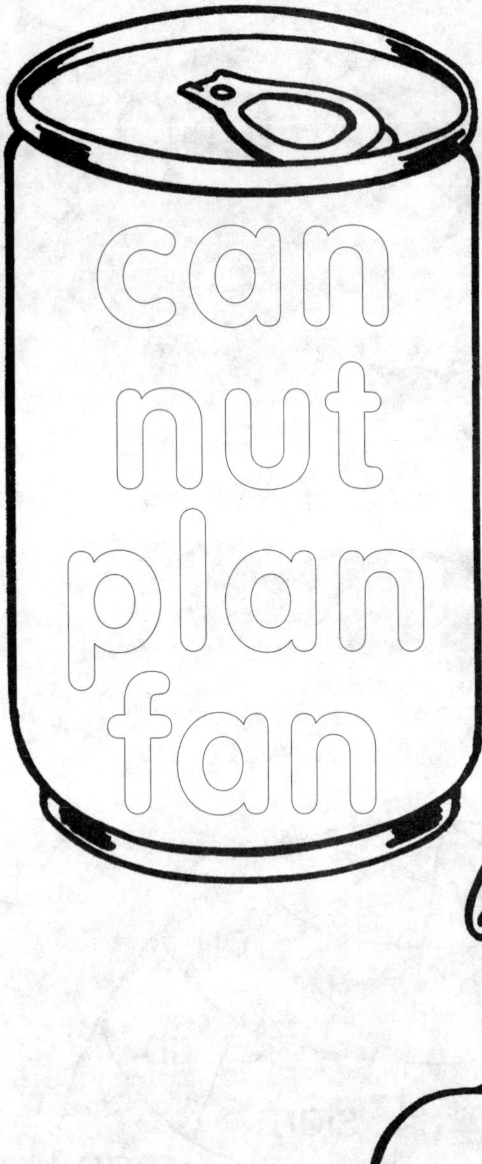

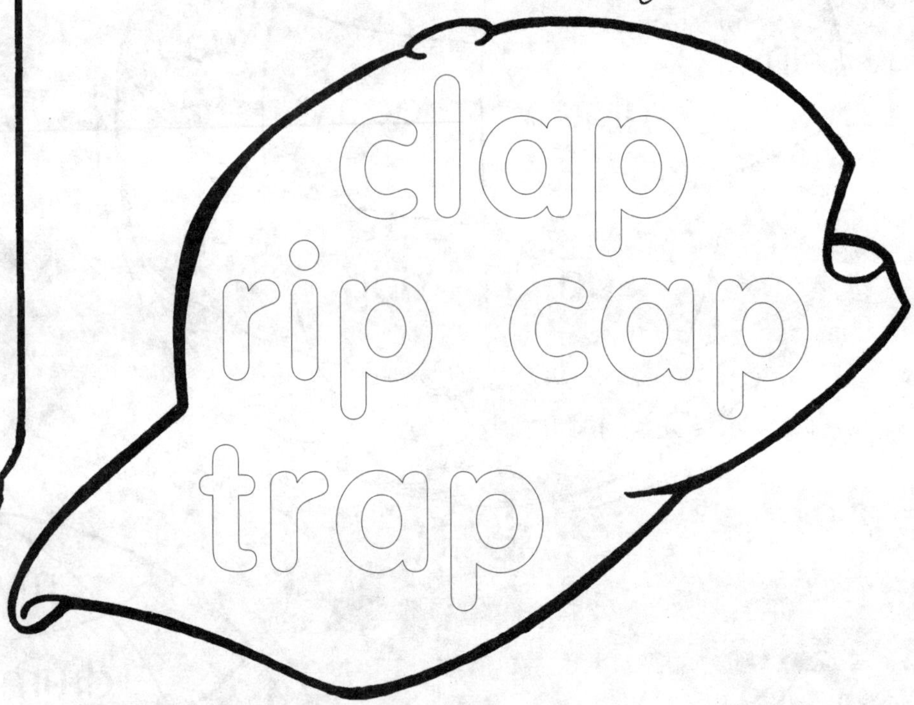

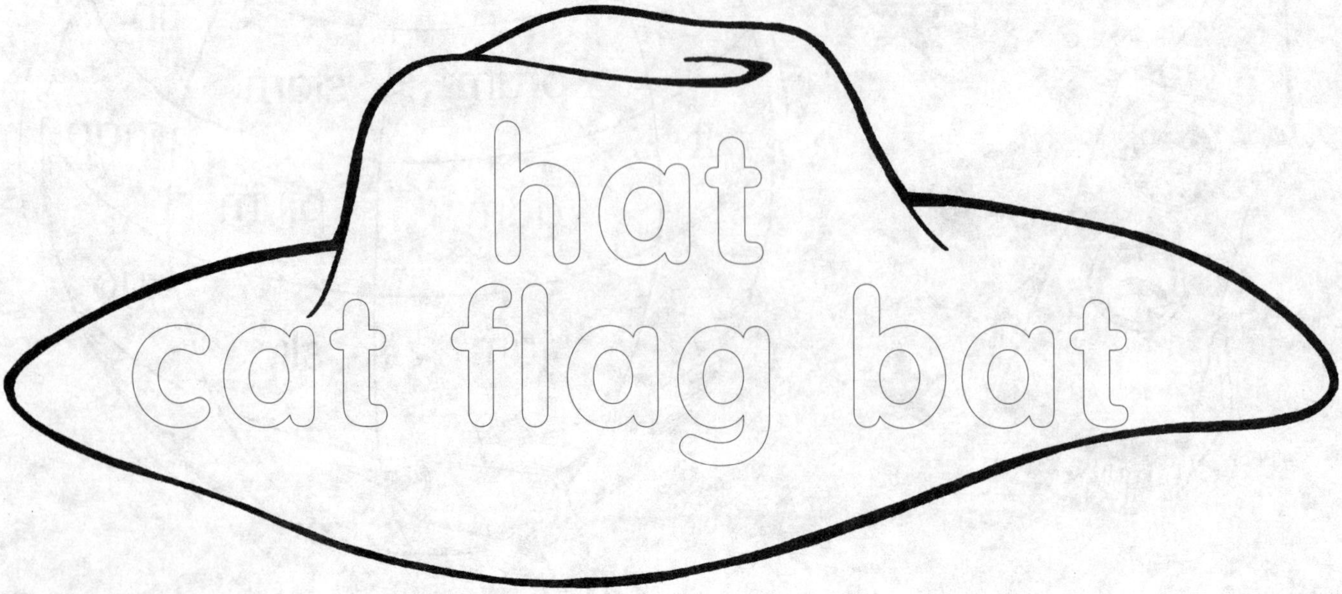

Words that rhyme

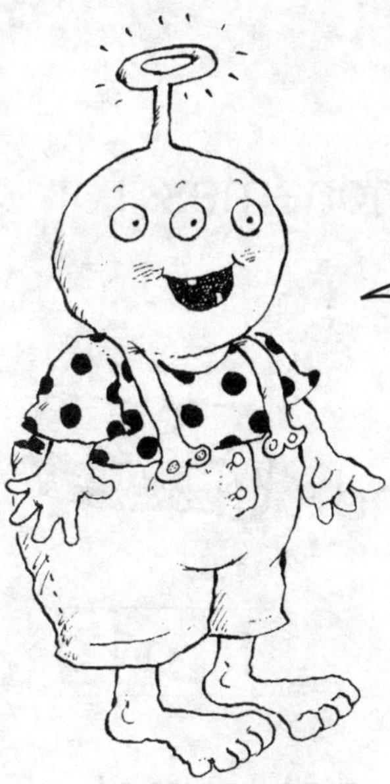

Blend the phonemes to read the words in the rockets. Can you hear the words with the same middle and end phonemes? These words rhyme. Join the words that rhyme from left to right. The first two words have been joined for you.

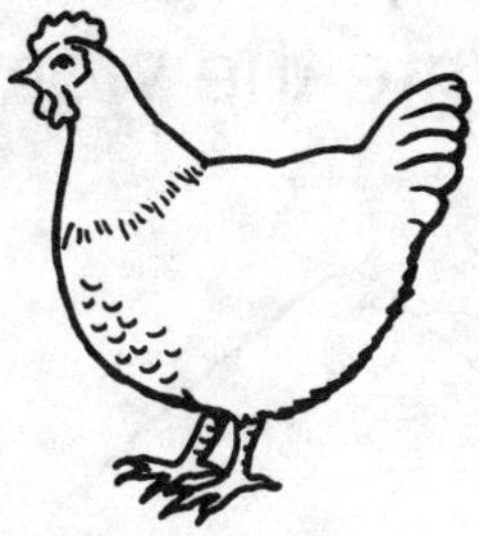

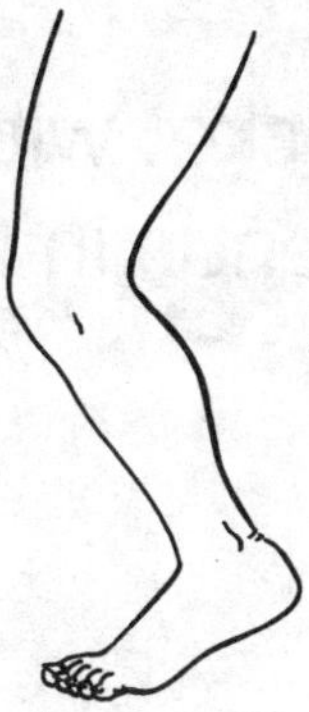

10

red ten shed fed

hen bed men peg

leg beg keg pen

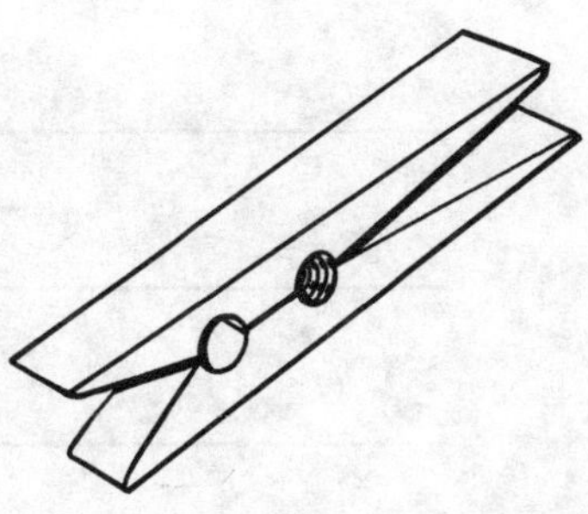

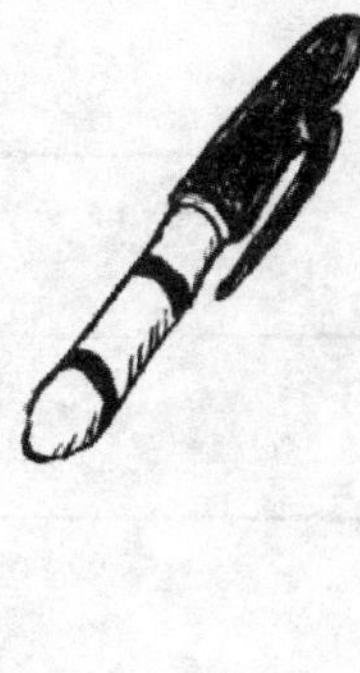

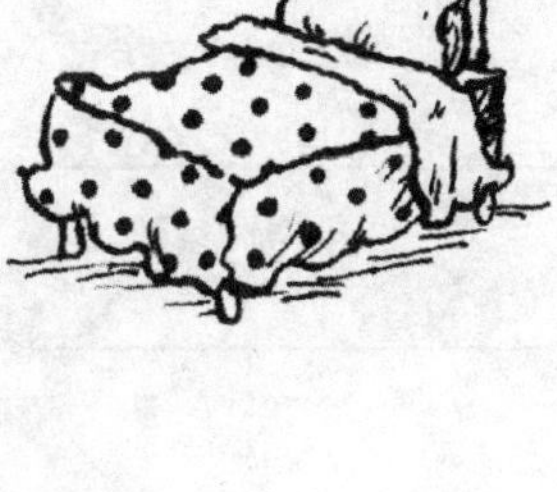

Words that rhyme

Words that rhyme have the same middle and end phonemes. For example:

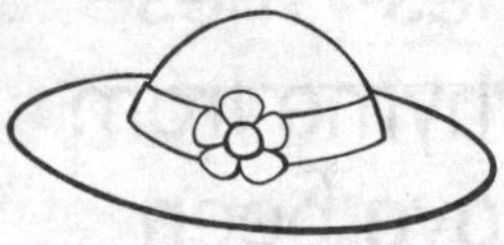 and 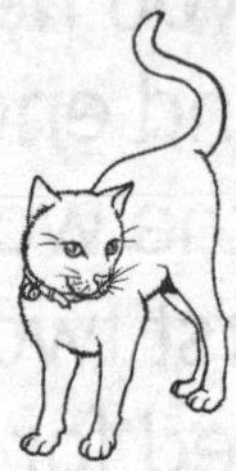

| h | a | t |

| c | a | t |

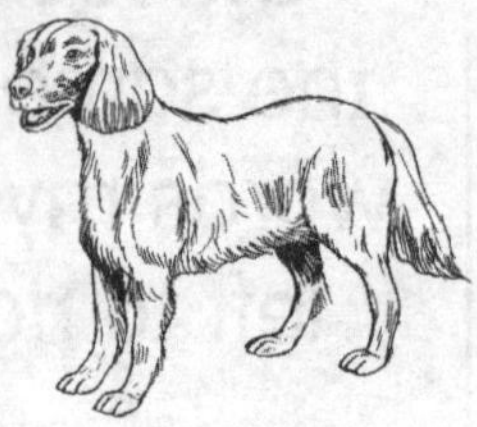 and 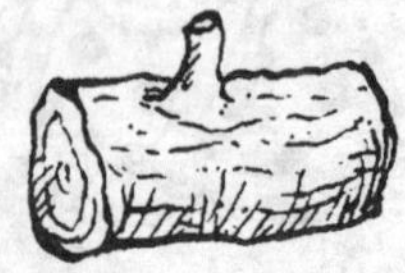

| d | o | g |

| l | o | g |

Use a phoneme from each rocket with the i in the planet to make words that rhyme with the blends in the stars. Write the words on the lines.

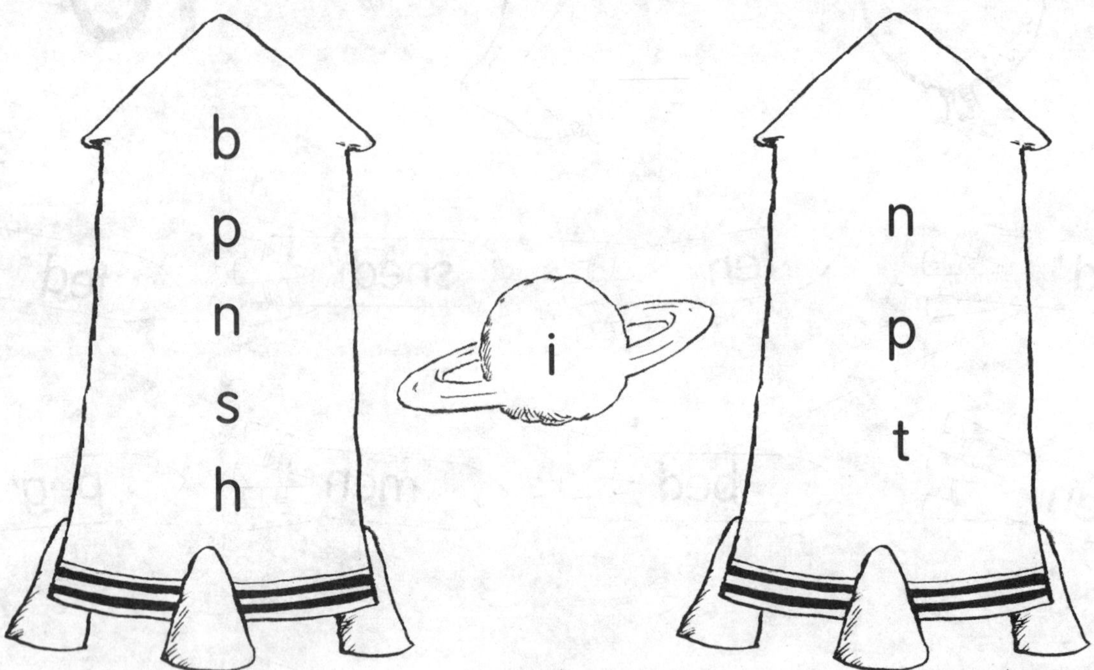

ip

in

it

______ ______ ______

______ ______ ______

______ ______ ______

______ ______ ______

______ ______ ______

Words that rhyme

Look at the pictures and say what they show. Can you hear the words with the same middle and end phonemes? These are words that rhyme. Write the first phoneme of each word. Join those that rhyme to the stars in the middle.

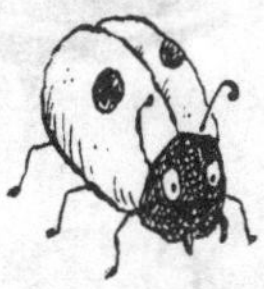

____ ox

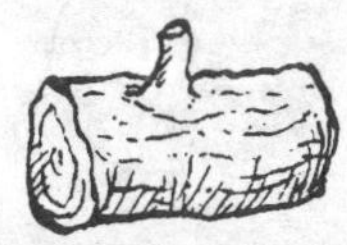

____ og

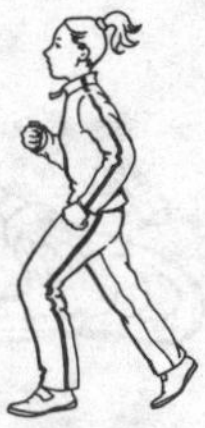

____ og

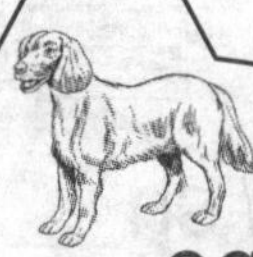

____ og

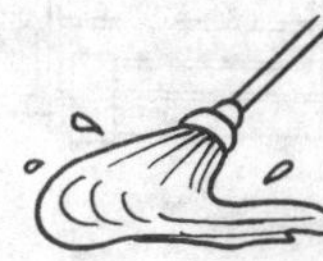

____ op

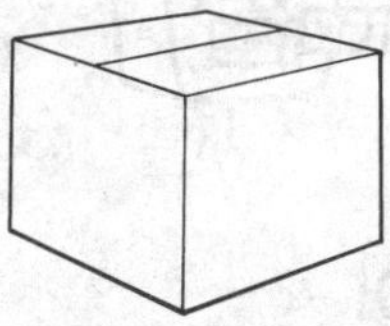

____ ox

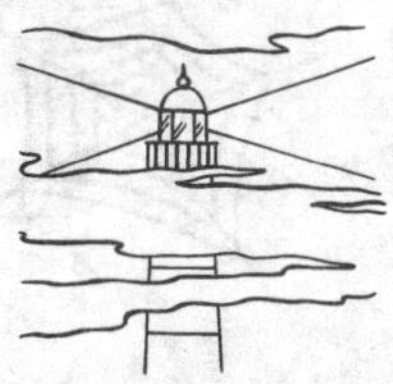

____ og

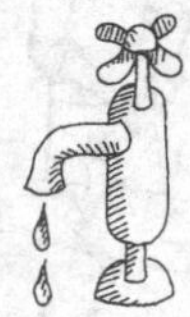

____ ap

★★★★★★★★★★★★★★★★★★★★★★★★★

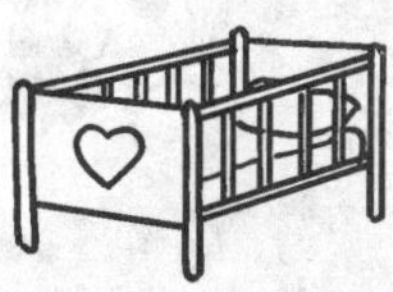

____ ot

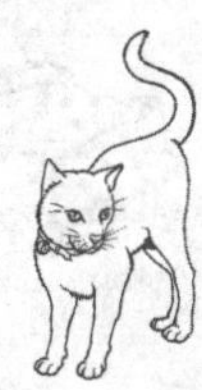

____ at

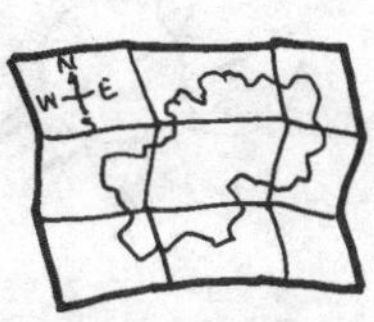

____ ap

____ ot

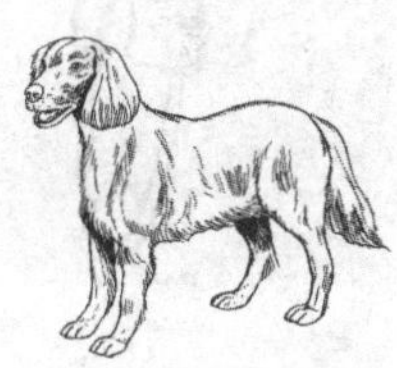

____ og

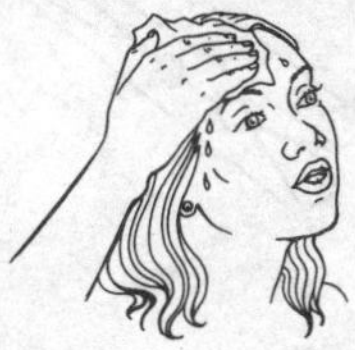

____ ot

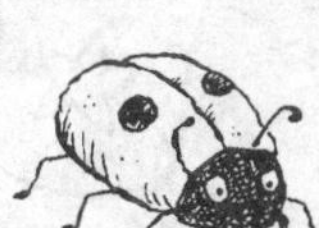

____ ug

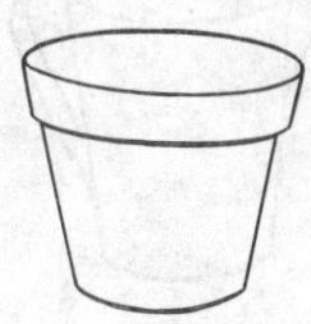

____ ot

Words that rhyme

Write in the middle and end phonemes. Blend the phonemes and say the words. Circle the pictures that rhyme with the word in the star.

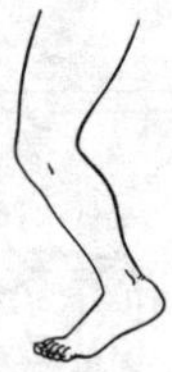

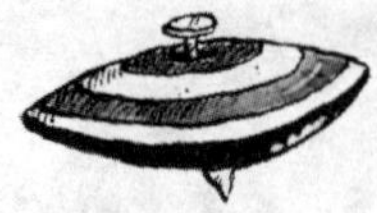

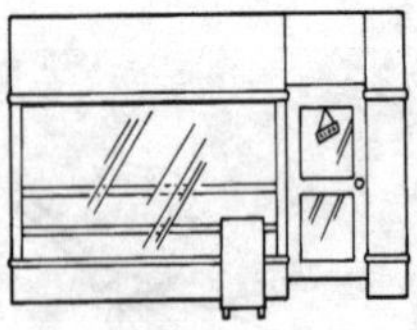

l ___ ___

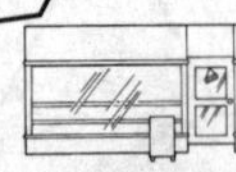

sh ___ ___

t ___ ___

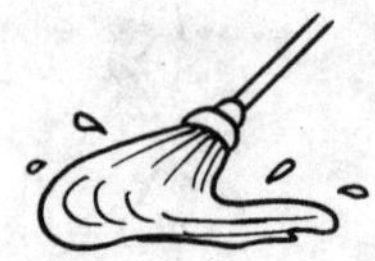

b ___ ___

m ___ ___

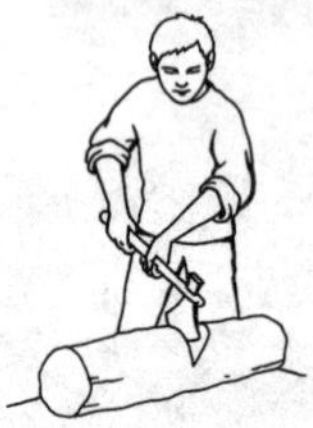

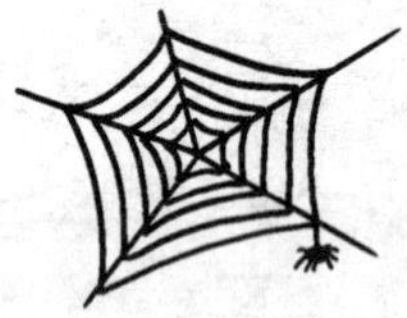

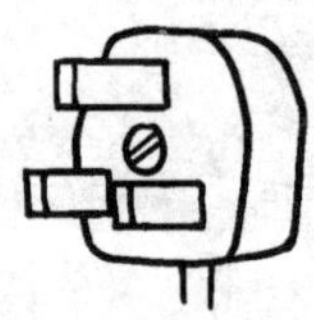

ch ___ ___

w ___ ___

pl ___ ___

★ ★

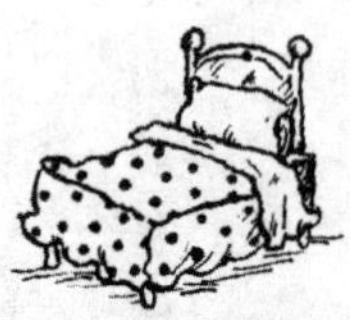

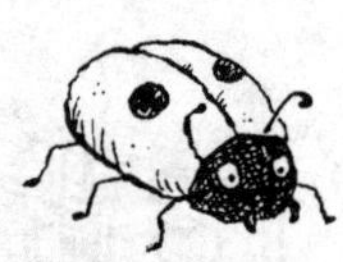

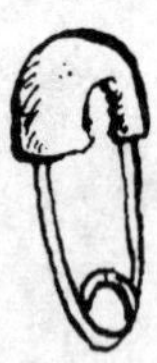

b ___ ___

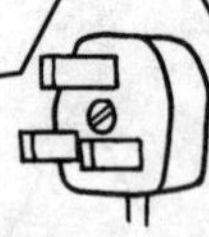

pl ___ ___

b ___ ___

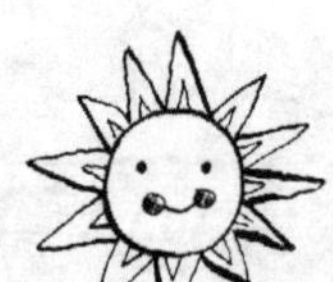

p ___ ___

s ___ ___

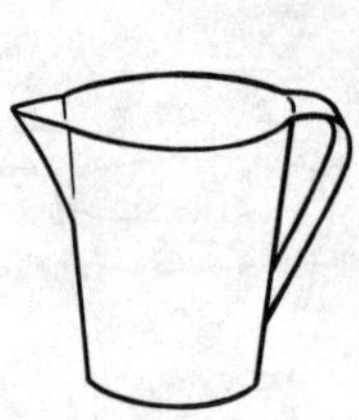

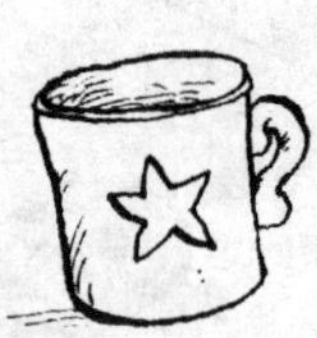

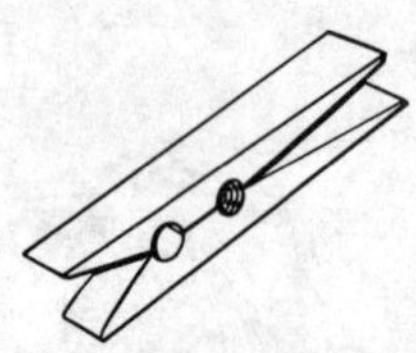

j ___ ___

m ___ ___

p ___ ___

Words that rhyme

Look at the pictures in the stars and read the word. Can you hear the middle and end phonemes? Look at the words at the bottom of the page. Write the words with the same middle and end phonemes in the spaceships next to the pictures.

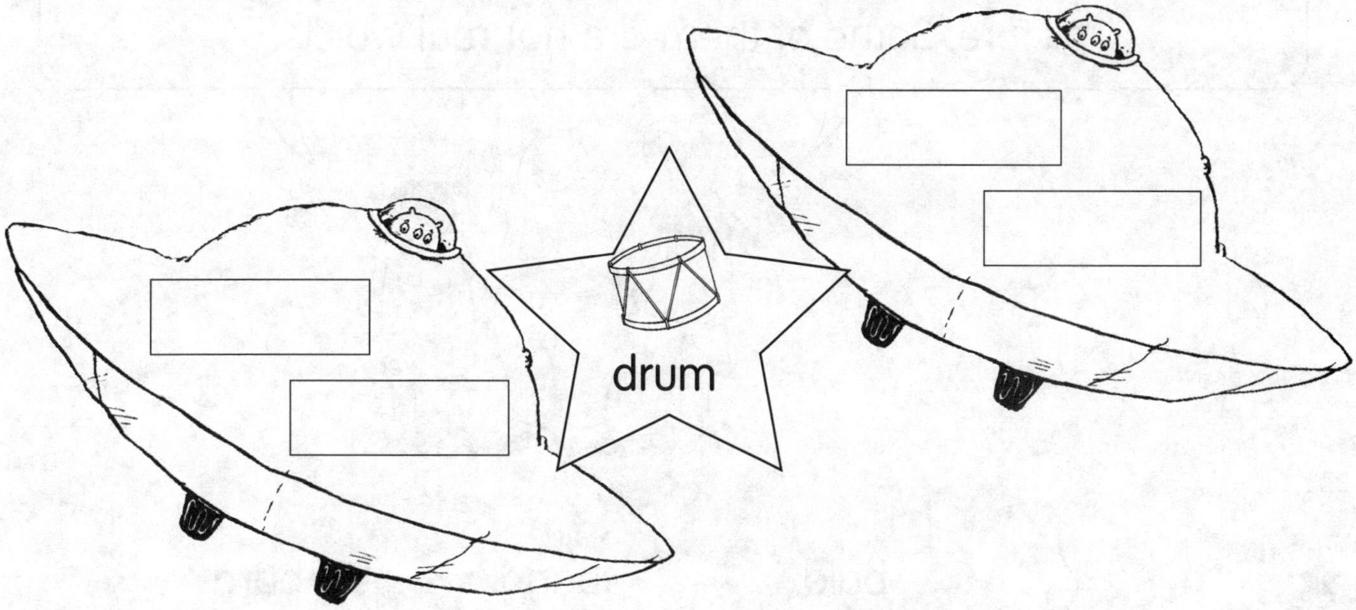

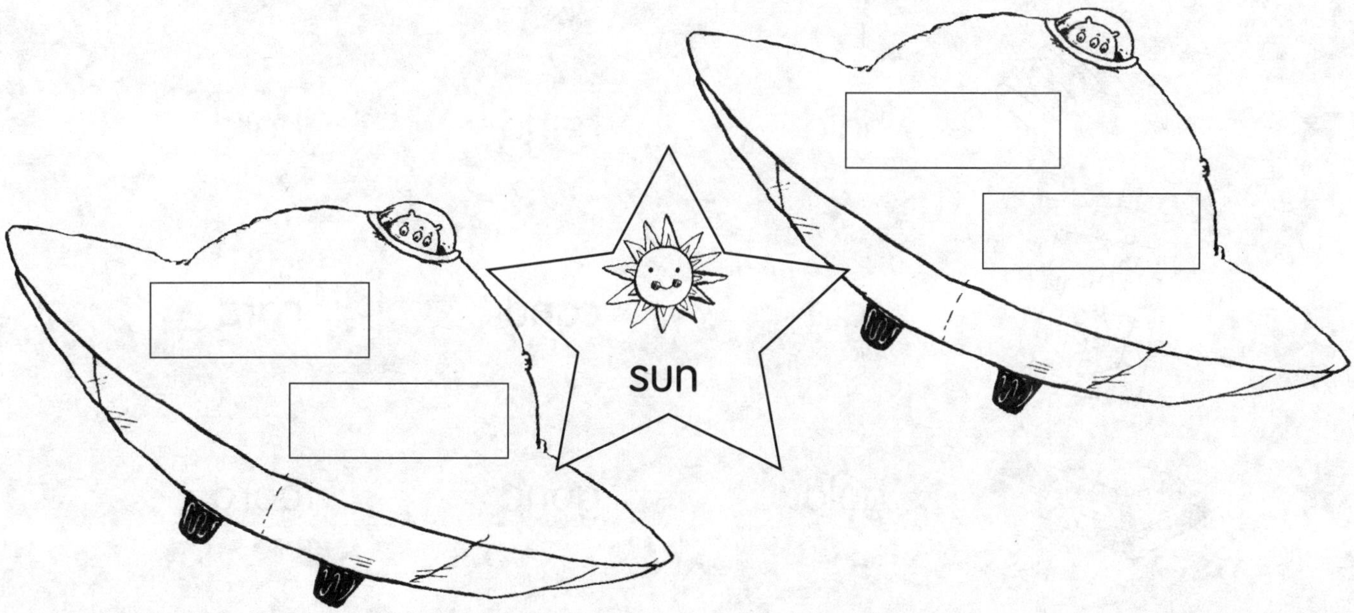

bun	plum	gum	fun
run	gun	sum	mum

Words that end in ld, nd and rd

Look at the pictures and say what they show. Blend the phonemes and say the words. Can you hear the phonemes at the ends of the words? Circle the correct word for each picture. Some of them are not real words.

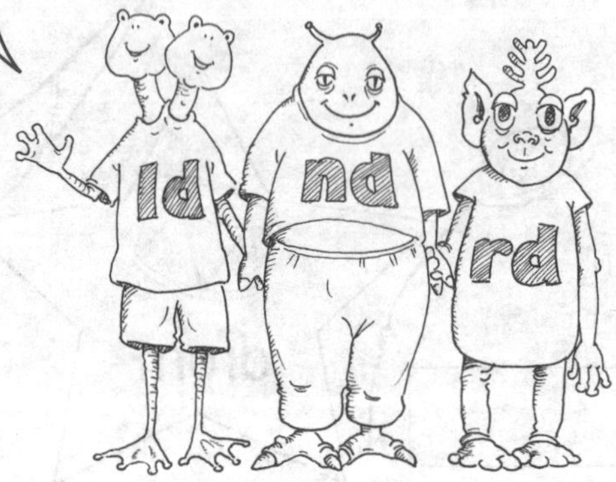

1 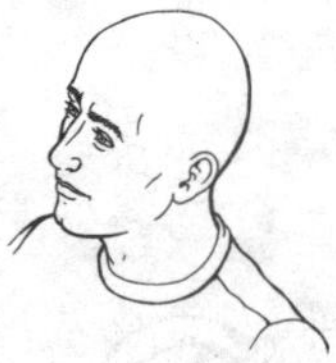 bald band bard

2 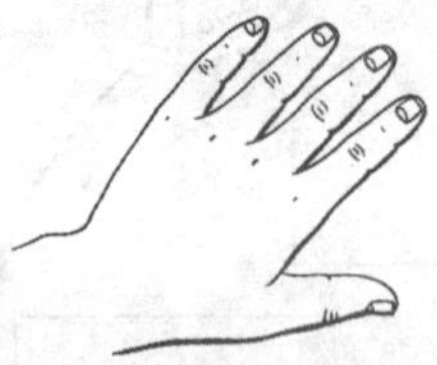 hald hand hard

3 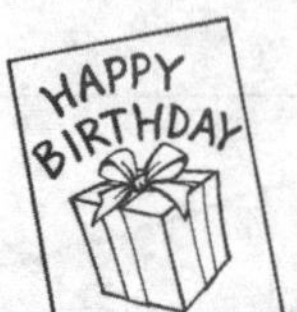

cald cand card

4 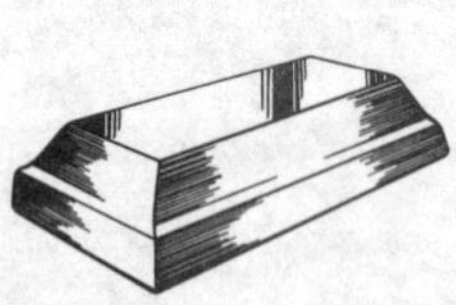 gold gond gord

5 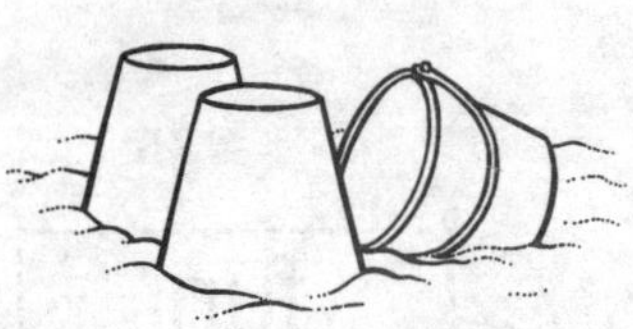 sald sand sard

6 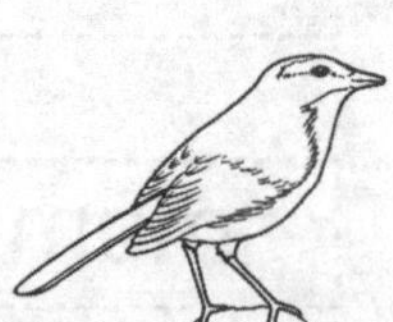 bild bind bird

Words that end in lk, nk and rk

Blend the phonemes to read the words at the bottom of the page. Look at the pictures and say what they show. Write the words by the pictures. One has been done for you.

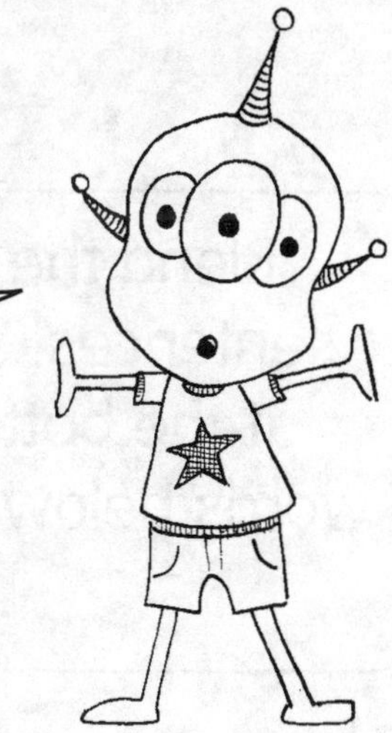

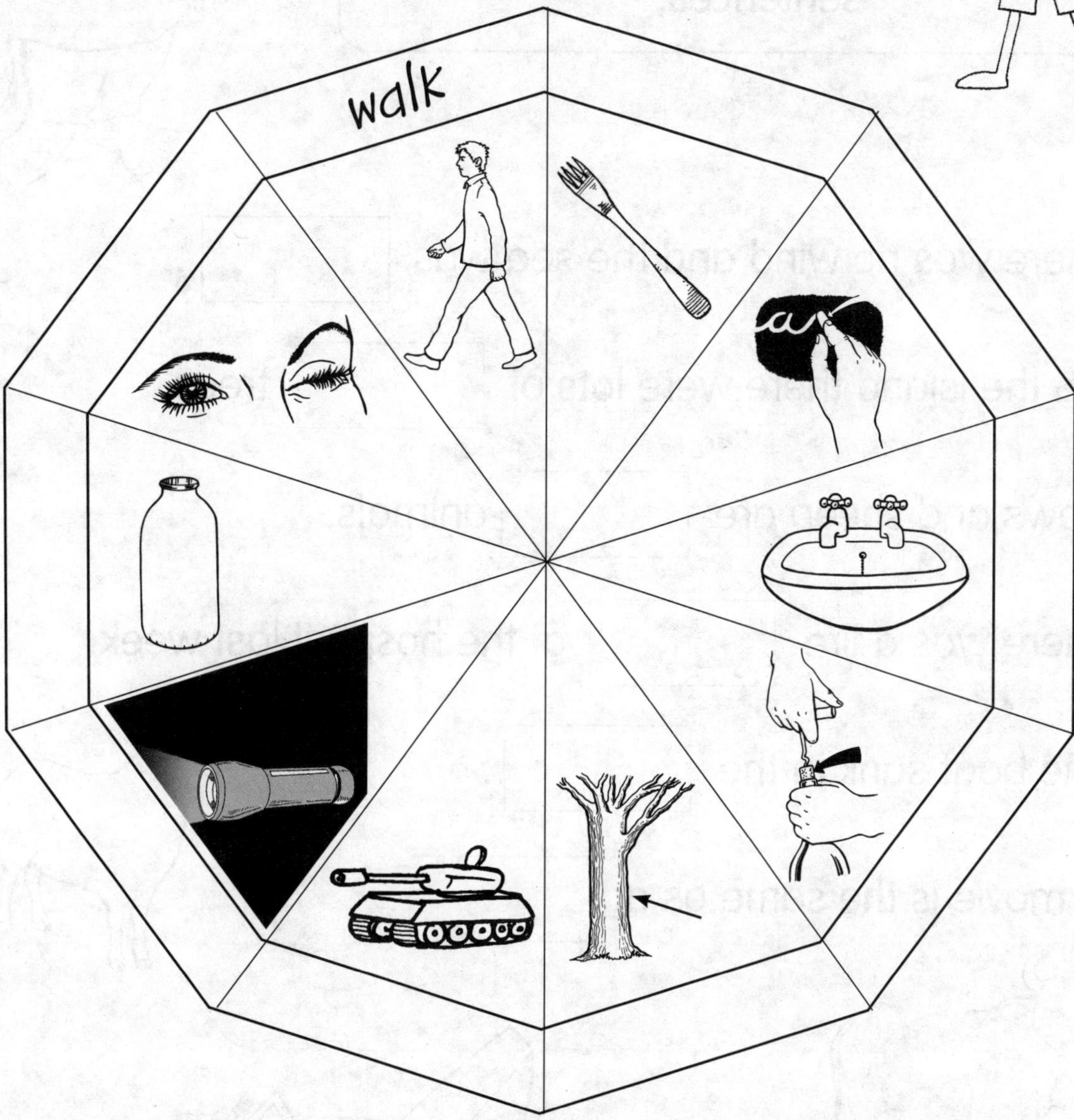

trunk	chalk	tank
cork	dark	milk
sink	fork	wink

Words that end in lm and rm

Blend the phonemes and read the sentences. Say the words in the boxes at the bottom of the page. Write the words below in the correct boxes to form sentences.

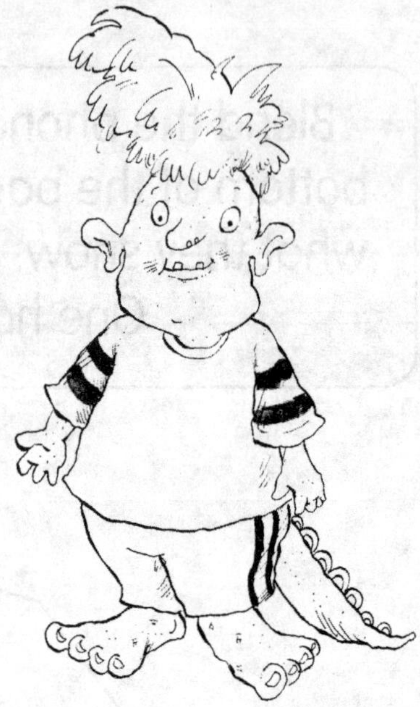

1. There was no wind and the sea was ______ .
2. On the island there were lots of ______ trees.
3. Cows and sheep are ______ animals.
4. There was a fire ______ at the hospital last week.
5. The boat sank in the ______ .
6. A movie is the same as a ______ .

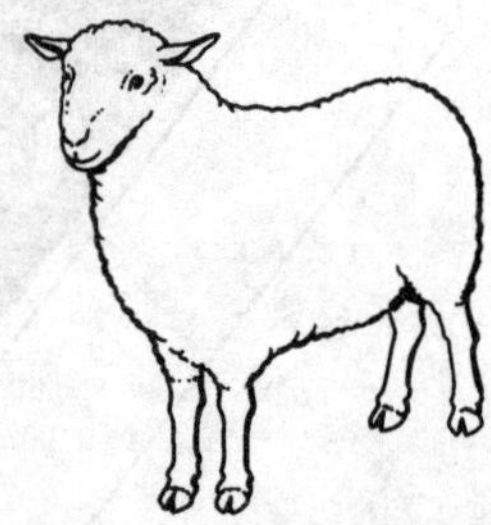

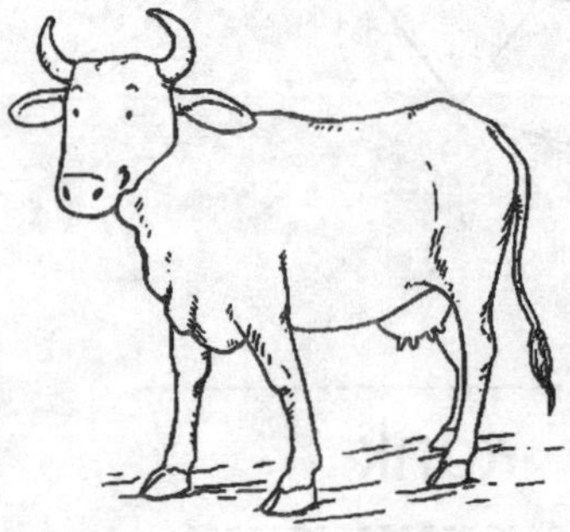

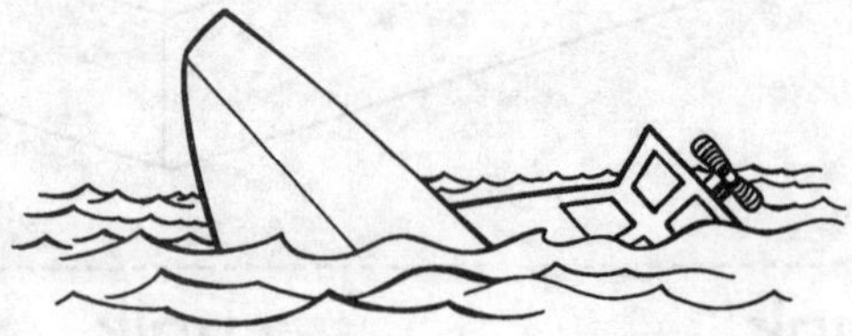

film	alarm	calm	palm	storm	farm

Words that end in lp, mp, rp and sp

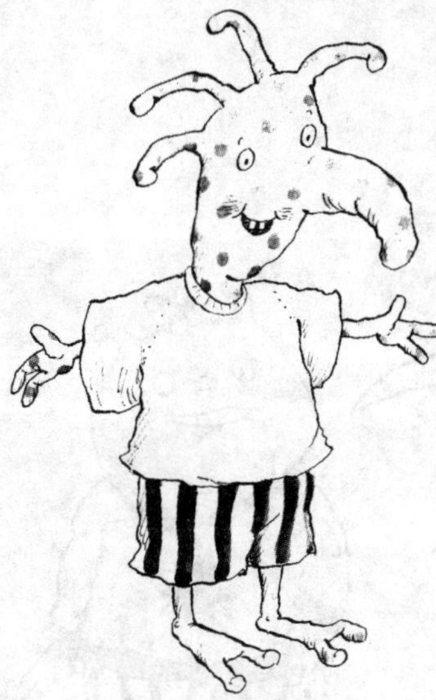

Blend the phonemes to read the words in the rockets. Write the words in the spaceships so that they rhyme.

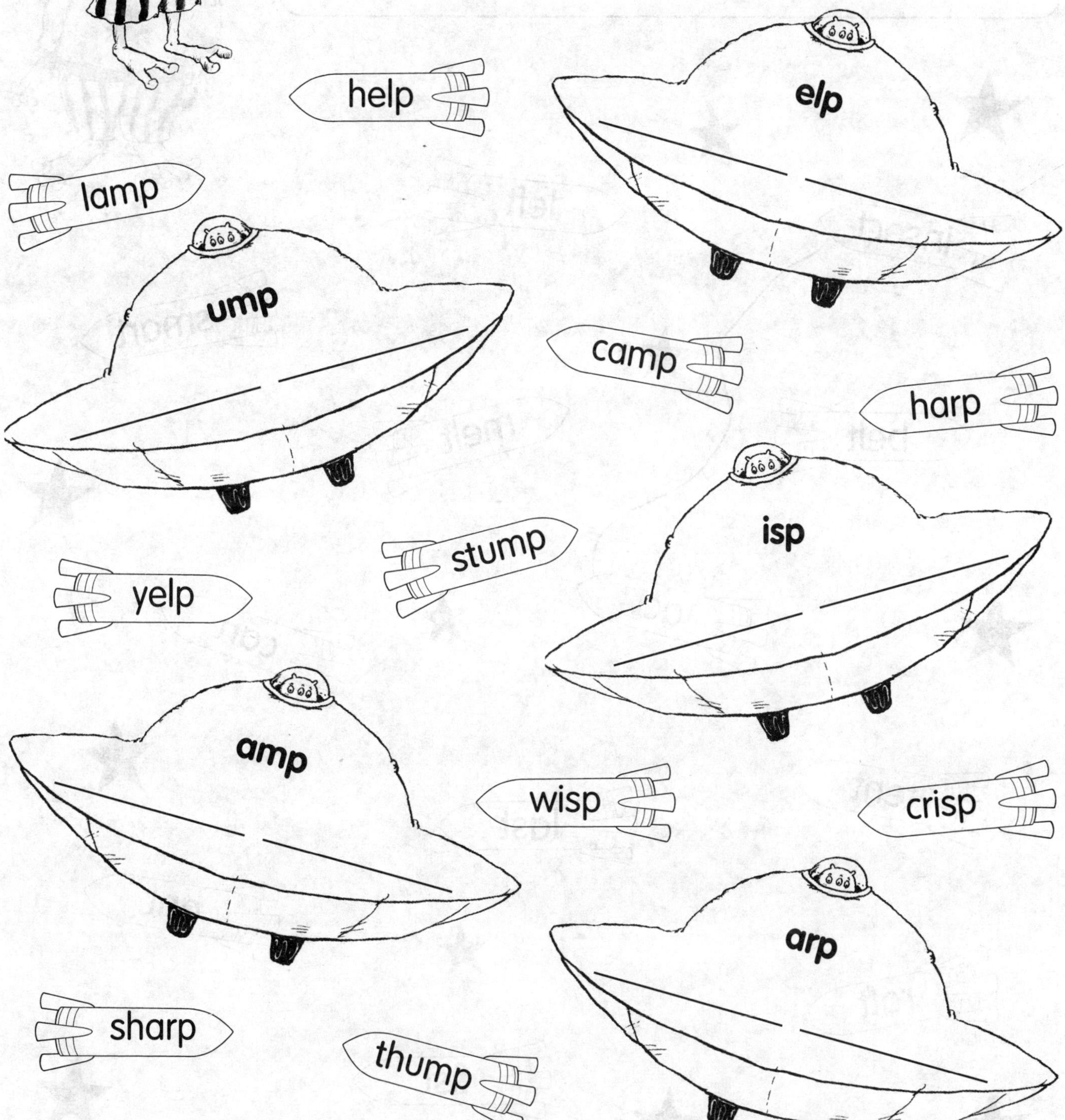

Words that end in ct, ft, lt, nt, rt and st

Read the words in the rockets. Can you hear the blends at the end of the words? Join the pairs of words which have the same final blends. One pair has been joined for you.

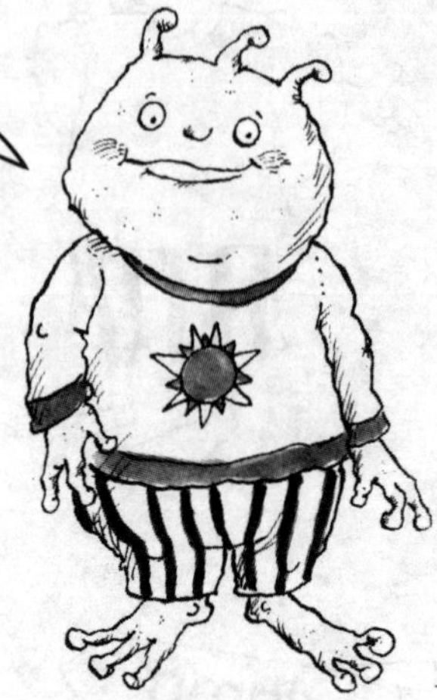

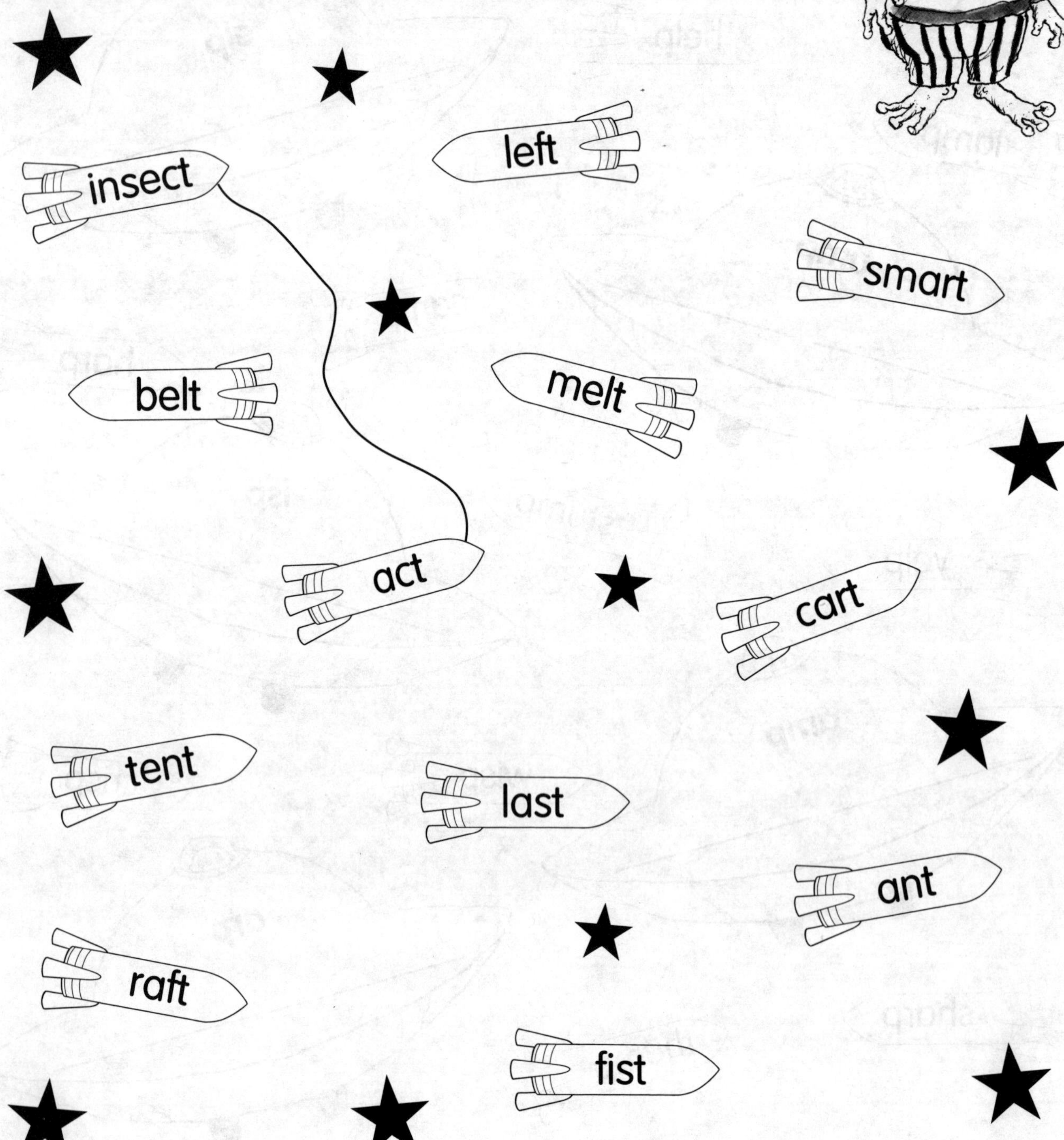

Words that end in nch, rch and tch

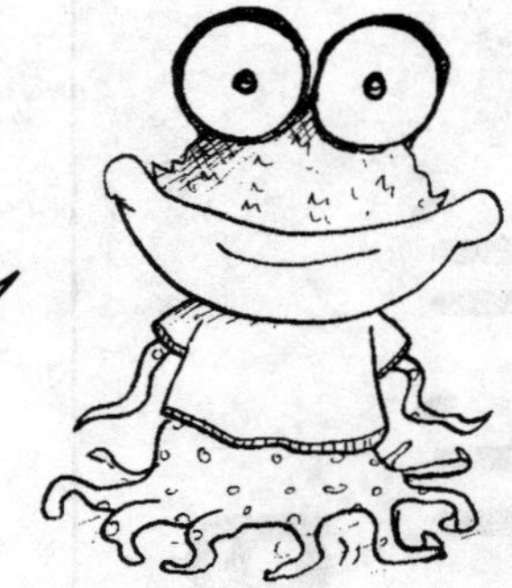

Look at the pictures and say what they show. Blend the phonemes to read the words in the planets. Can you hear the phonemes at the end of the word? Circle the correct picture for each word.

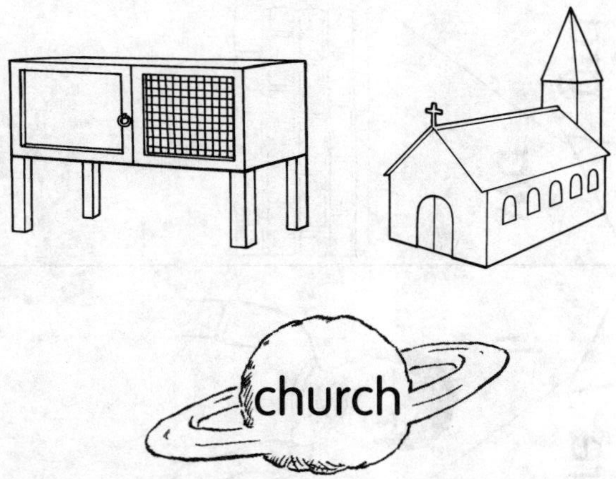

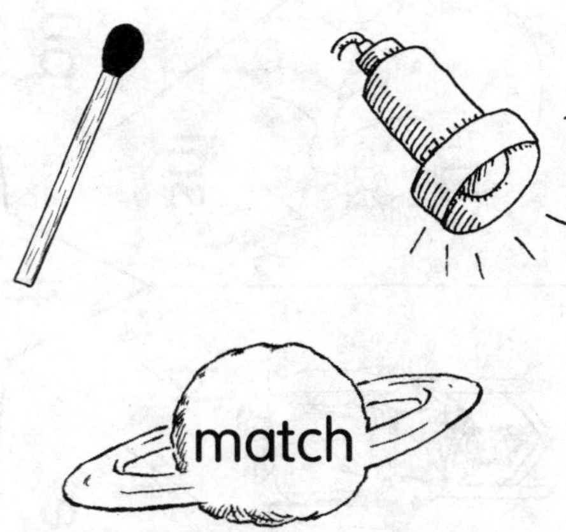

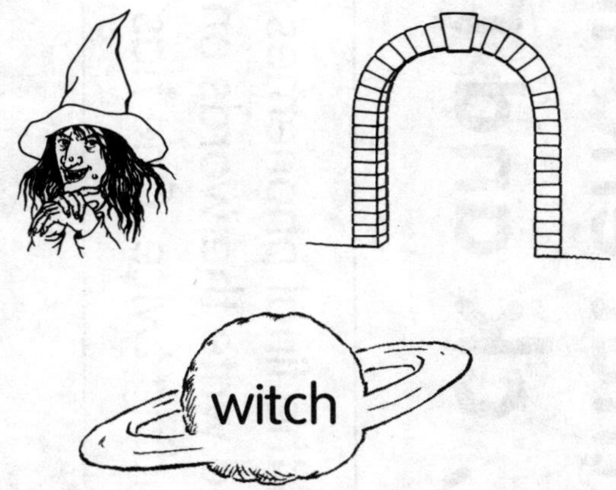

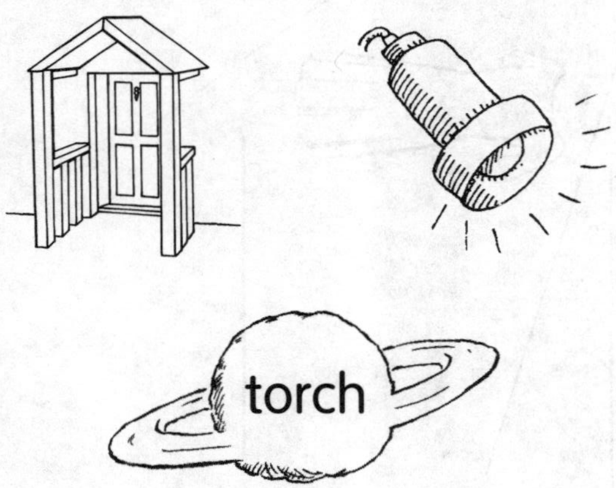

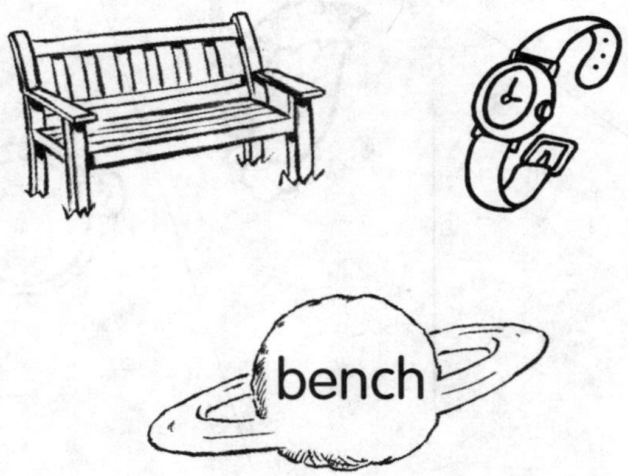

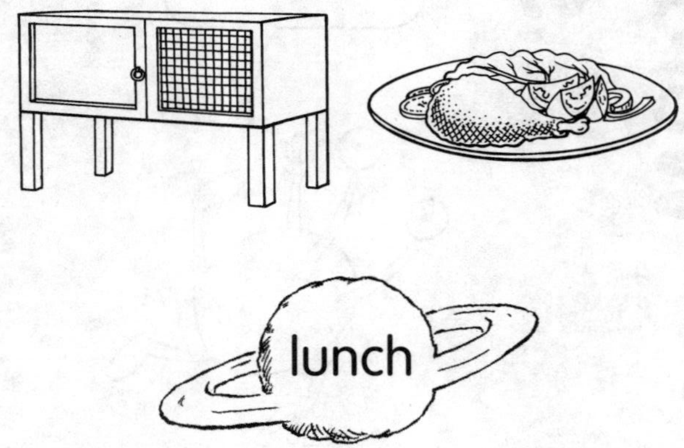

Words that end in ff, ll, ss, ck and ng

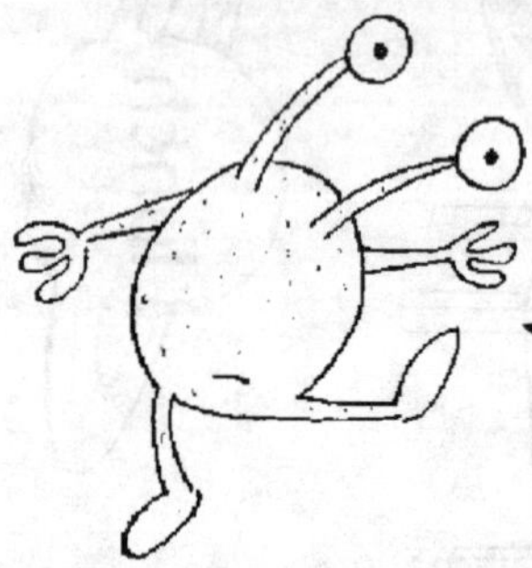

Add the final phonemes to these letter strings and write the words on the lines. Use each ending twice. One has been done for you.

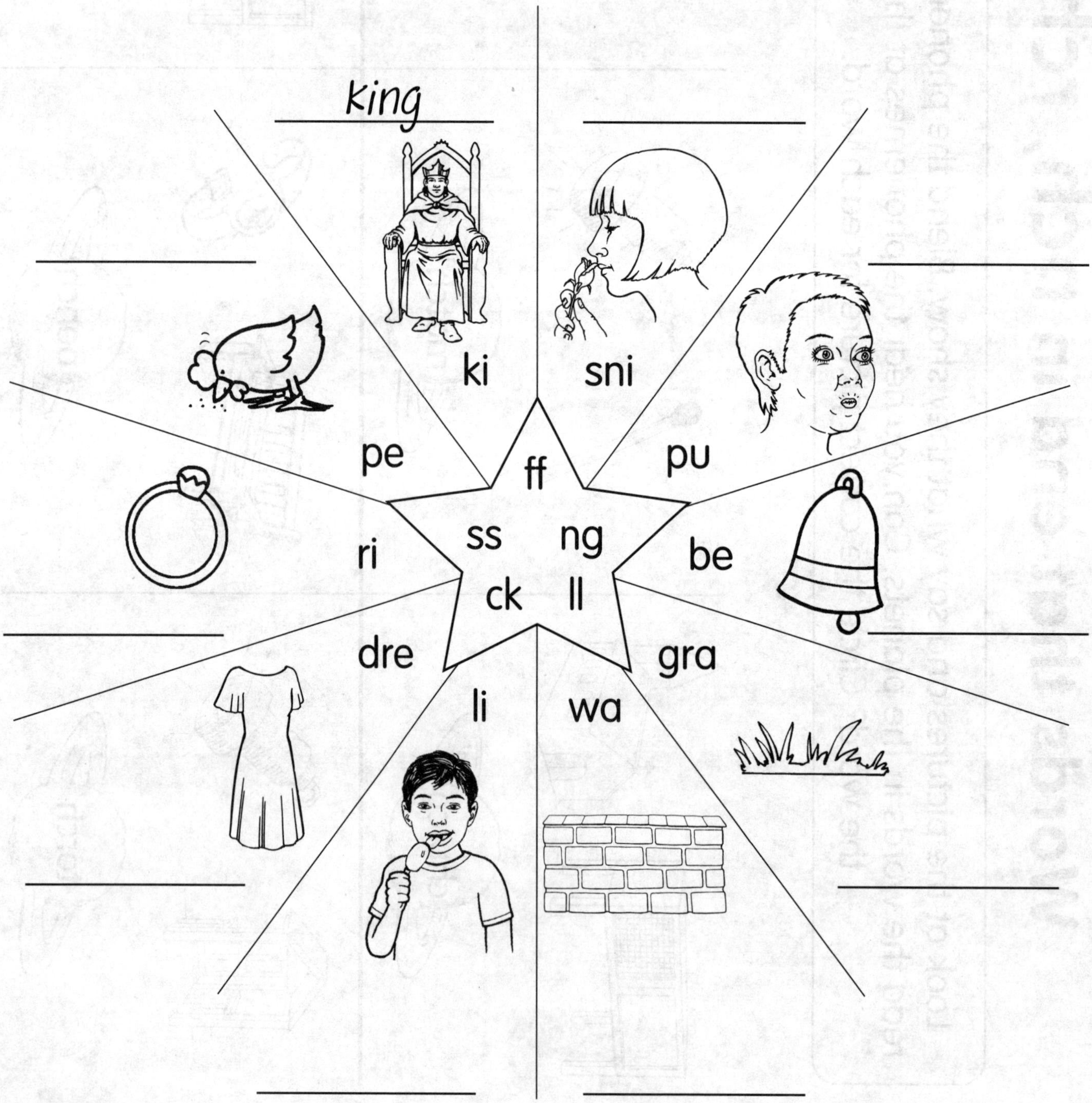

Words that end in ck

Blend the phonemes to read the words in the word bank. Can you hear **ck** at the end of the words? Write the words in the pictures so that they rhyme.

Word bank

black check pack suck quick pick block
rock duck shock lick snack deck neck luck

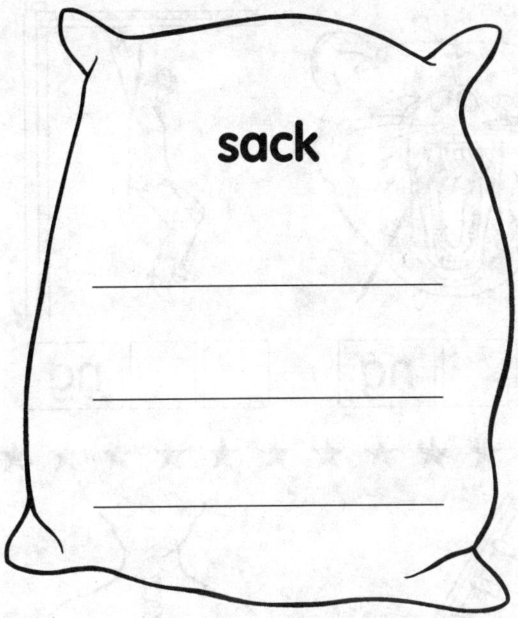

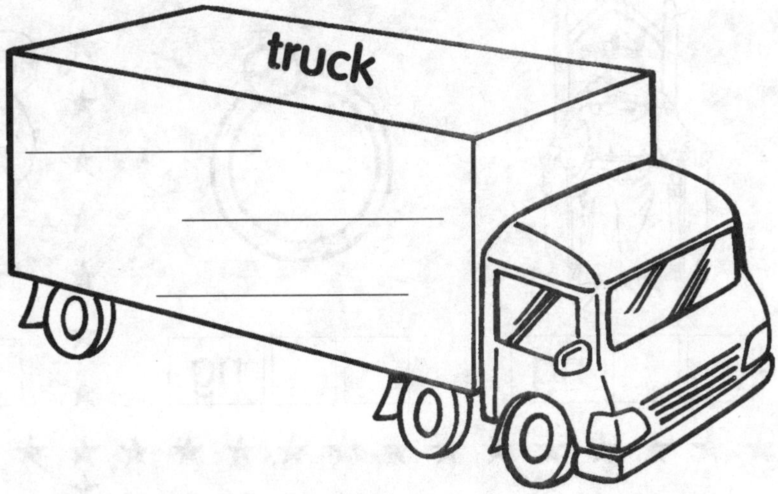

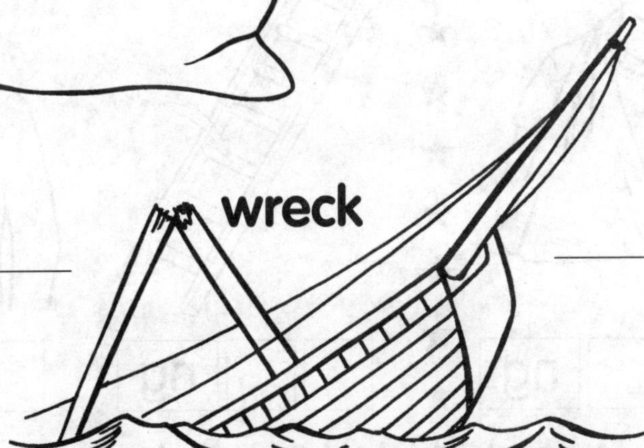

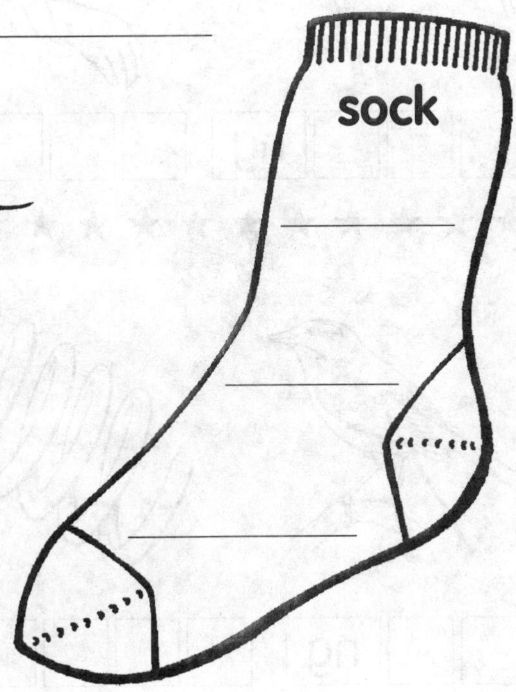

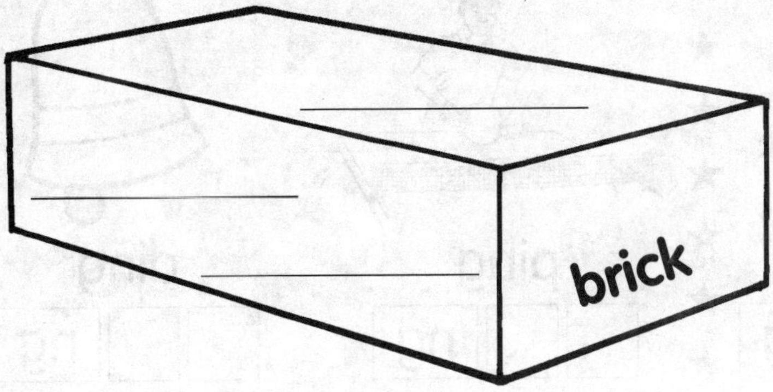

Words that end in **ng**

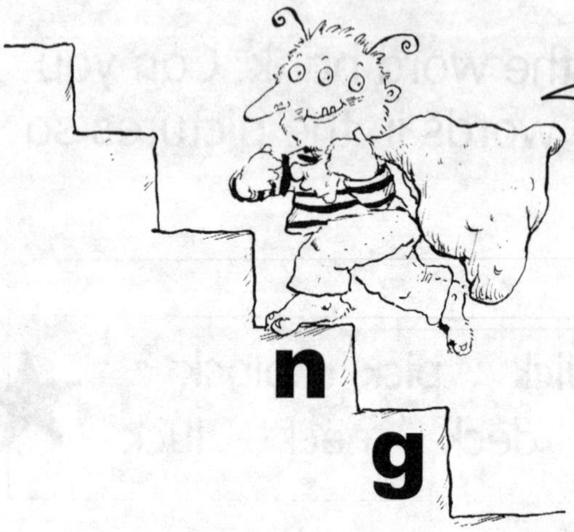

Look at the pictures and say what they show. Write the missing phonemes to make pairs of rhyming words. All the words end in **ng**.

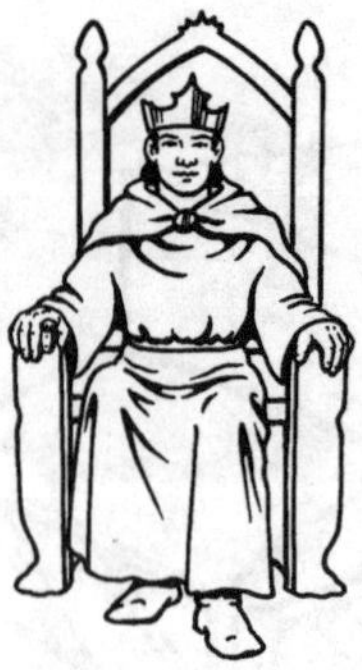

[ ] [ ] ng

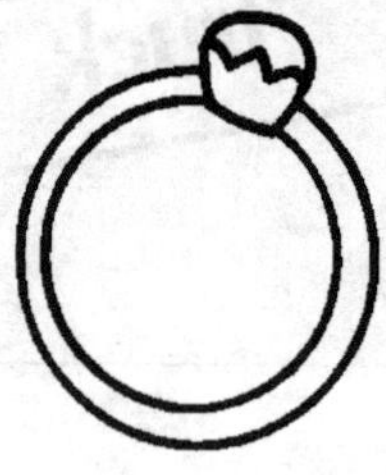

[ ] [ ] ng

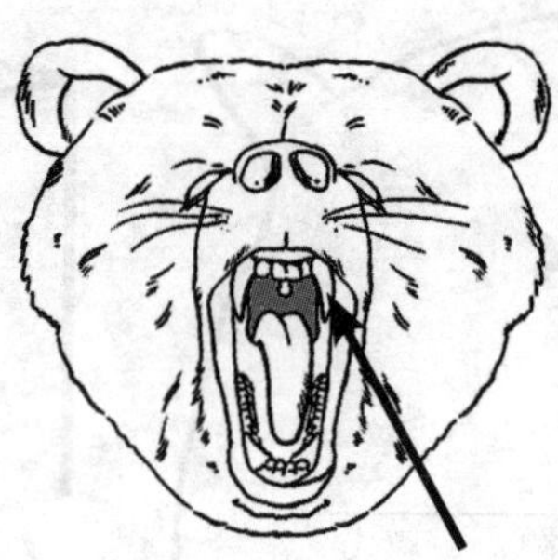

[ ] [ ] ng

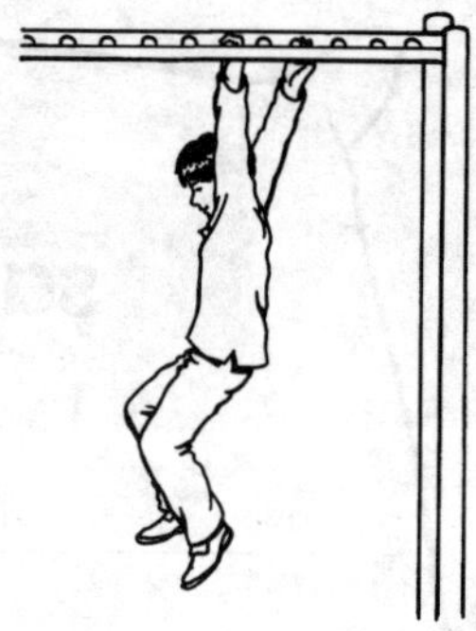

[ ] [ ] ng

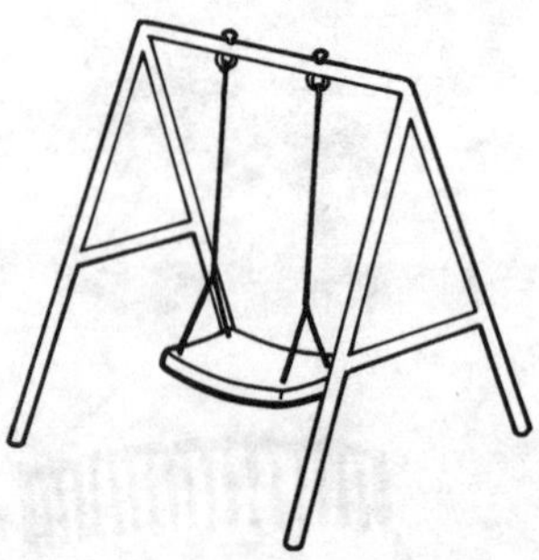

[ ] [ ] [ ] ng

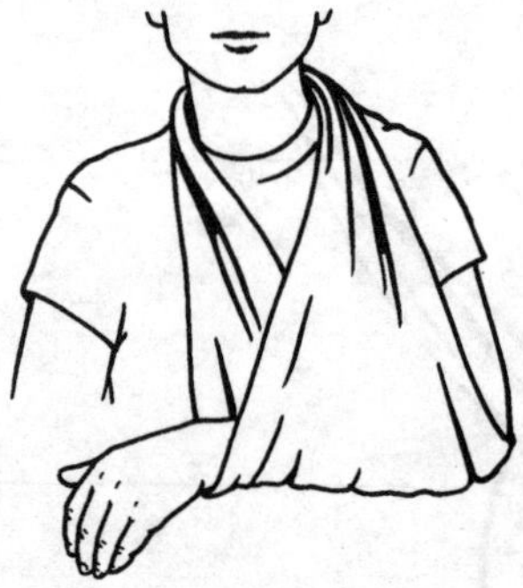

[ ] [ ] [ ] ng

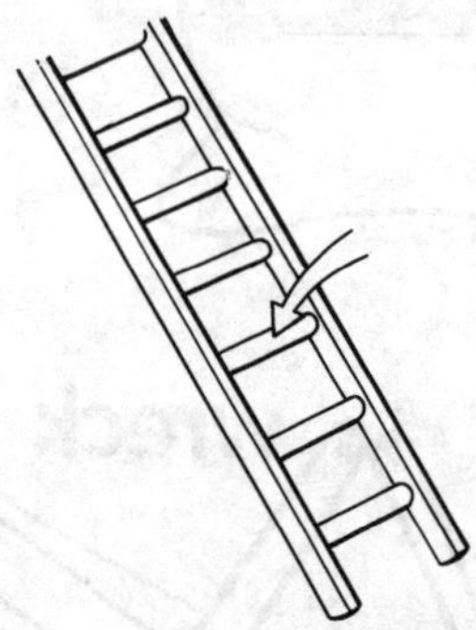

[ ] [ ] ng

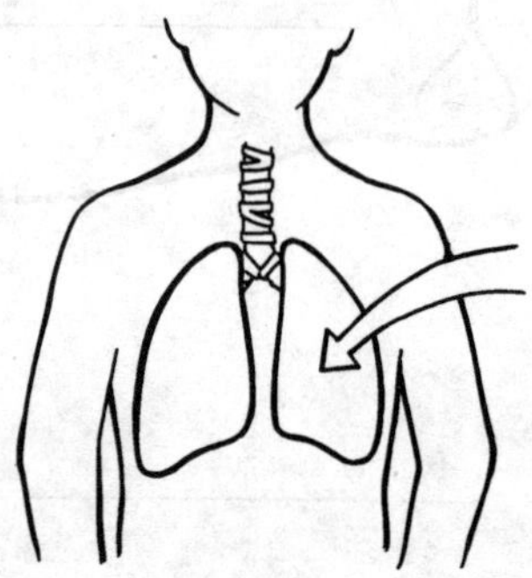

[ ] [ ] ng

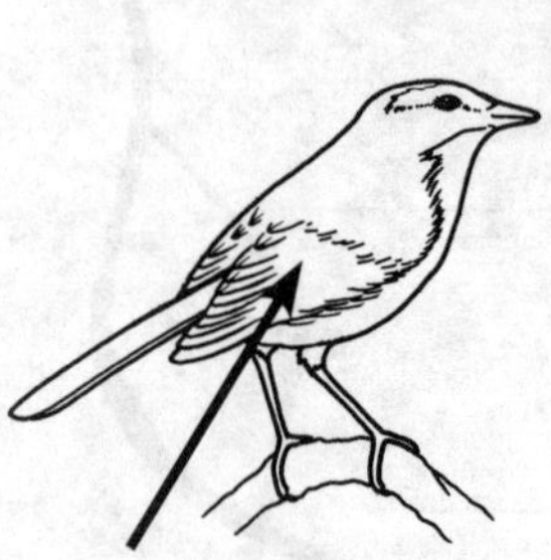

[ ] [ ] ng

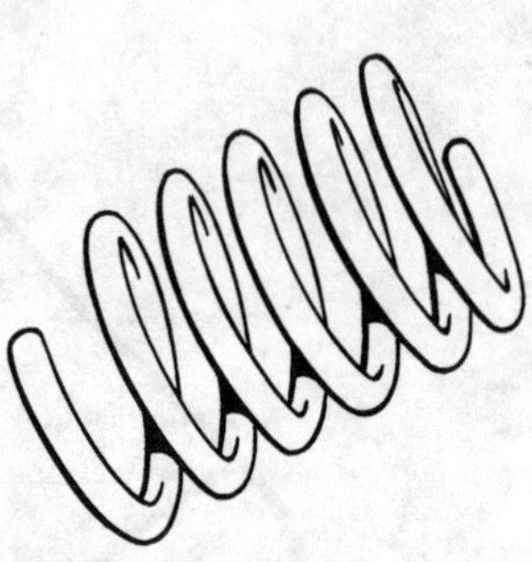

[ ] [ ] [ ] [ ] ng

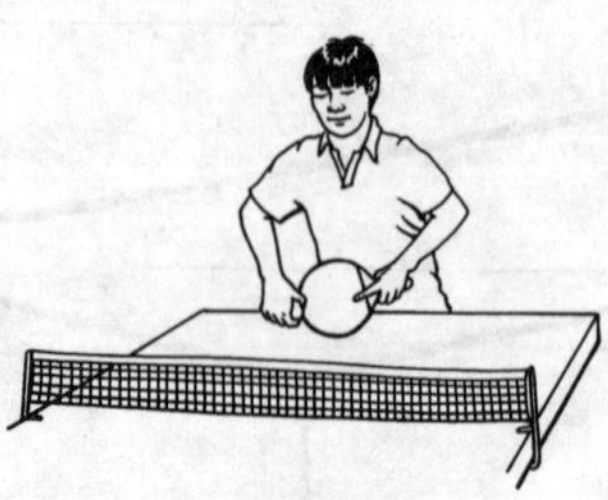

ping

[ ] [ ] ng

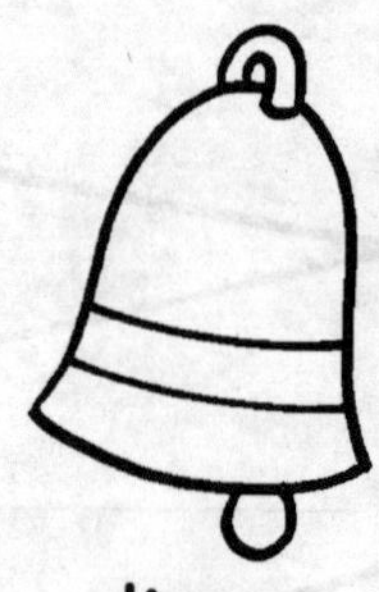

ding

[ ] [ ] ng

Hard and soft g

Blend the phonemes to read these words:

g a t e

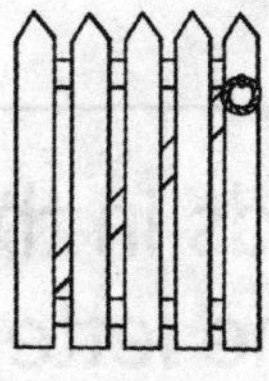

c a g e

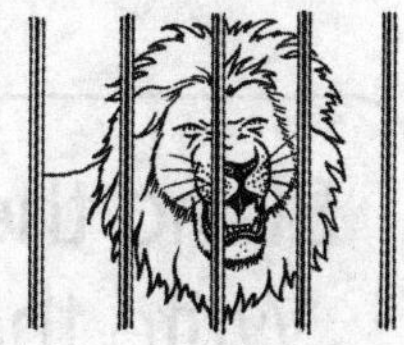

b a g

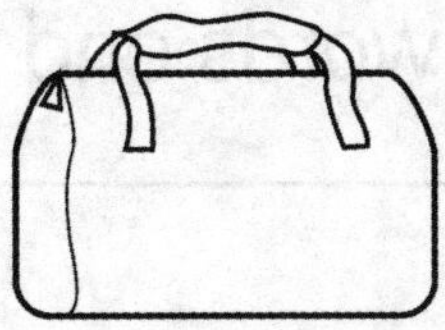

g e m

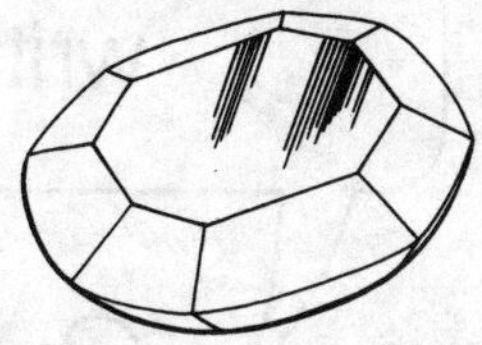

Can you hear the different **g** phonemes? The words ***g**ate* and *ba**g*** have a **hard g**. The words *cage* and ***g**em* have a **soft g**. This sounds like the phoneme **j**.

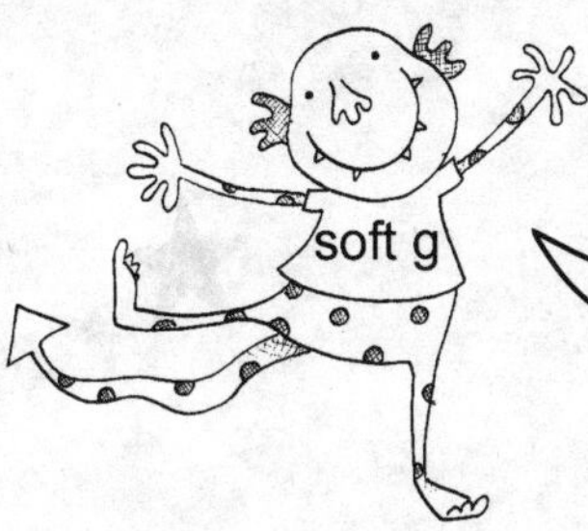

Blend the phonemes to read these words. Colour the **hard g** phoneme green. Colour the **soft g** phoneme red.

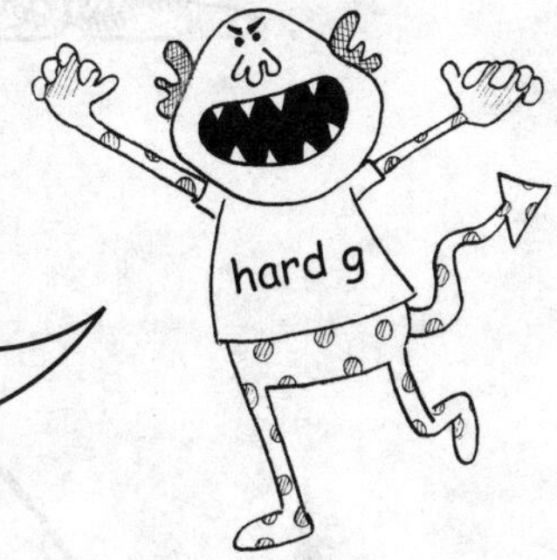

go page girl

dog germ bag

garage cage

The ai phoneme spelt ay

The **ai** phoneme can be spelt **ay**, for example, *hay*, *say* and *may*.

Blend the phonemes to read the words in the word bank. Write them in this rocket puzzle. Some letters have been written in to help you. All the words end in **ay**.

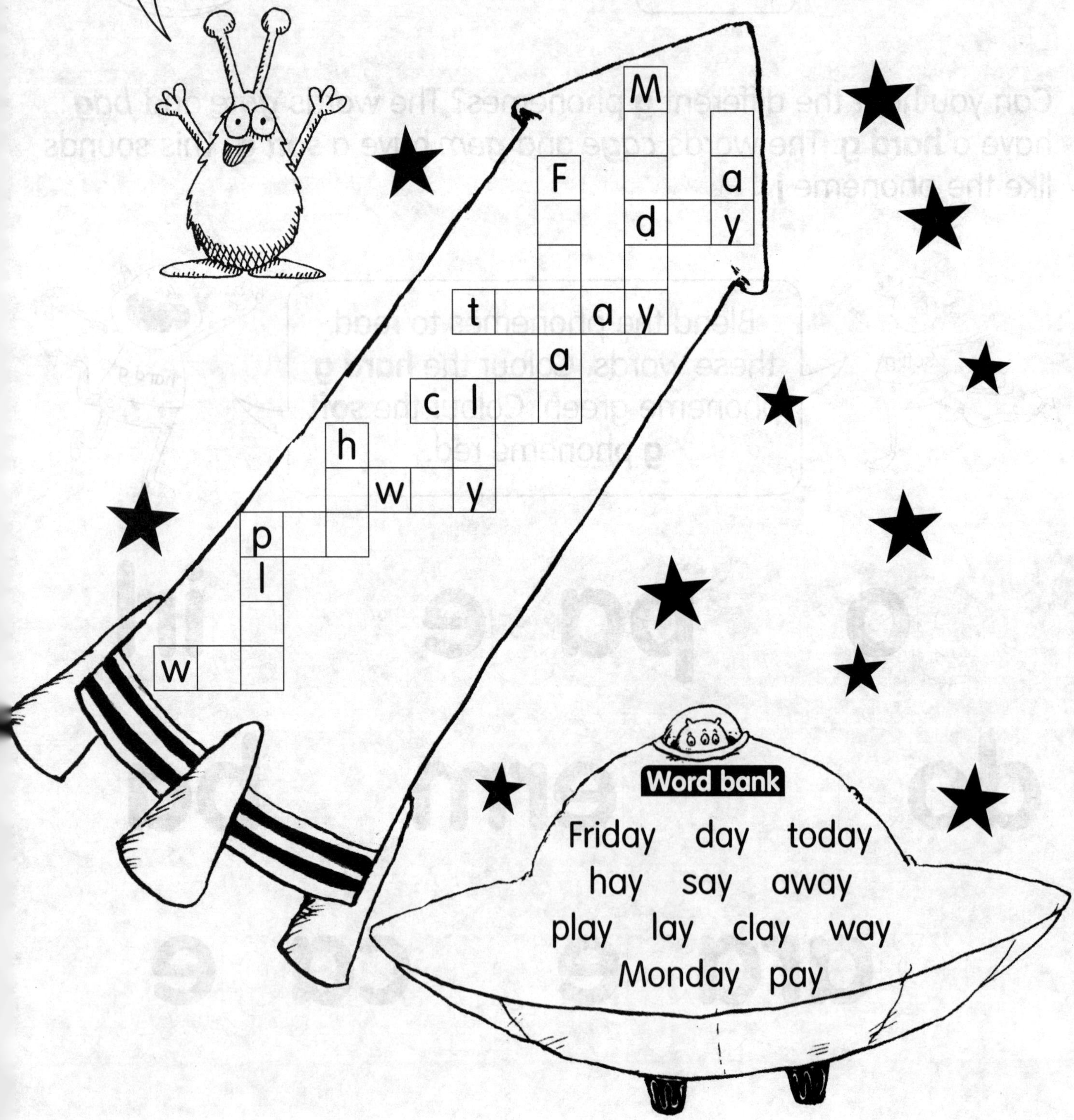

The ai phoneme

Blend the phonemes to read these words: *make, day* and *rain*. They are not spelt the same, but can you hear that they all have the **ai** phoneme? This phoneme can be spelt **ai, ay** and **a-e**.

Look at these pictures and read the words.
Circle the pictures with the **ai** phoneme.
Remember, it can be spelt **ai, ay** or **a-e**.

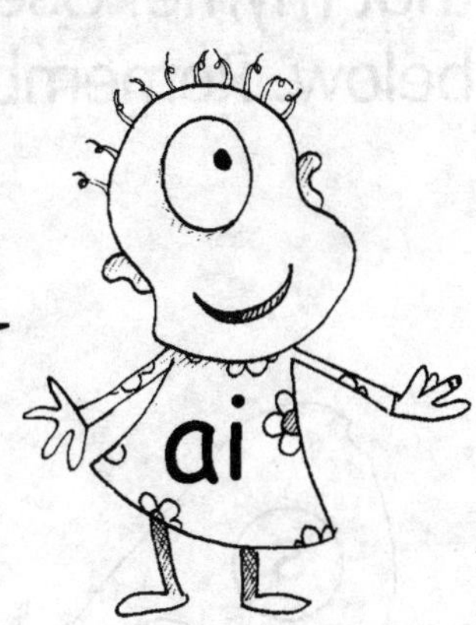

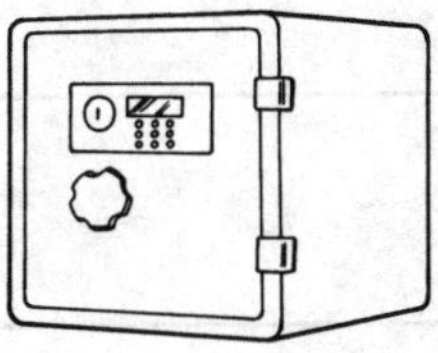
safe

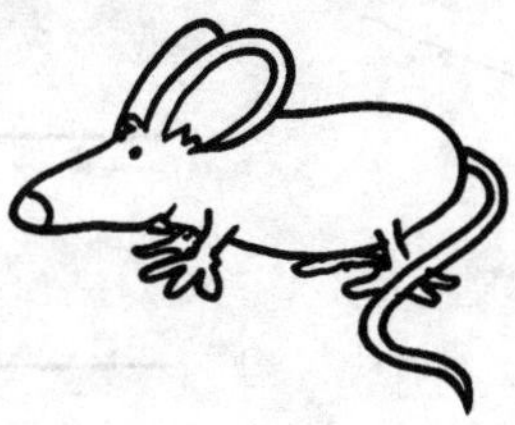
rat

rain

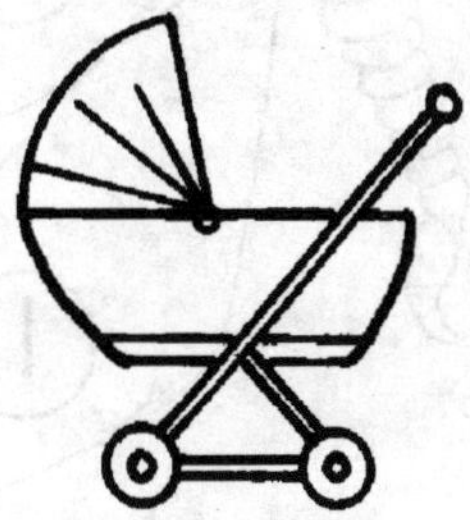
pram

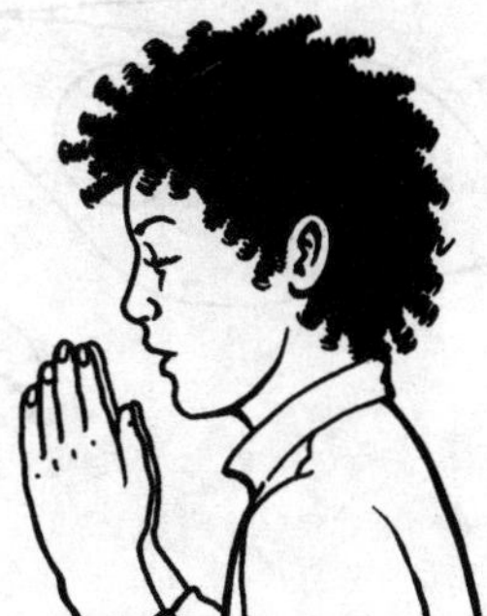
pray

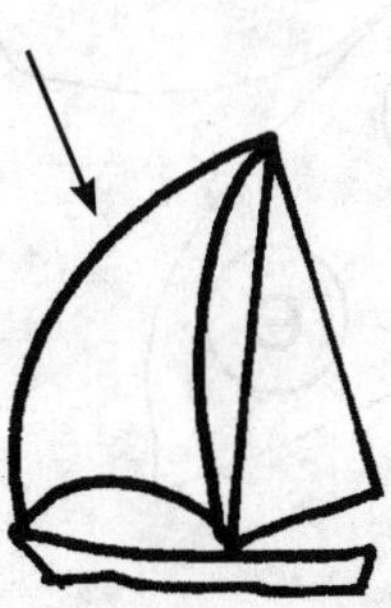
sail

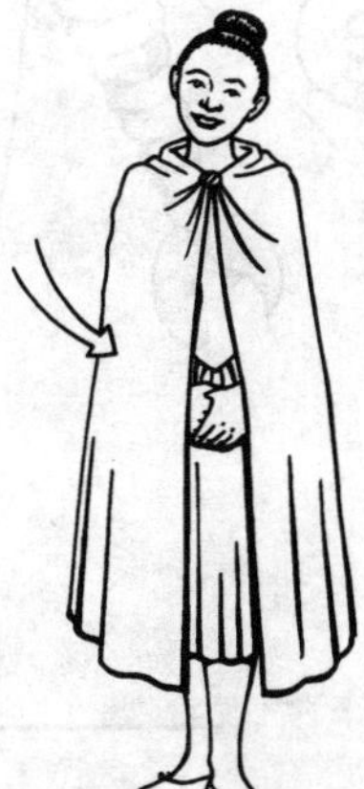
cape

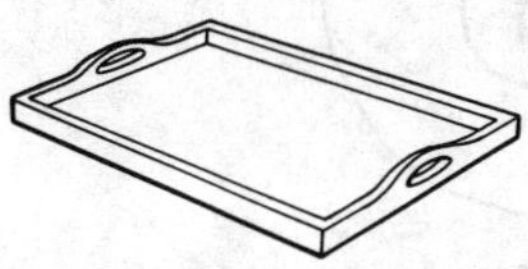
tray

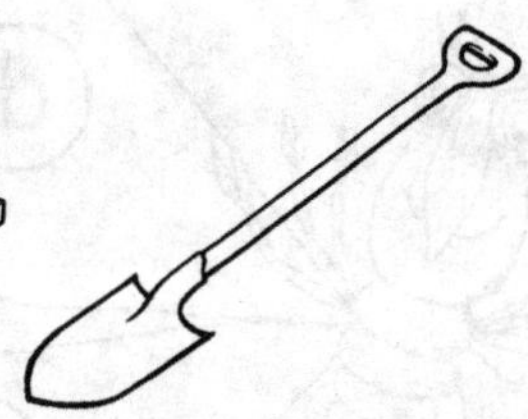
spade

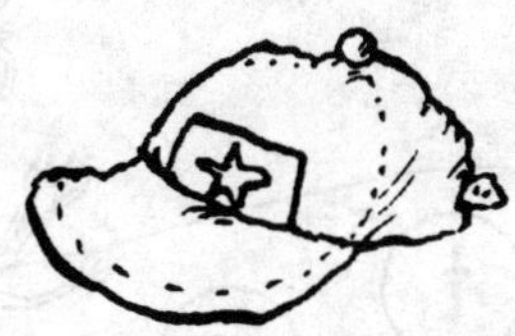
cap

Words that rhyme using the ai phoneme

Look at the letters in the wings of the alien insects. They spell words that rhyme. Use them to write two rhyming words on the lines below. Remember, the **ai** phoneme can be spelt **ai**, **ay** or **a-e**.

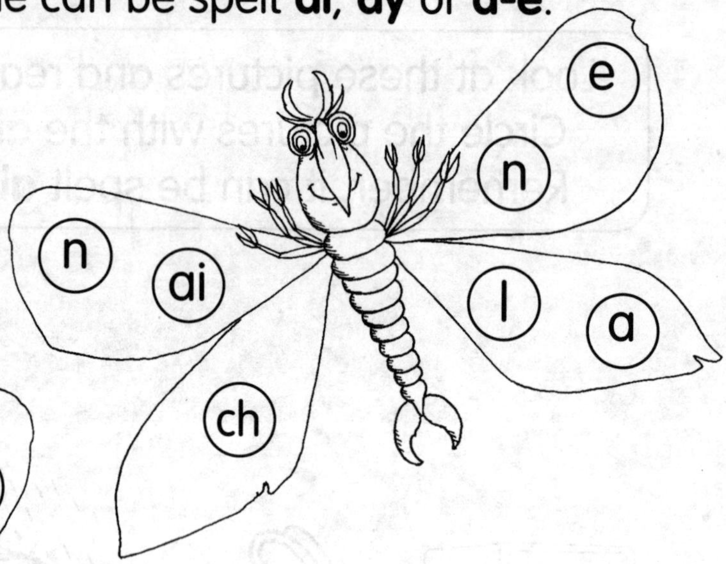

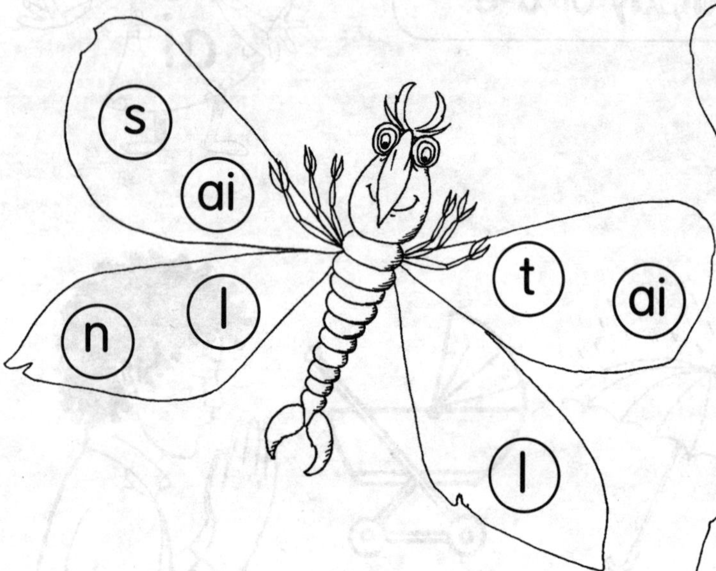

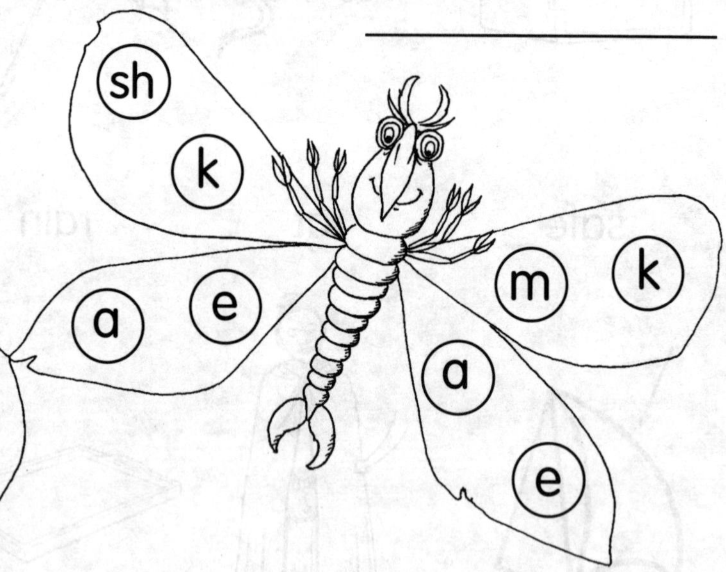

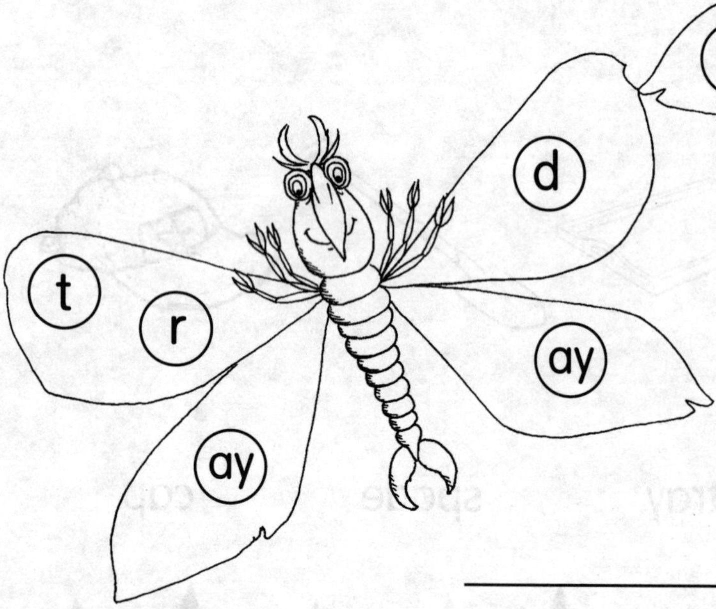

The ee phoneme

Blend the phonemes to read these words: *he, see* and *leaf*. They are not spelt the same but can you hear that they all have the **ee** phoneme? This phoneme can be spelt **ee, ea** or **e**.

Blend the phonemes to read these words. Colour the words with the **ee** phoneme. Remember, it can be spelt **ee**, **ea** or **e**. Be careful as some of the words are spelt with an **e** but do not have the **ee** phoneme.

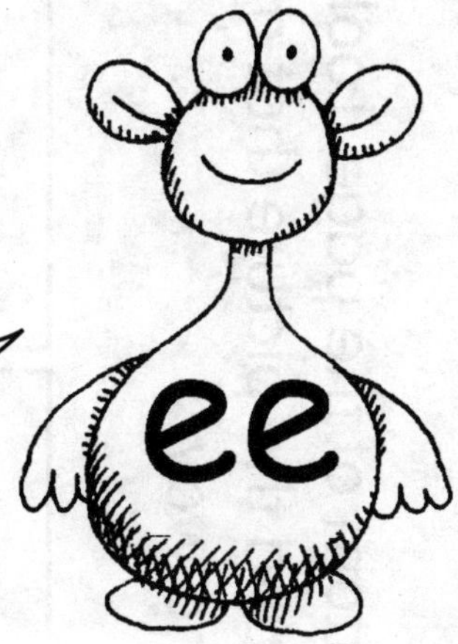

bed she me

green neck

sea eat bee

week pet

Words that rhyme using the ee phoneme

Blend the phonemes to read the words at the bottom of the page. Look at the pictures and say what they show. Write the words from the list around the picture that rhymes with the word. Words that rhyme are not always spelt in the same way.

bee	meat
seat	me
sea	sweet
tea	pea
three	treat
heat	see

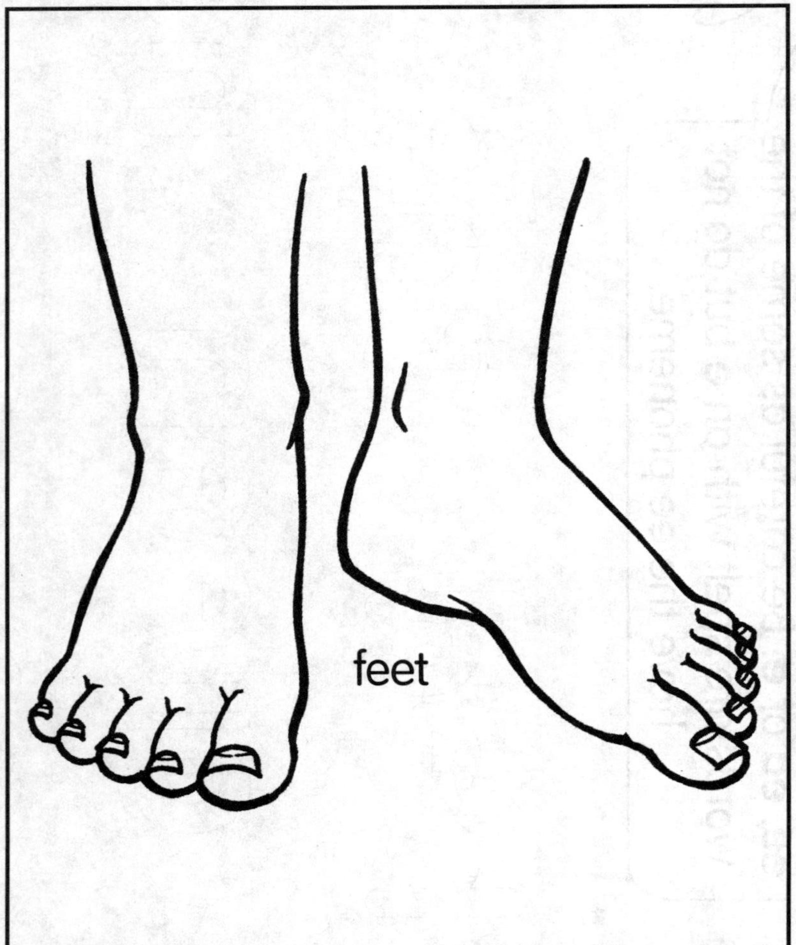

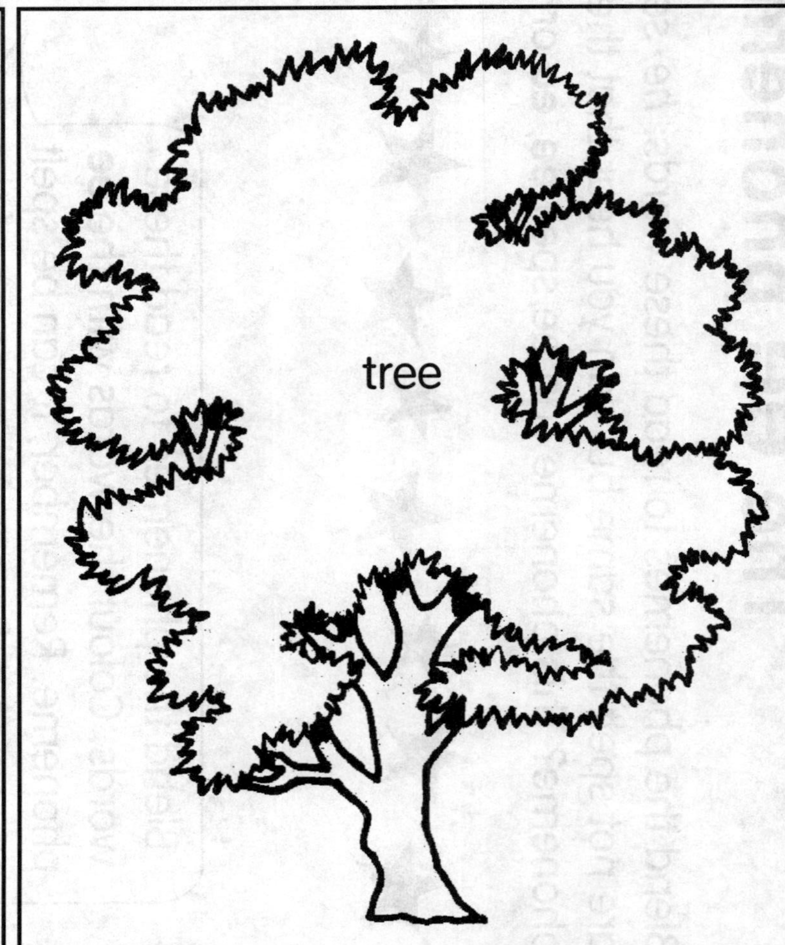

The igh phoneme

Blend the phonemes to read these words: *try, pie, line* and *sigh*. They are not spelt the same but can you hear that they all have the **igh** phoneme? This phoneme can be spelt **igh**, **y**, **ie** and **i-e**.

Blend the phonemes to read these letter strings. Look at the pictures and say what they show. On a separate piece of paper, write the letter strings together to make words with the **igh** phoneme. Draw the pictures next to the words.

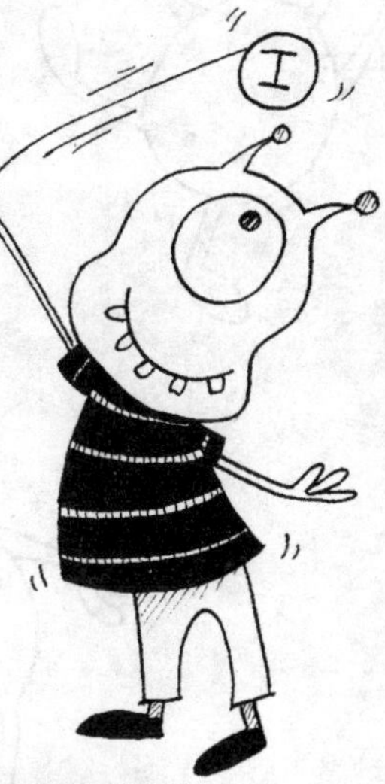

fr		ie	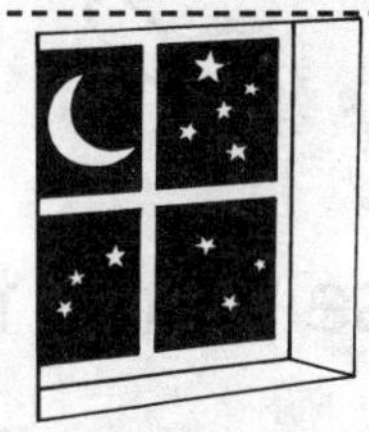
t		ight	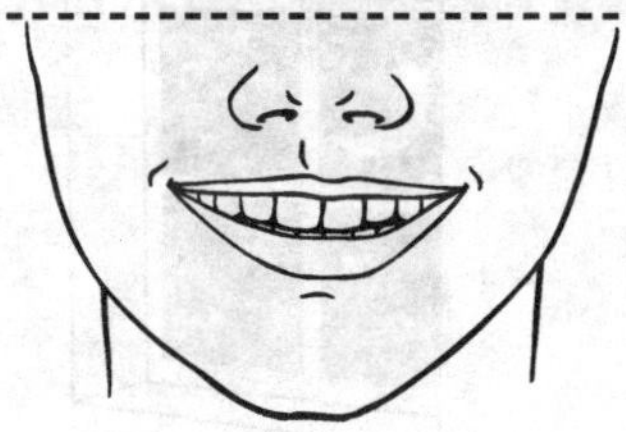
n	+	ile	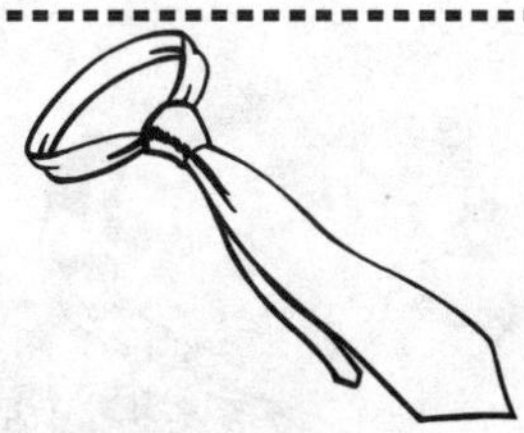
sm		y	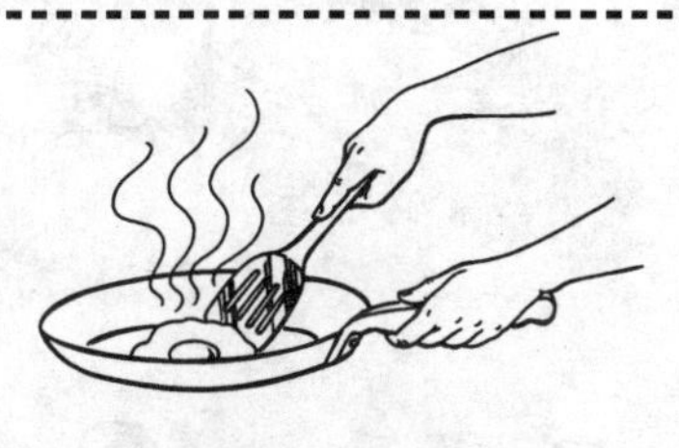
d		ive	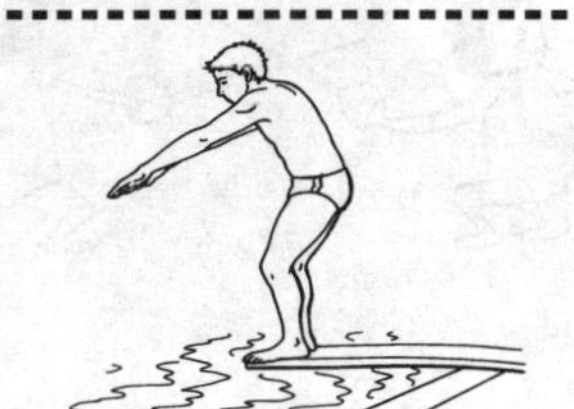

The **igh** phoneme

Blend the phonemes to read these words:

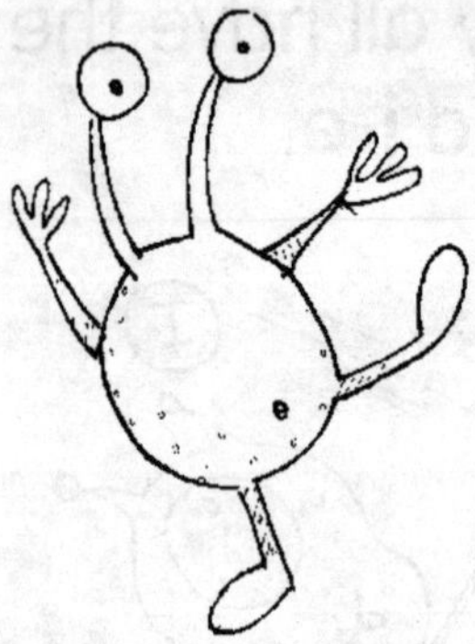

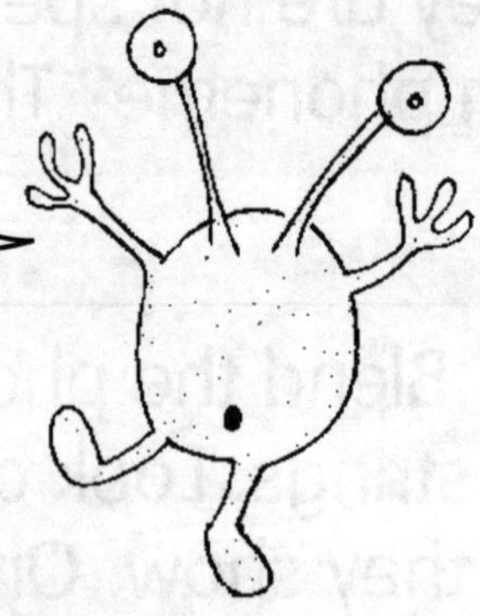

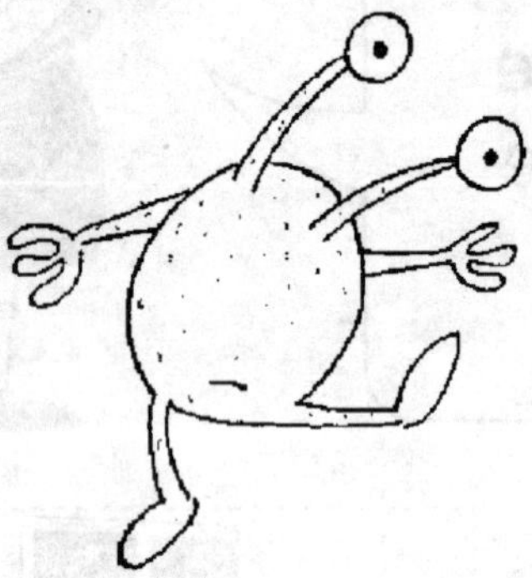

Join these words to the pictures.

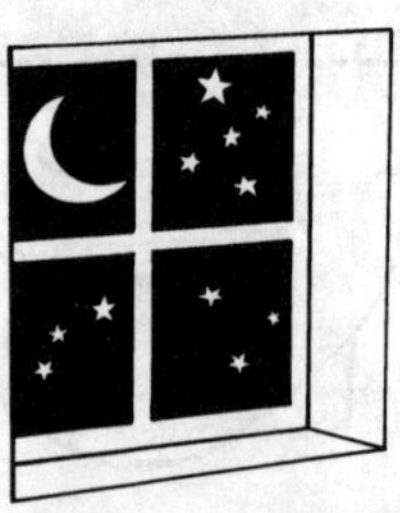

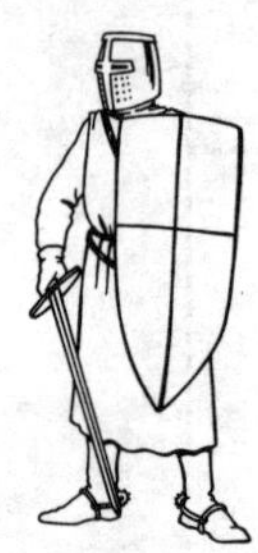

high

night

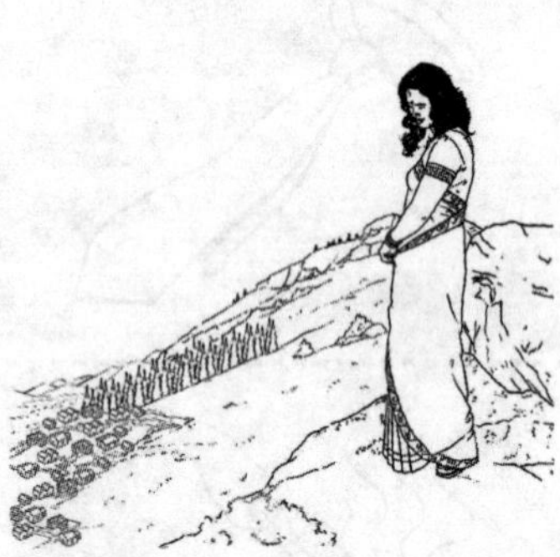

light

knight

right

fight

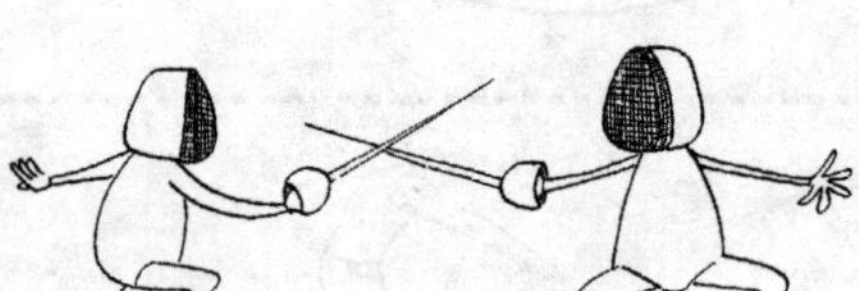

Words that rhyme using the **igh** phoneme

Read the word in the speech bubbles. In each letter puzzle there are four hidden words which rhyme with the word in the speech bubble. Circle the words. Words that rhyme do not have to be spelt in the same way.

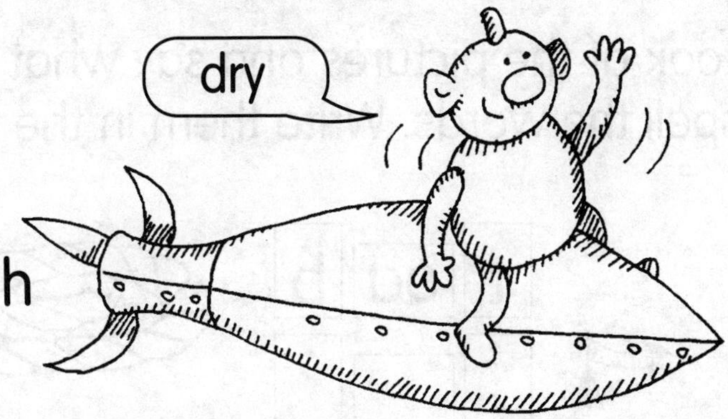

piecrytiehigh

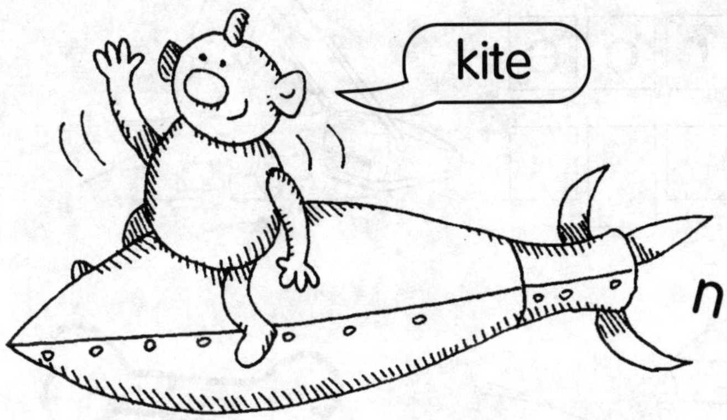

nightbitewhitefight

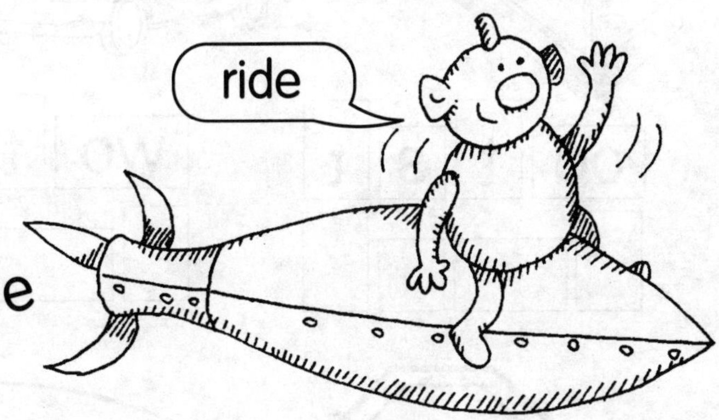

widesidetidehide

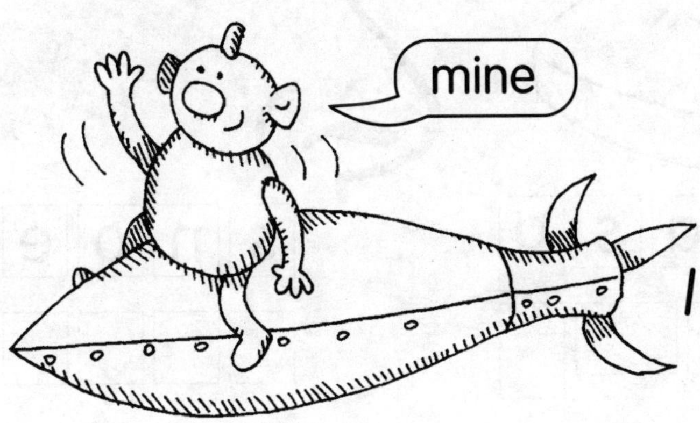

linefinenineshine

The oa phoneme

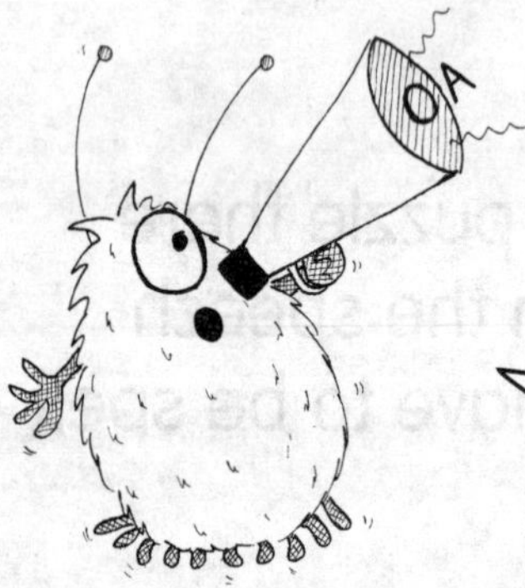

Blend the phonemes to read these words: *no*, *low*, *home* and *foam*. They are not spelt the same but can you hear that they all have the **oa** phoneme? This phoneme can be spelt **oa**, **ow**, **o** or **o-e**.

Look at the pictures and say what they are. Use the phonemes to spell the words. Write them in the boxes.

t oa b

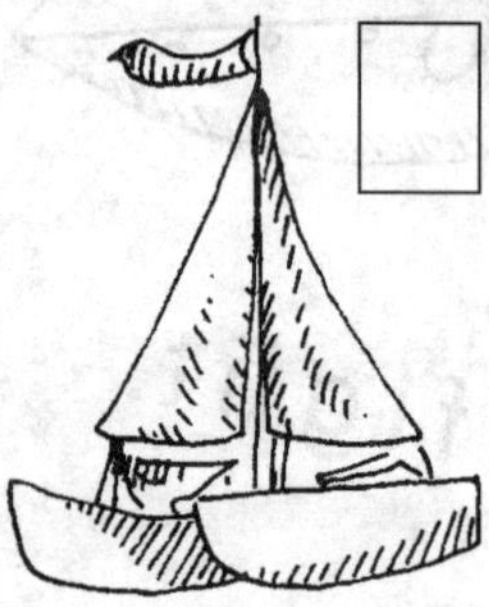

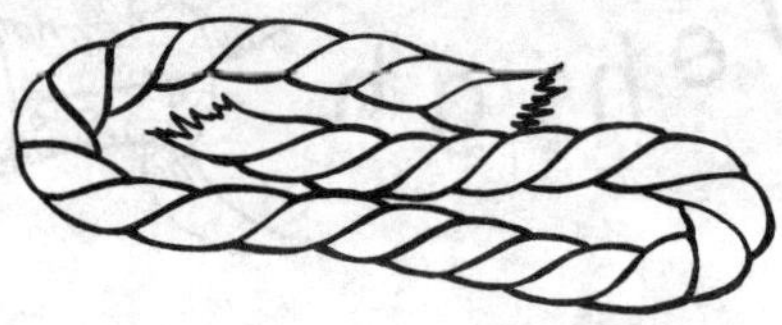

ow m

p r o e

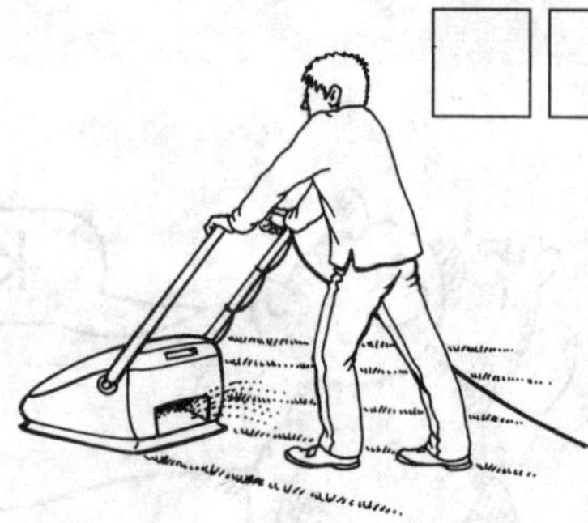

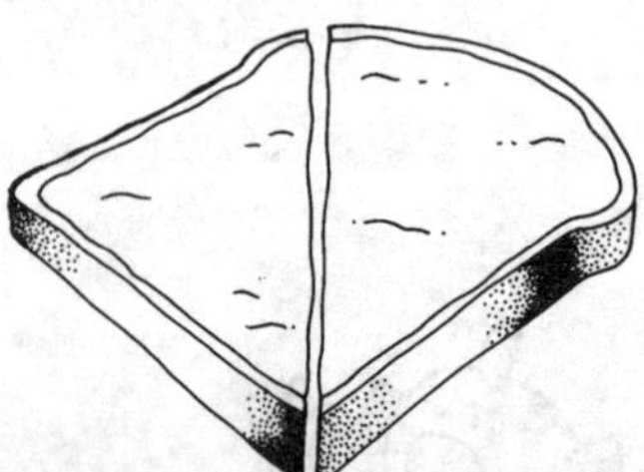

oa t s t

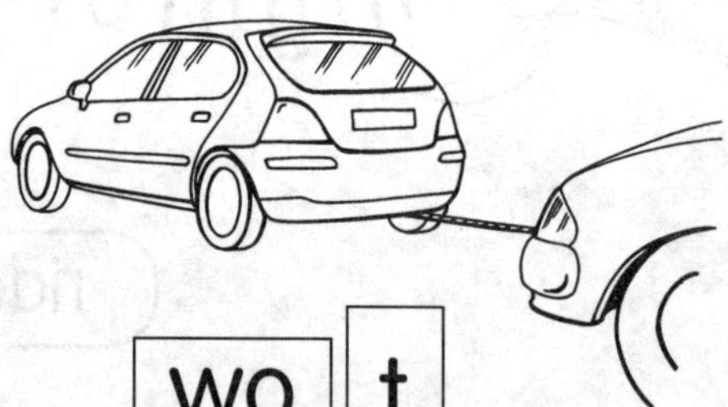

wo t

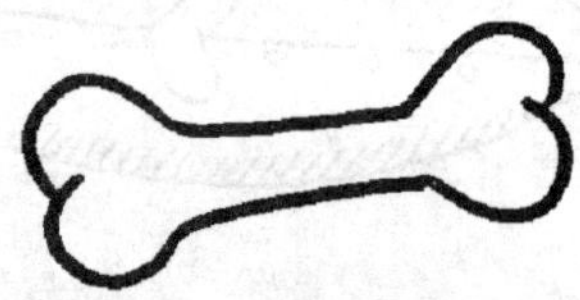

b n o e

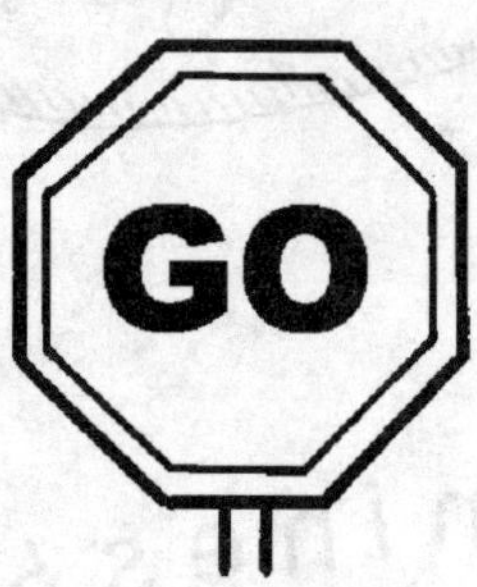

o g

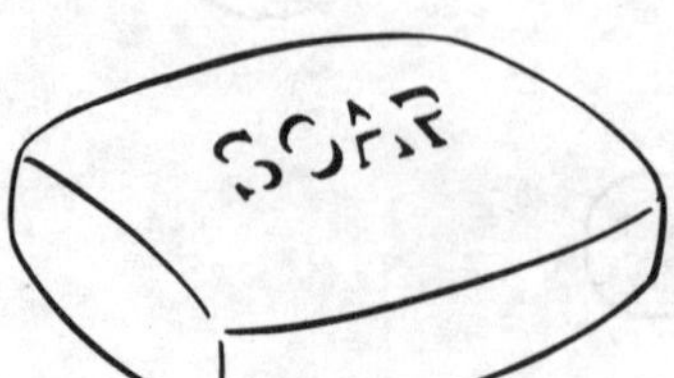

oa s p

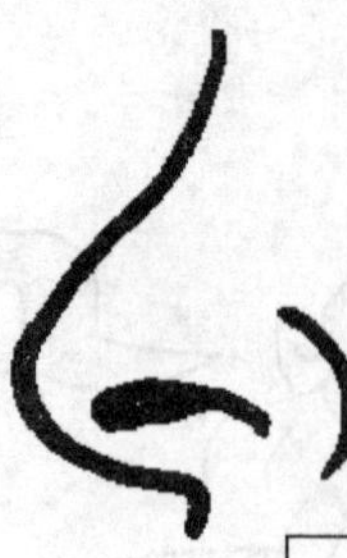

s n o e

Words that rhyme using the oa phoneme

Look at the pictures. Blend the phonemes and say the words. Can you hear some words that rhyme? Write the words in the boxes in groups that rhyme.

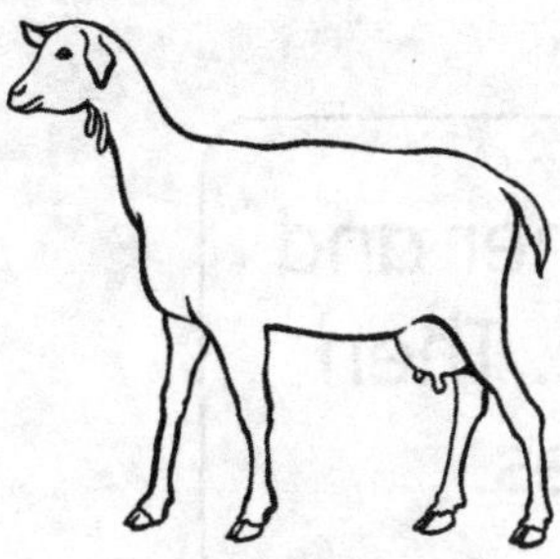

goat

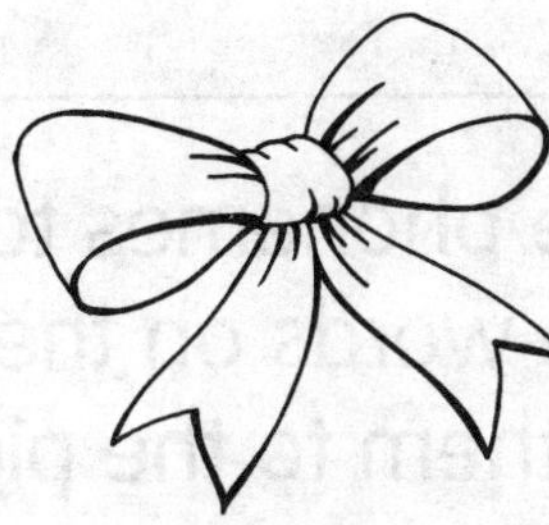

bow

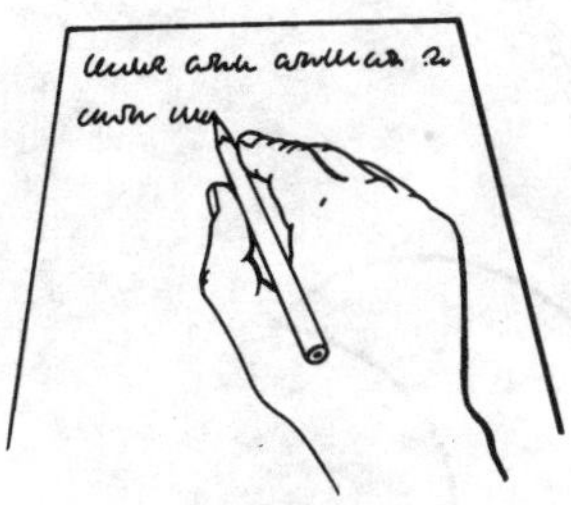

note

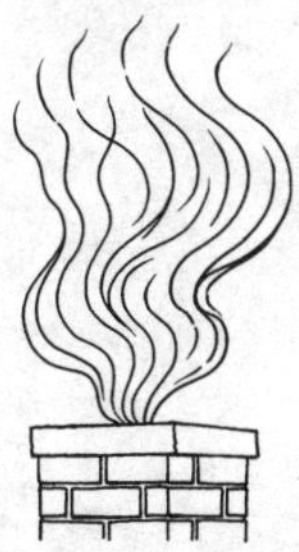

smoke

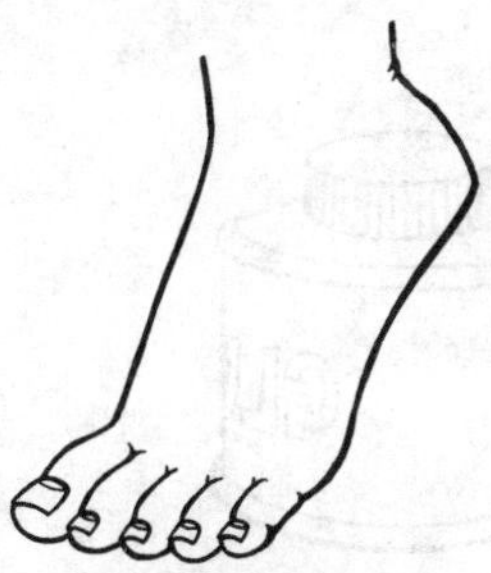

toe

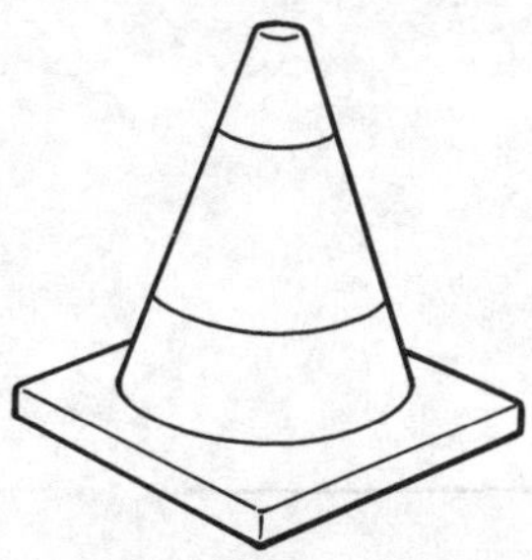

cone

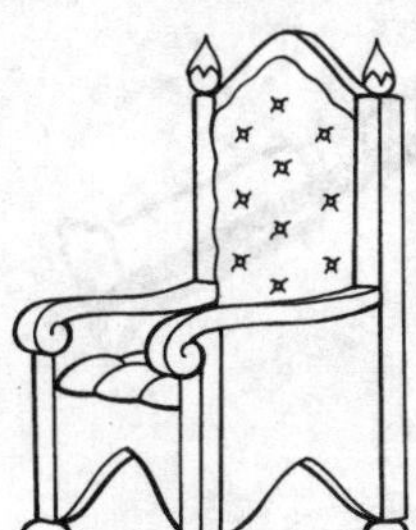

throne

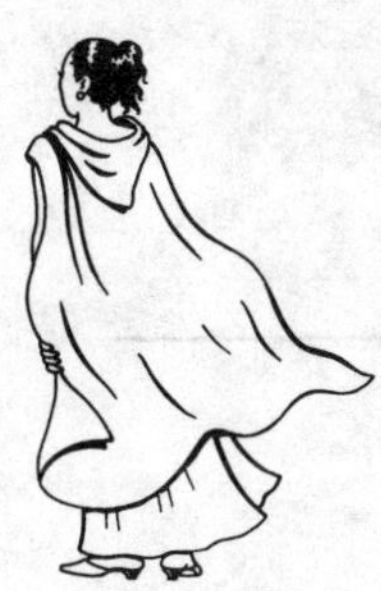

cloak

Words that rhyme with **boat**

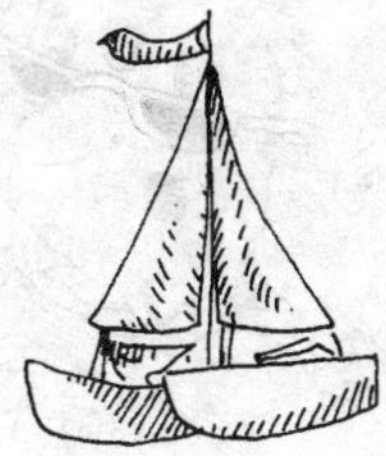

__________ __________

Words that rhyme with **bone**

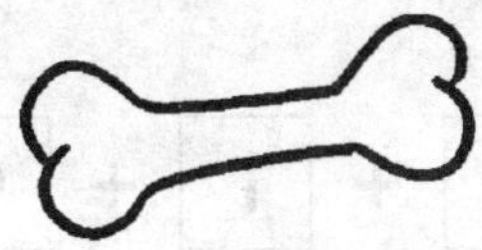

__________ __________

Words that rhyme with **blow**

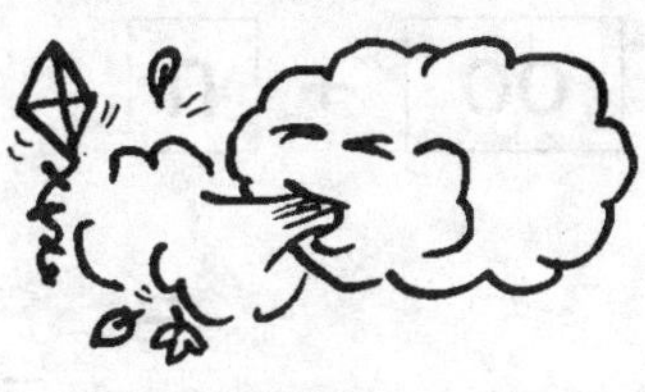

__________ __________

Words that rhyme with **oak**

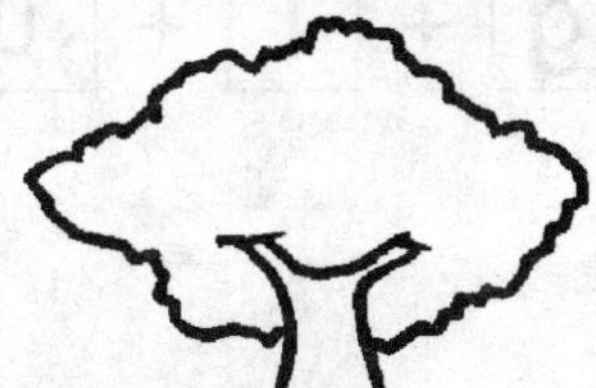

__________ __________

The long oo phoneme

Blend the phonemes to read these words: *shoot, rule, blew* and *blue*. They are not spelt the same but can you hear that they have the same long **oo** phoneme? This can be spelt **oo**, **o-e**, **ew** or **ue**.

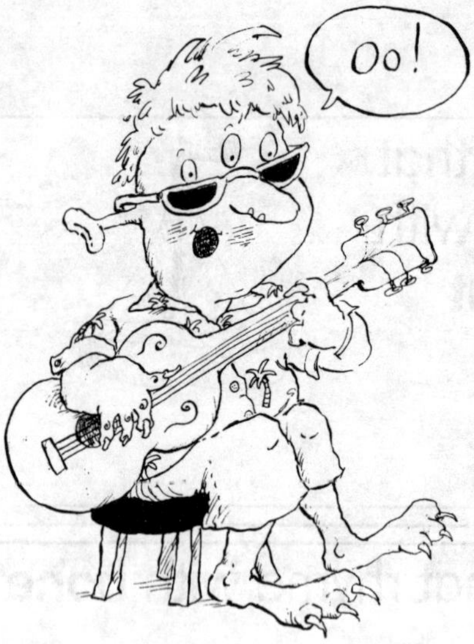

Join these phonemes together and write the words on the line. Then join them to the pictures.

s + c + r + ew

= ______________________

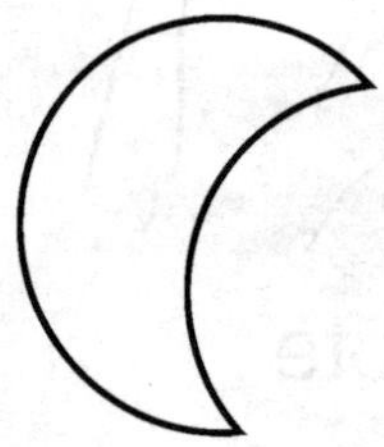

m + oo + n

= ______________________

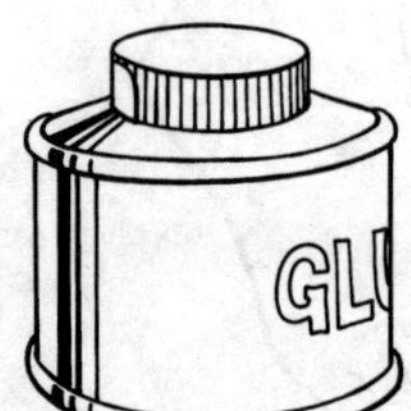

g + l + ue

= ______________________

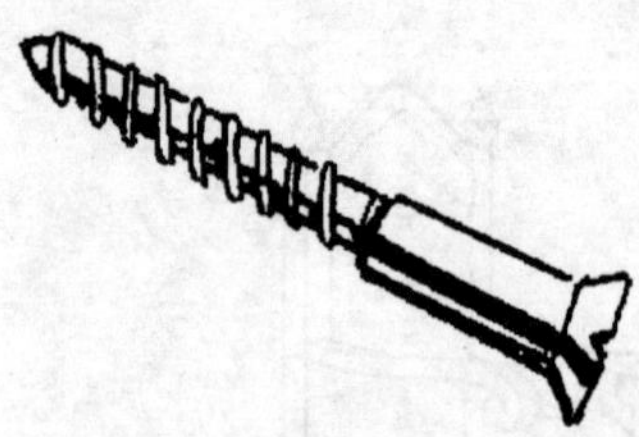

sh + a + m + p + oo

= ______________________

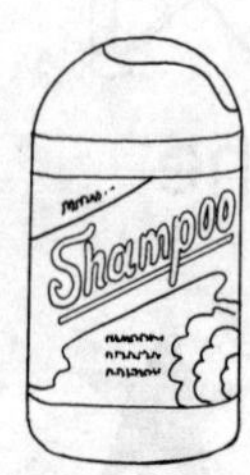

Words that rhyme using the long OO phoneme

Blend the phonemes to read the words.
Can you hear some words that rhyme?
Join the rhyming words together.
Remember, the rhyming words may
not be spelt in the same way.

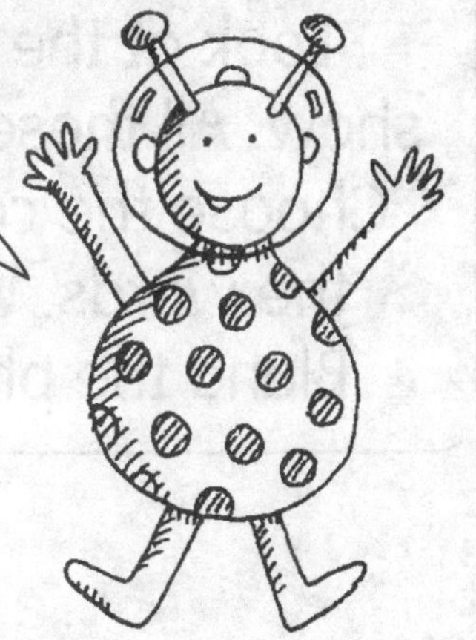

blue	broom	flute
pool	too	room
spoon	rule	food
rude	moon	boot

Words with **ar**

Look at the pictures and say what they show. All these words have the phoneme **ar**. Choose the correct phonemes to complete the words. Write the words on the lines. Blend the phonemes to read the words.

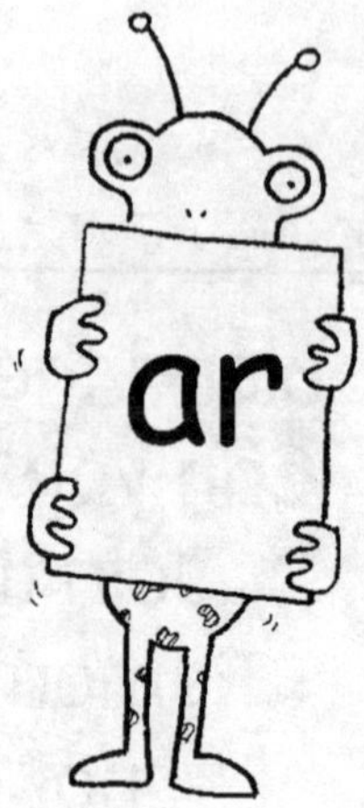

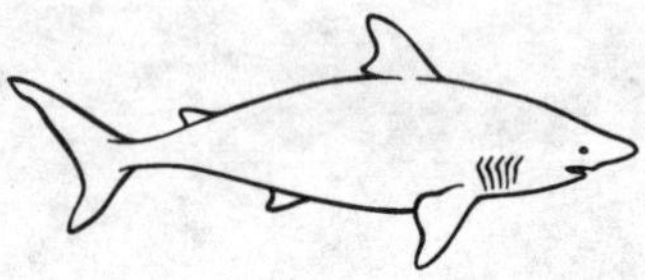 → sh | ar | t ______________________

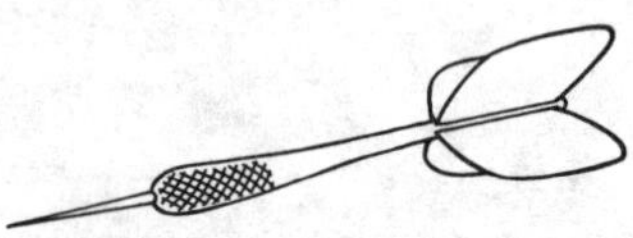 → d | ar | k ______________________

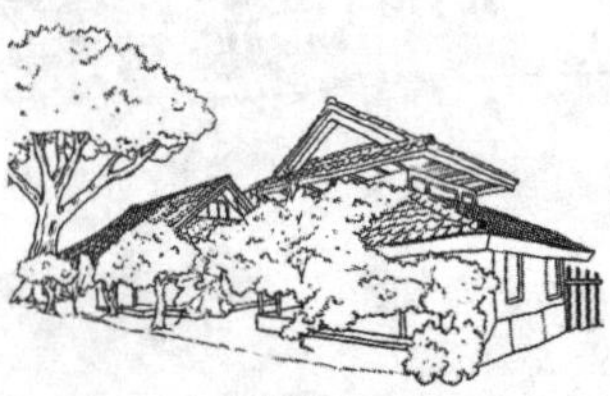 → f | ar | d ______________________

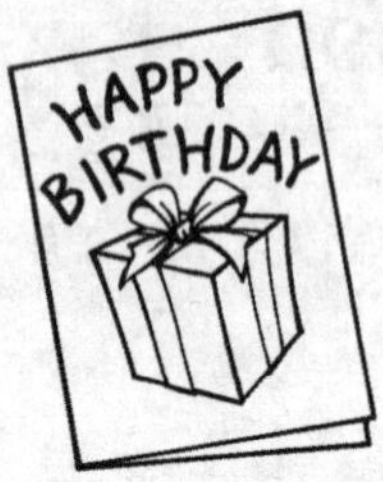

→ c | ar | n ______________________

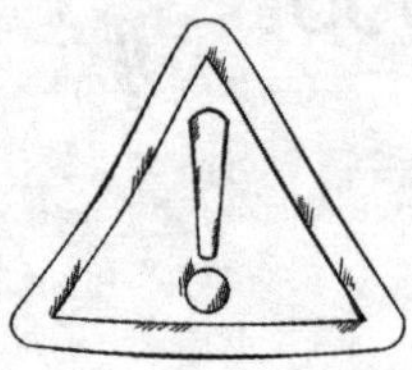 → w | ar | n ______________________

Words with aw

Blend the phonemes to read this word: *saw*. Can you hear the **aw** sound?

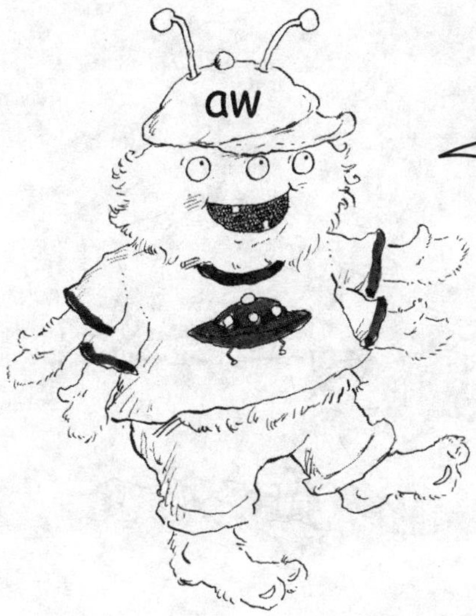

Look at the pictures and say what they show. They all have **aw**. Write the **aw** letter strings in the words below. Then blend the phonemes to read each word.

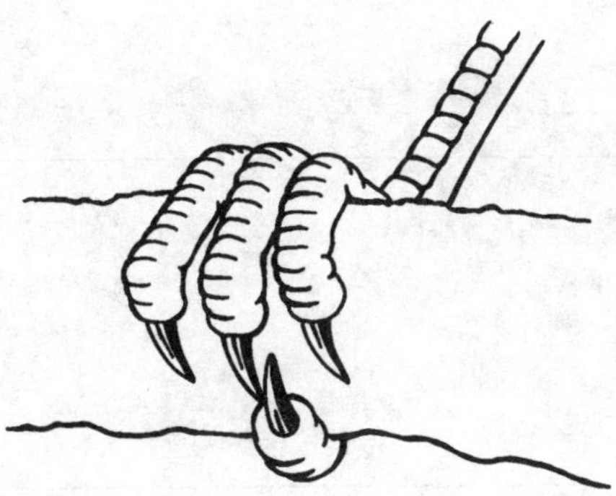

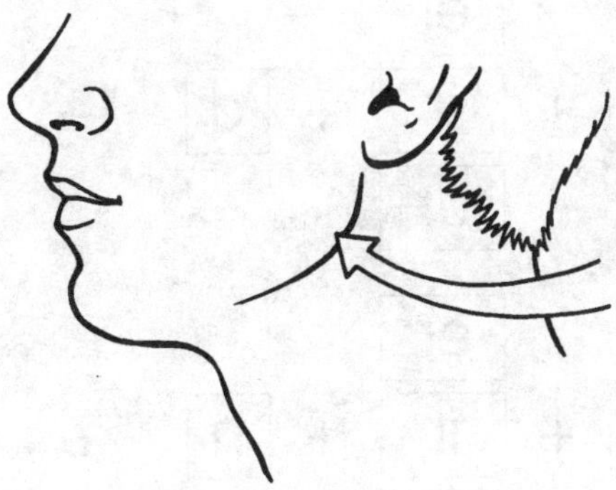

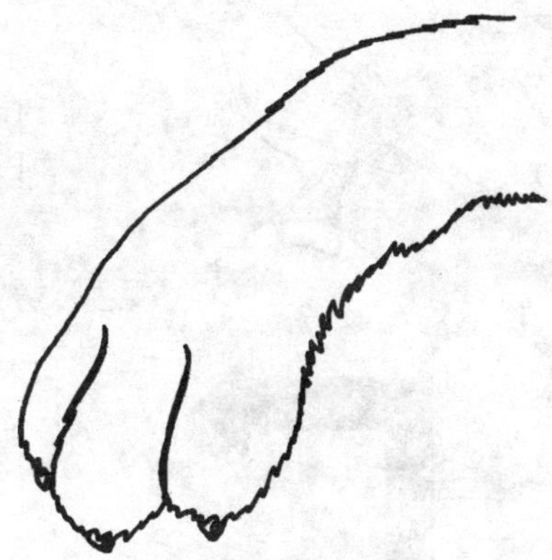

c l ___   j ___   p ___

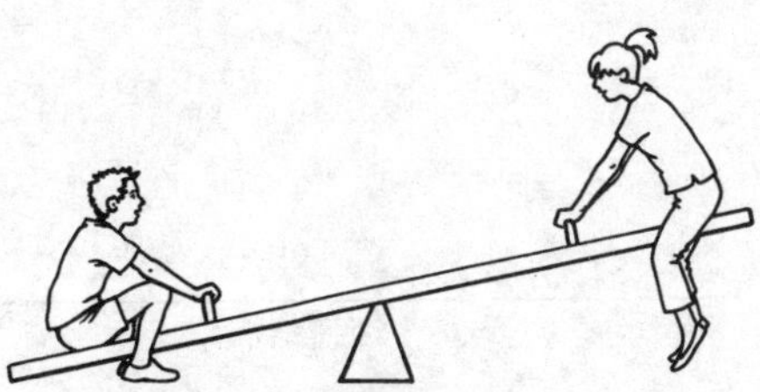

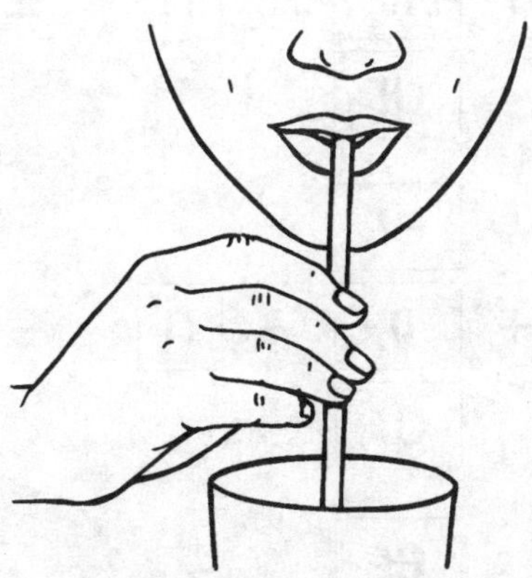

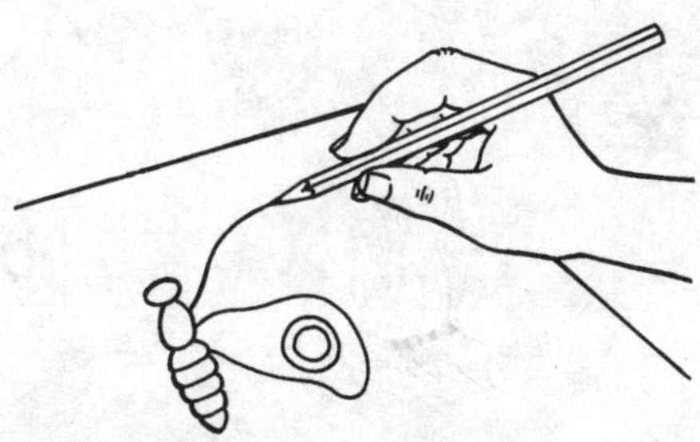

see- s ___   s t r ___   d r ___

aw   aw   aw   aw   aw   aw

The ur phoneme

Blend the phonemes and say these words: *her*, *girl* and *fur*. Can you hear the **ur** phoneme? It can be spelt **ur**, **er** or **ir**.

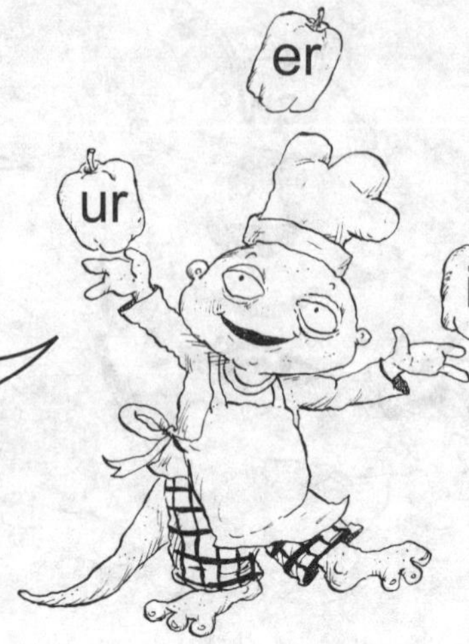

Choose the correct spelling of the phonemes for these words. Write the words on the lines. Blend the phonemes to read the words.

1 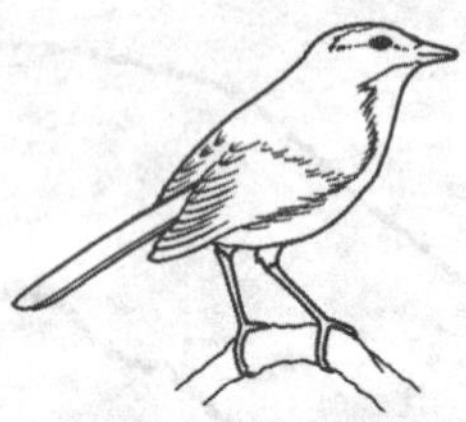

er
b + ir + d = ______________
ur

2 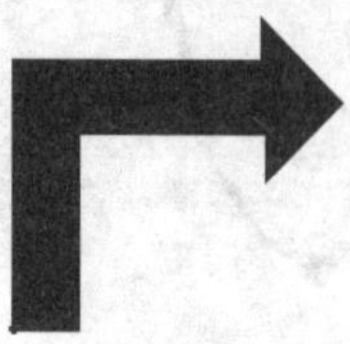

er
t + ir + n = ______________
ur

3 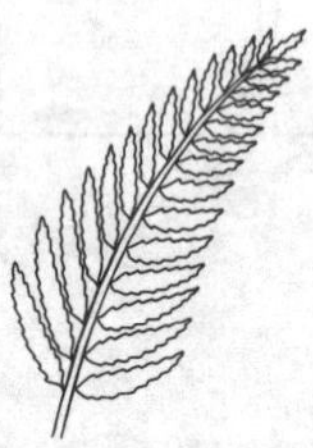

er
f + ir + n = ______________
ur

4 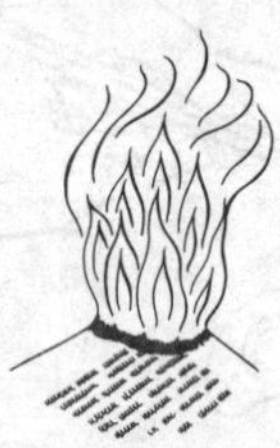

er
b + ir + n = ______________
ur

5 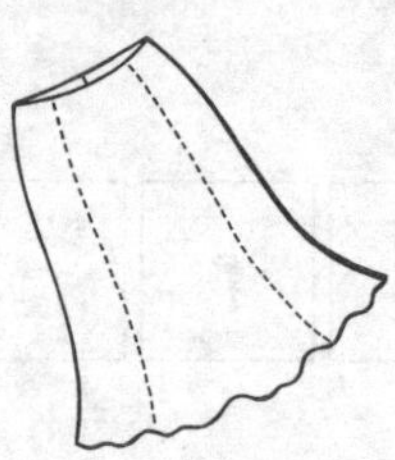

er
sk + ir + t = ______________
ur

Words with ea

Blend the phonemes to read these words: *sea* and *neat*. Can you hear the **ee** phoneme? This phoneme can be spelt **ea**.

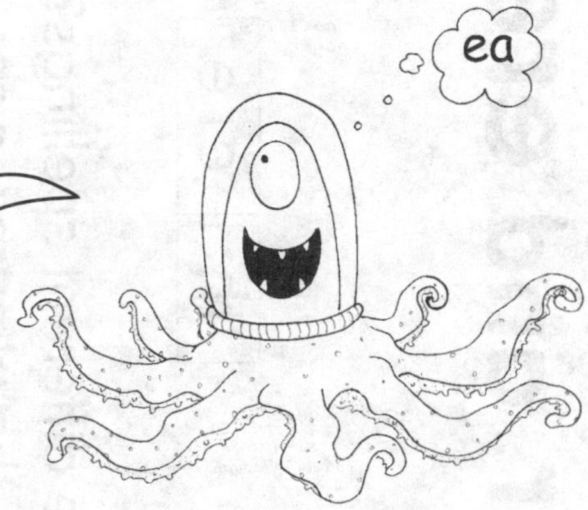

Look at the pictures. Blend the phonemes to read the words. Colour the pictures with the **ee** phoneme spelt **ea**.

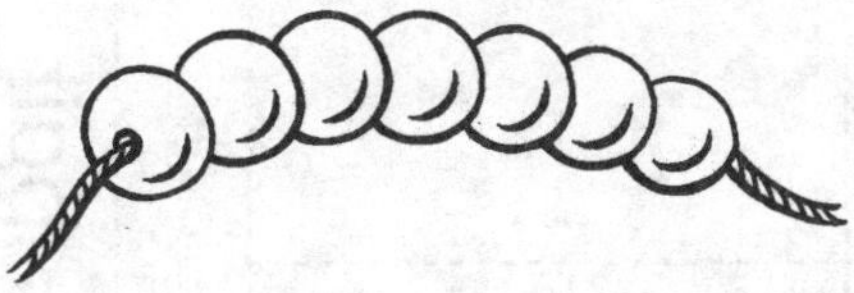

beads

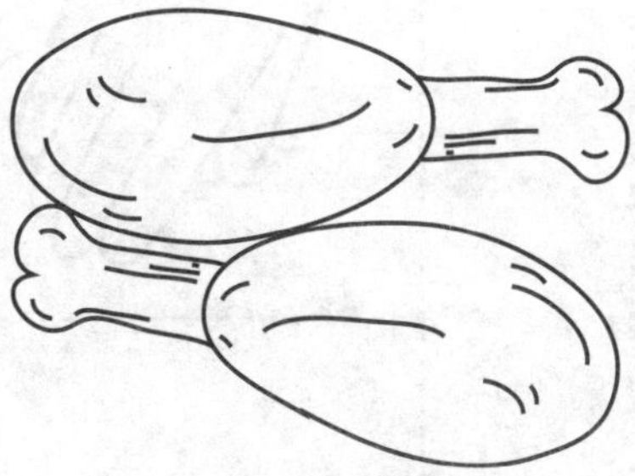

meat

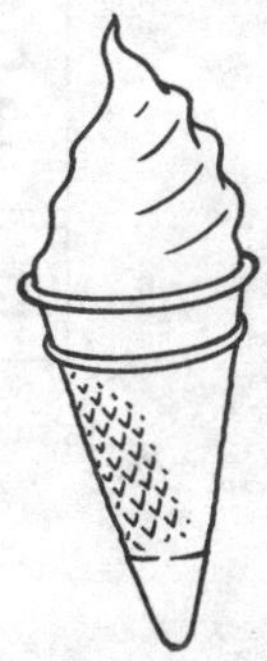

ice cream

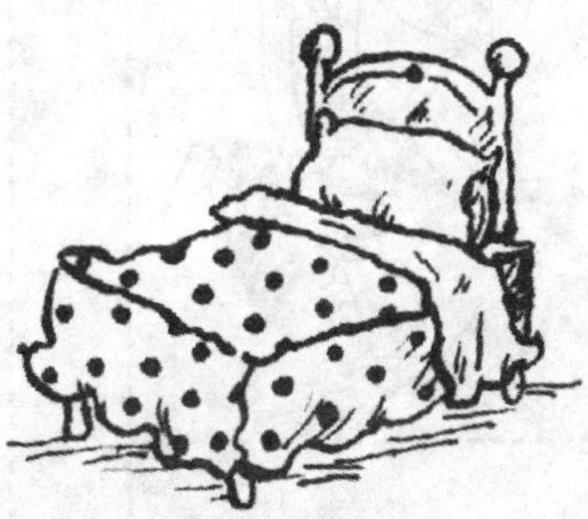

bed

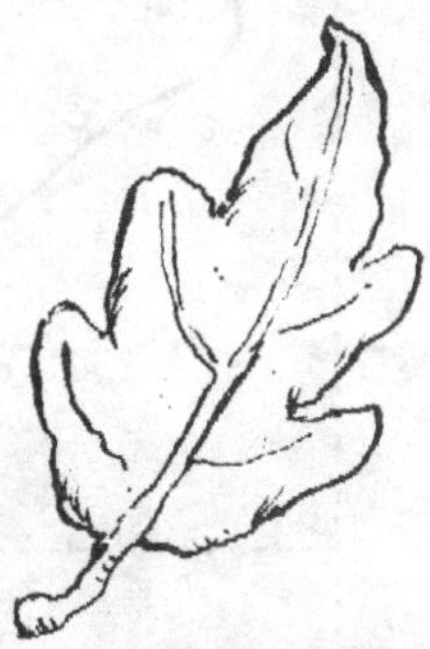

leaf

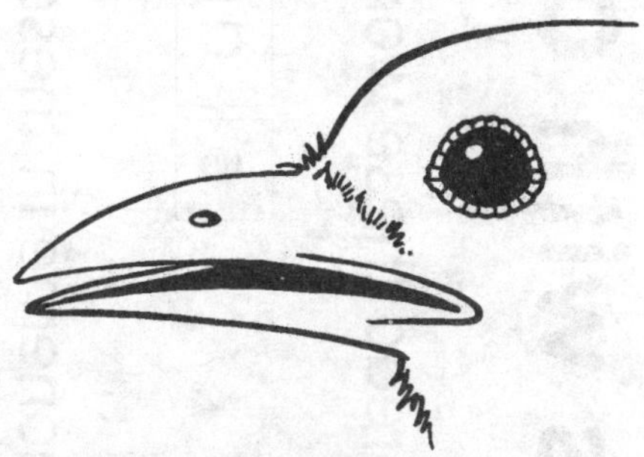

beak

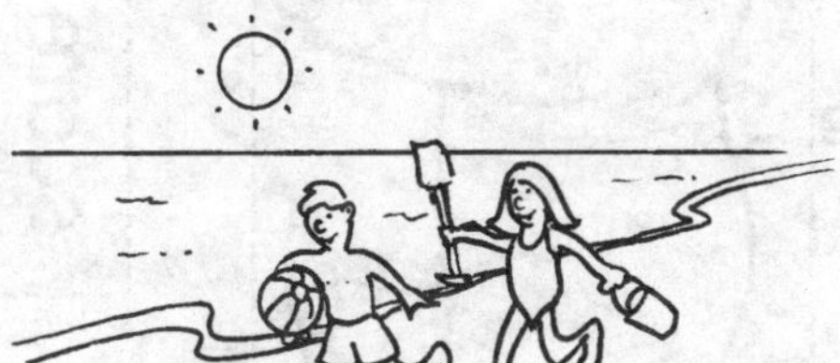

beach

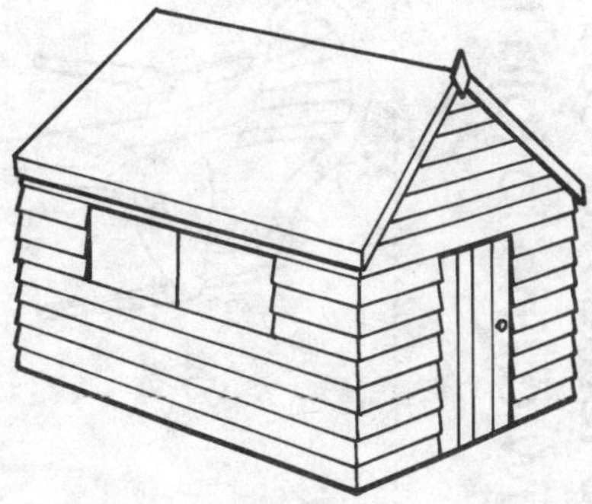

shed

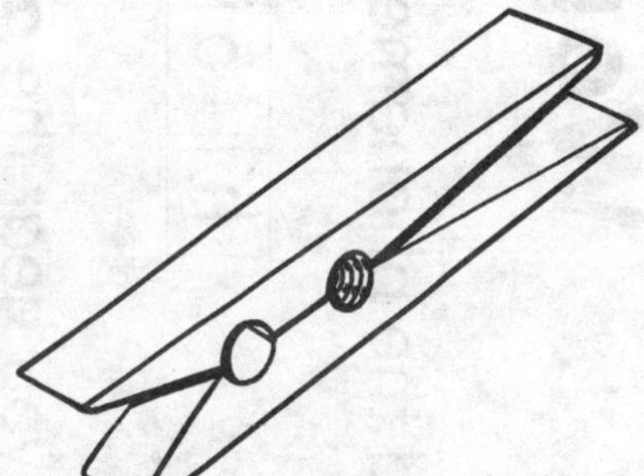

peg

Words with **air, are, ear** and **ere**

Blend the phonemes to read these words:

h	air

c	are

b	ear

th	ere

Can you hear the **air** phoneme in these words? Can you see the different spellings? Blend the phonemes to read the words at the bottom of the page. Match the pictures to the words and draw a line to join them together.

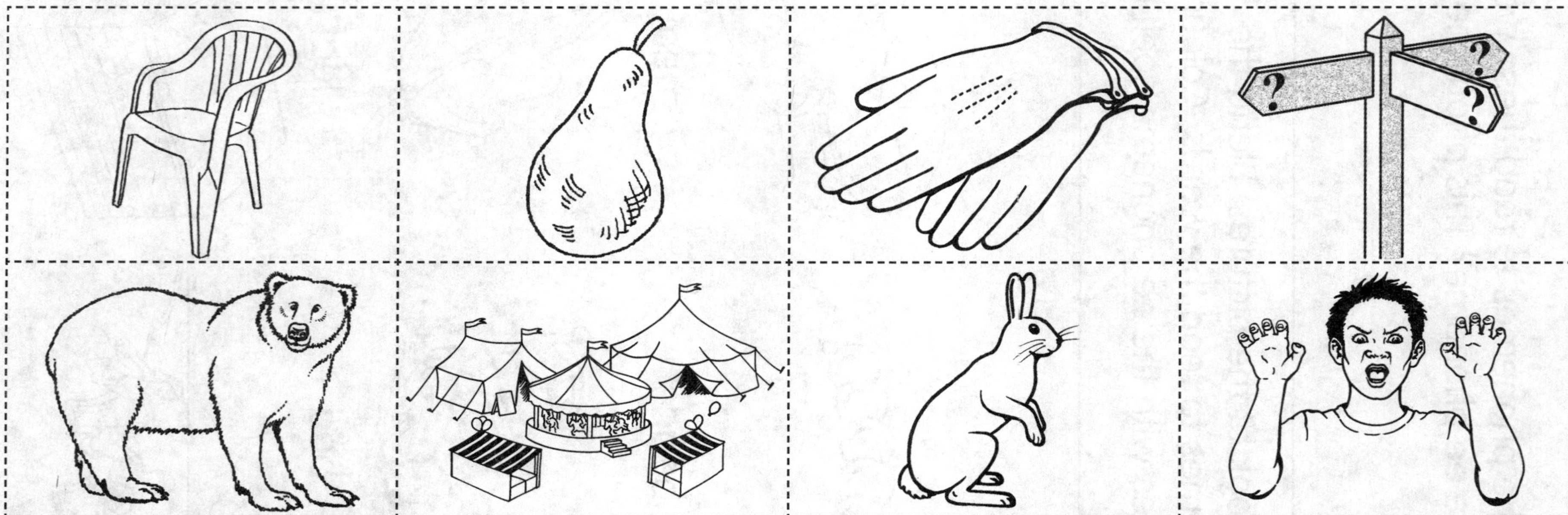

scare	pear	hare	chair	pair	where	bear	fair

Words with ow

Blend the phonemes to read these words:

t	ow	n

s	l	ow

Can you hear the difference?

Look at the pictures. Blend the phonemes to read the words. Colour those which rhyme with the **ow** phoneme in *town*. Circle those which rhyme with the **ow** phoneme in *slow*.

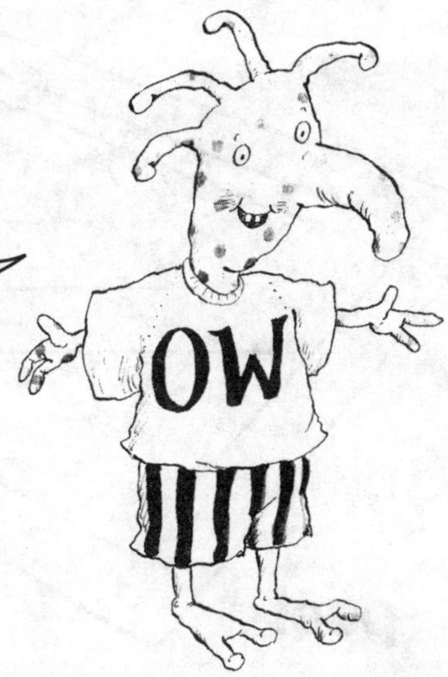

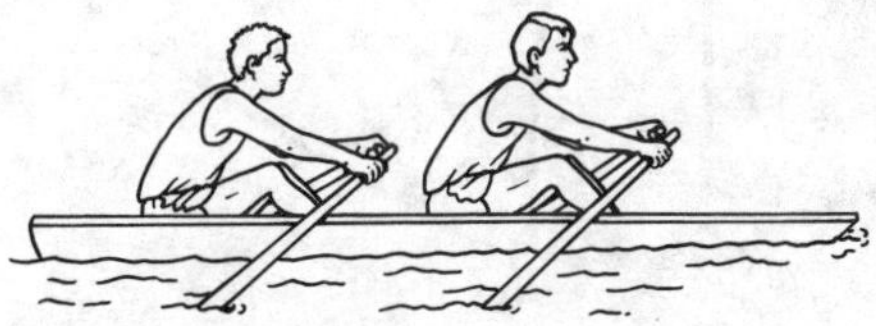

row

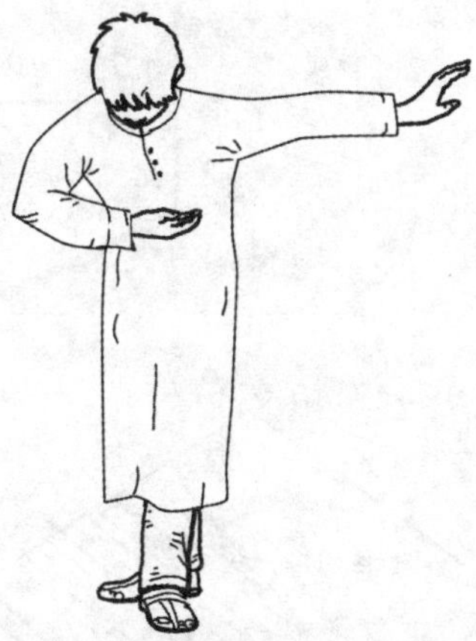

bow

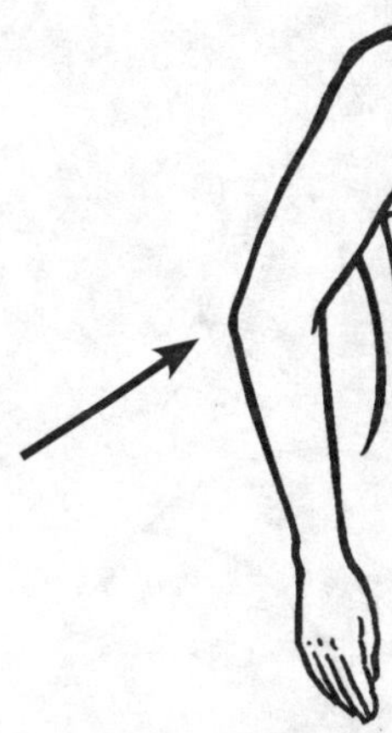

elbow

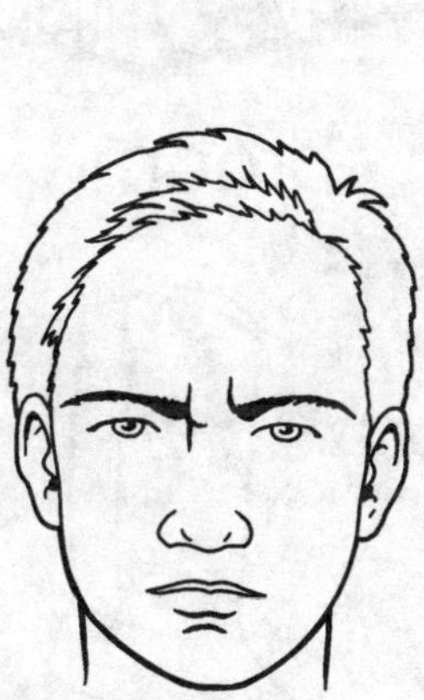

frown

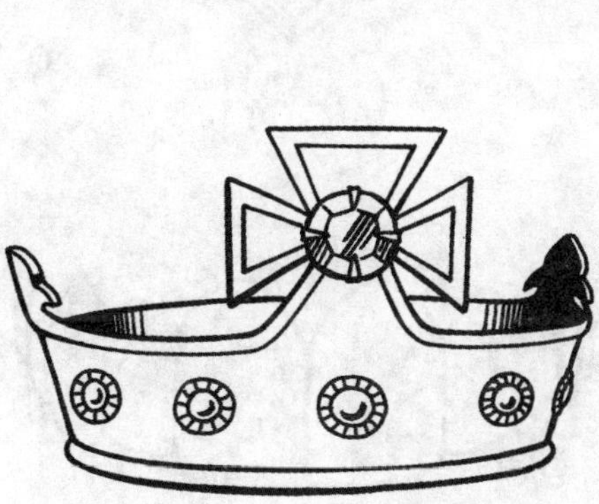

crown

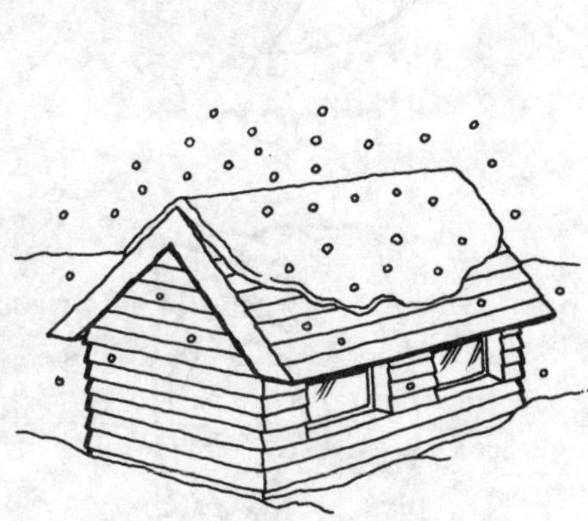

snow

Words with oo

Blend the phonemes to read these words: *good* and *room*. Can you hear the difference? Look at these pictures and read the words. Write words with a long **oo** phoneme in the pool and words with a short **oo** phoneme in the book.

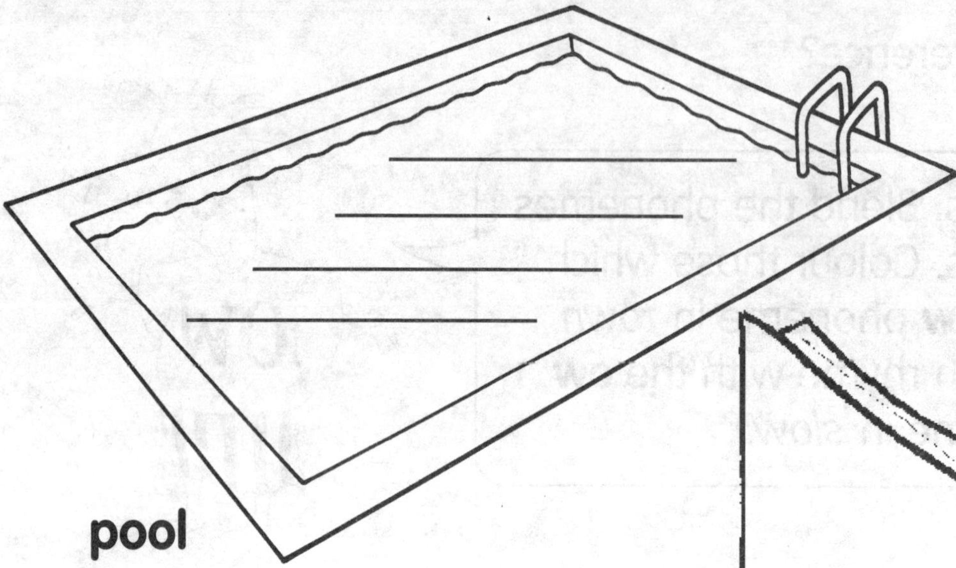

pool

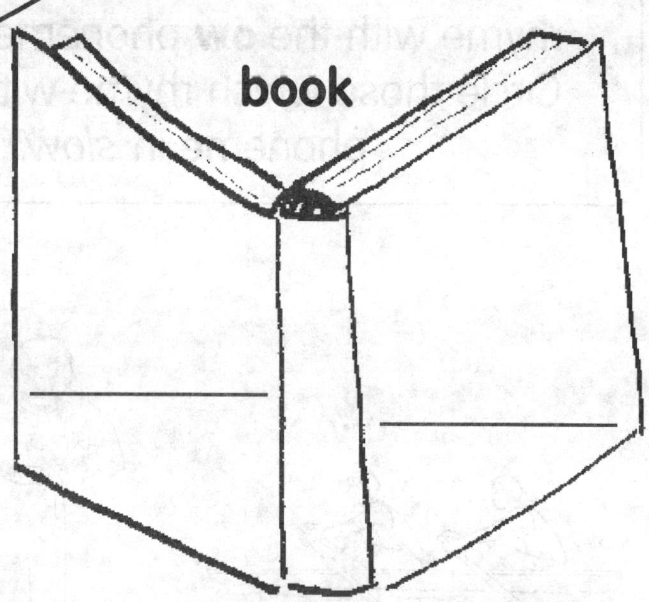

book

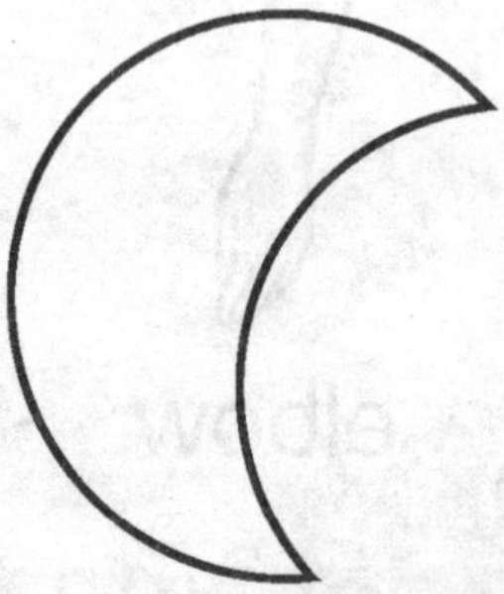

moon

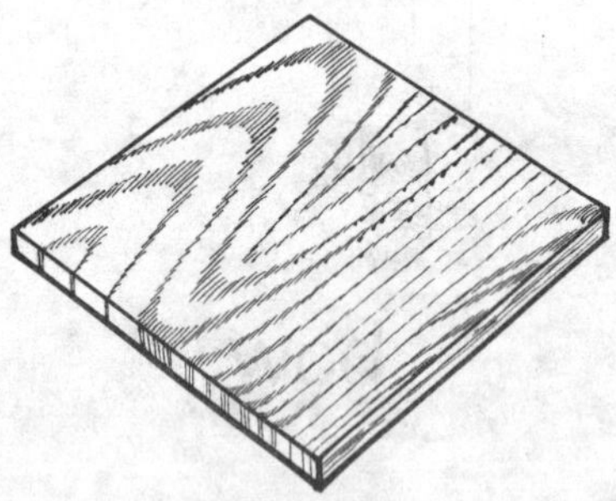

wood

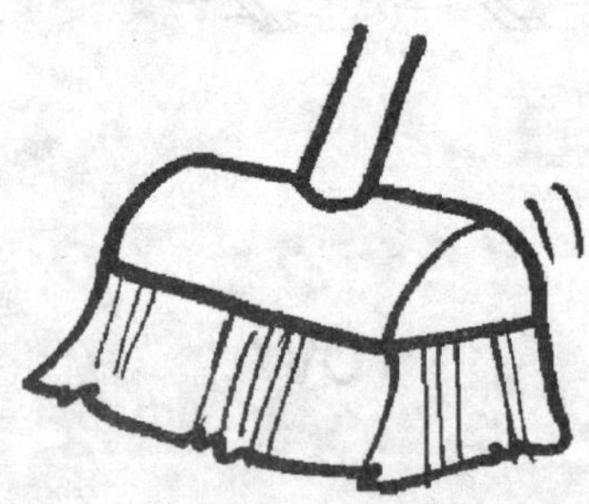

broom

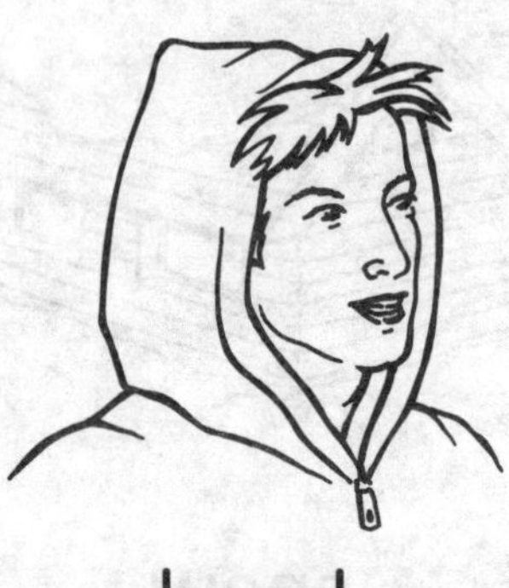

hood

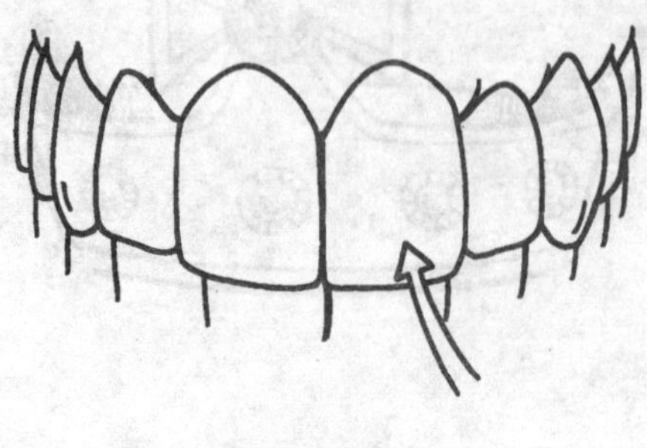

tooth

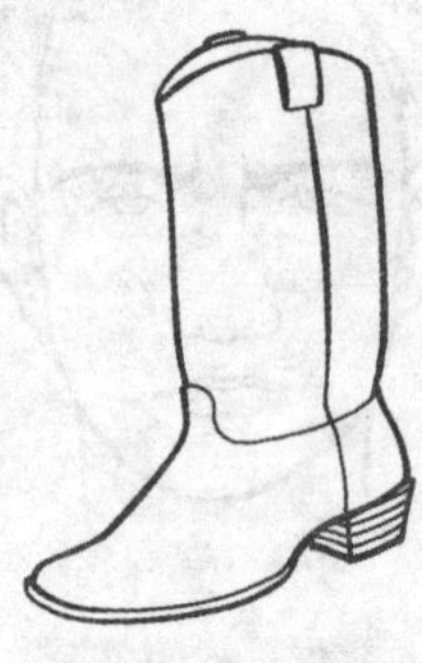

boot

The oi phoneme

Blend the phonemes to read these words: *boy* and *coil*. The phoneme **oi** can be spelt **oy**.

Blend the phonemes to read these words. Colour **oy** red. Colour **oi** blue.

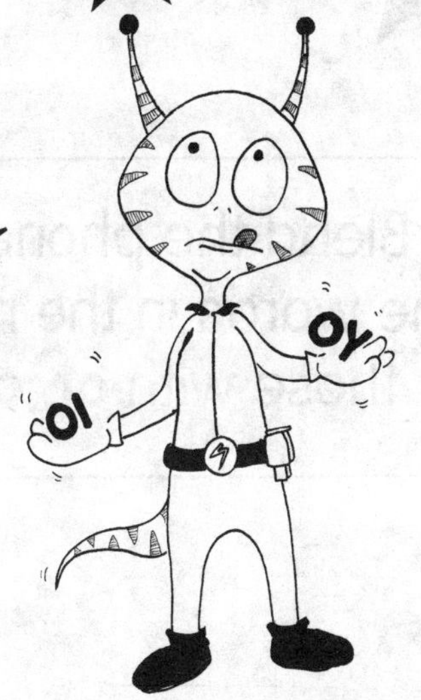

toilet

toy

coin

soil

boy

The or phoneme

Blend the phonemes to read these words: *for*, *floor* and *more*. The phoneme **or** can be spelt **or**, **oor** and **ore**.

Blend the phonemes to read the words in the rockets. Colour those with **or**, **oor** and **ore**.

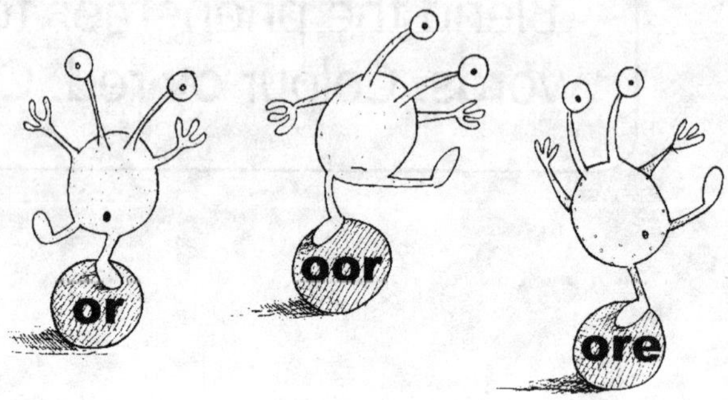

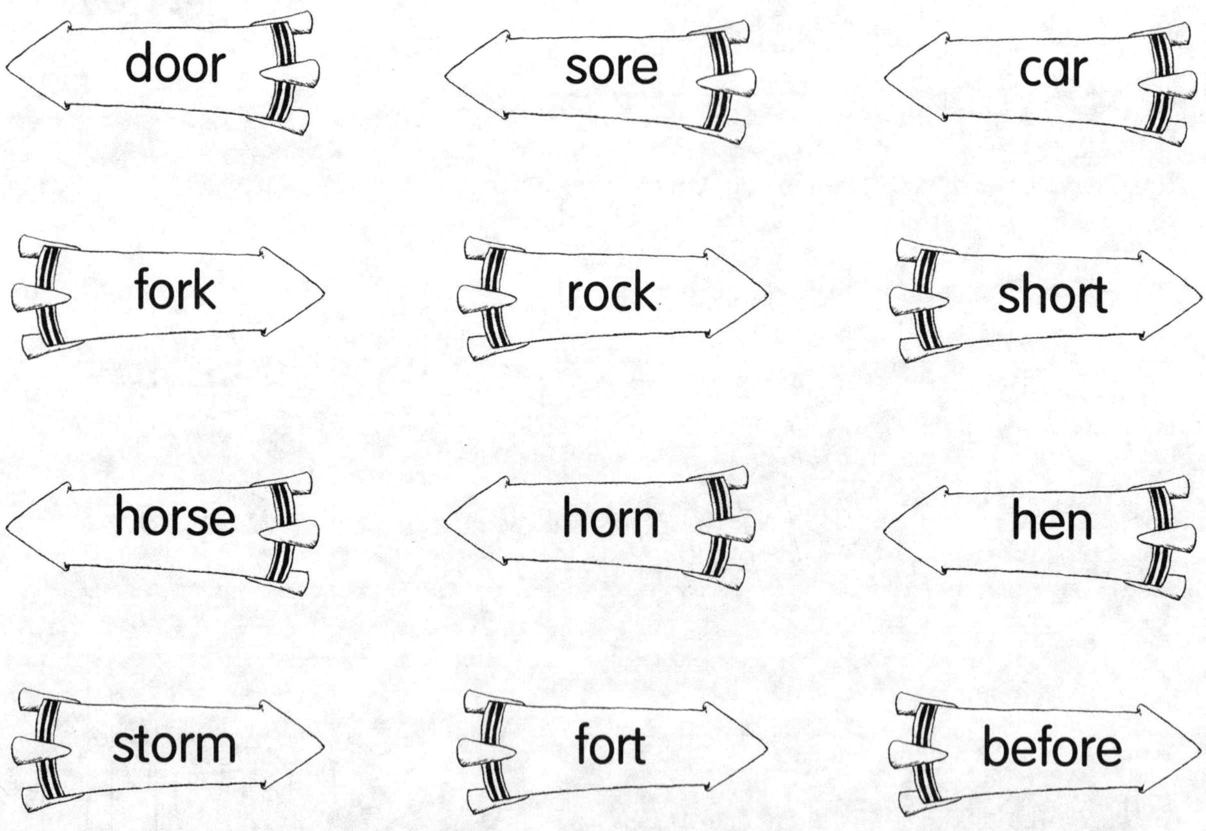

Plurals

Read the sentences. Change the words in the planets to plurals by adding **s**, for example, *brick* – *bricks*. Complete the sentences.

1. desk — In my class there are lots of ______________.
2. sack — We need ten ______________ for the sack race.
3. wing — A bird flaps its ______________ to fly.
4. hand — I have two ______________ and two feet.
5. neck — Giraffes have long ______________.
6. ball — I like to throw and catch ______________.
7. tent — Our ______________ got wet in the rain.
8. queen — Kings and ______________ wear crowns.

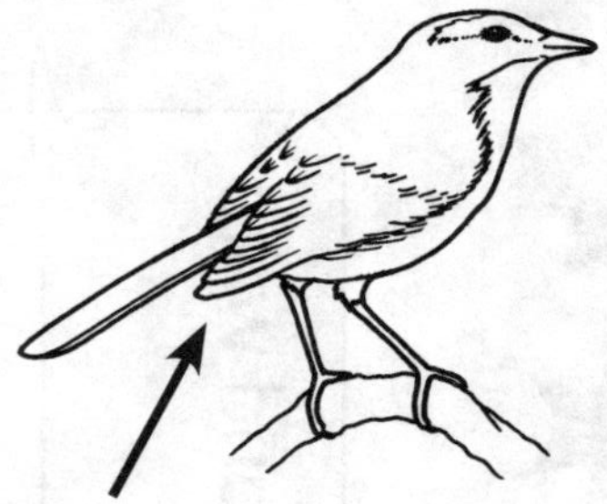

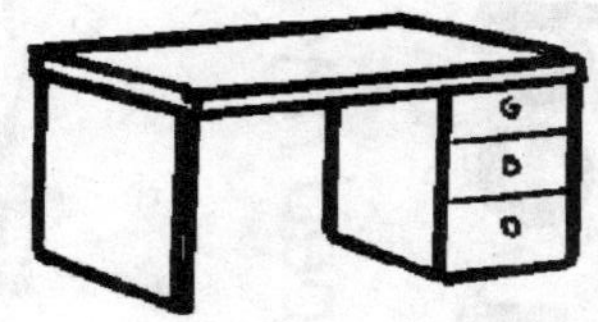

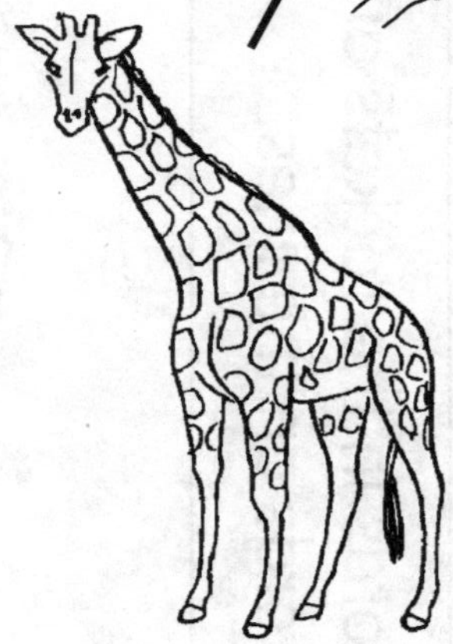

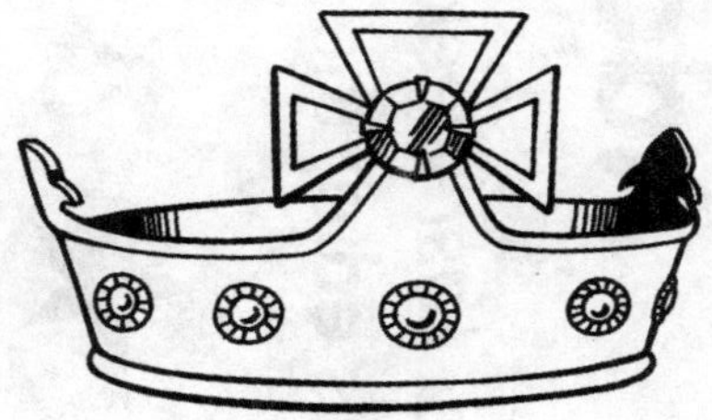

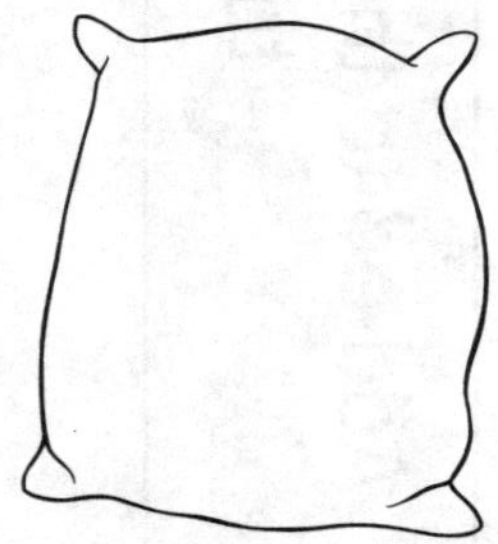

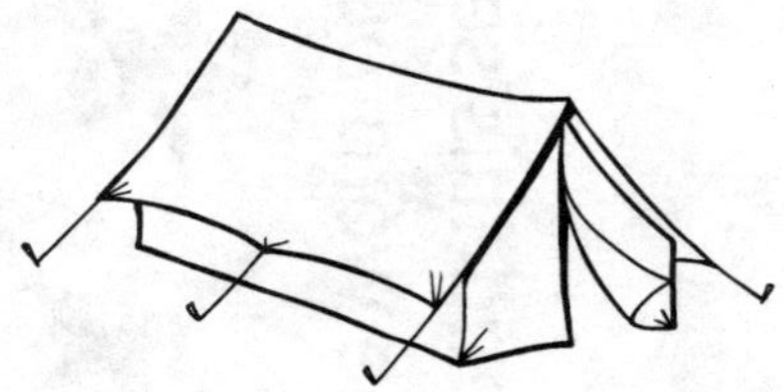

Adding **ed**

Read this sentence: *Last week I bumped my head*. Can you see that the word *bump* has **ed** at the end?

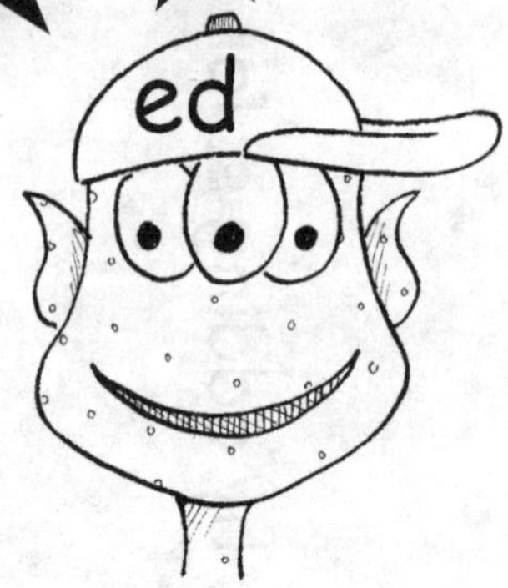

Add **ed** to the words in the rockets and write the words on the lines.

jump → __________

help → __________

lock → __________

ask → __________

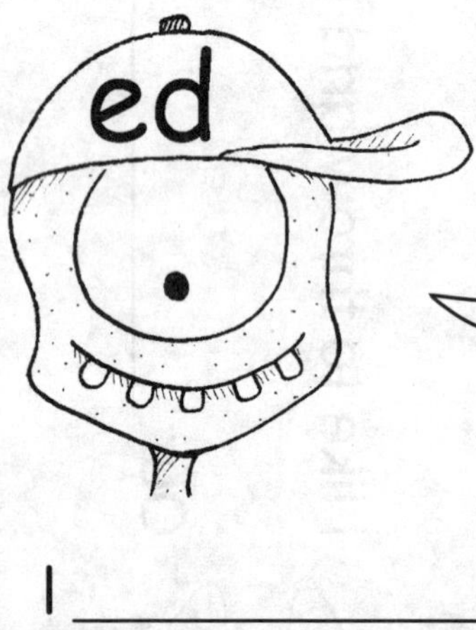

Now write the above words with **ed** in these sentences.

1. I ______________ up and down on my bed.
2. I ______________ my mum bake a cake.
3. My dad ______________ the door with a key.
4. I ______________ my mum if I could go out to play.

Adding **ing**

Read this sentence: *I am going home soon.* Can you see that the word *go* has **ing** at the end?

Add **ing** to the words in the spaceships and write the words on the lines.

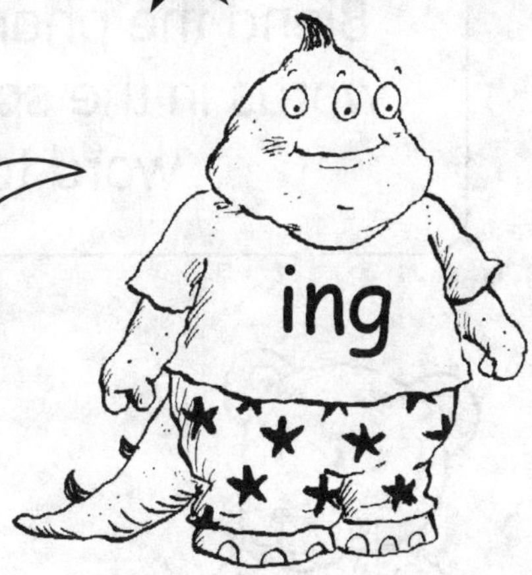

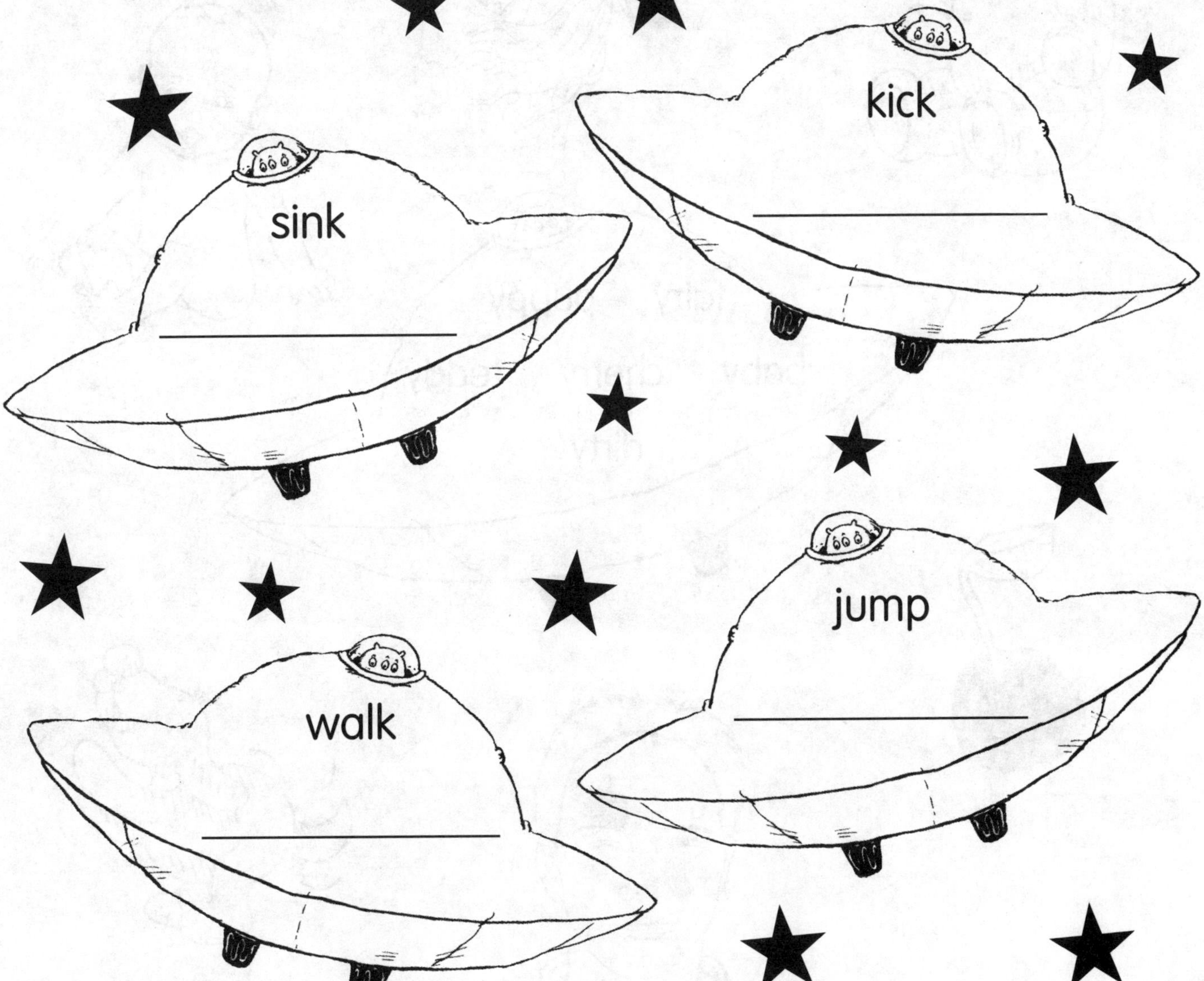

Words that end in y

Blend the phonemes to read these words: *hairy* and *teddy*. Can you hear the phoneme **ee** at the end? This phoneme can be spelt with a **y**.

Blend the phonemes to read the words in the spaceship. Join each word to a picture.

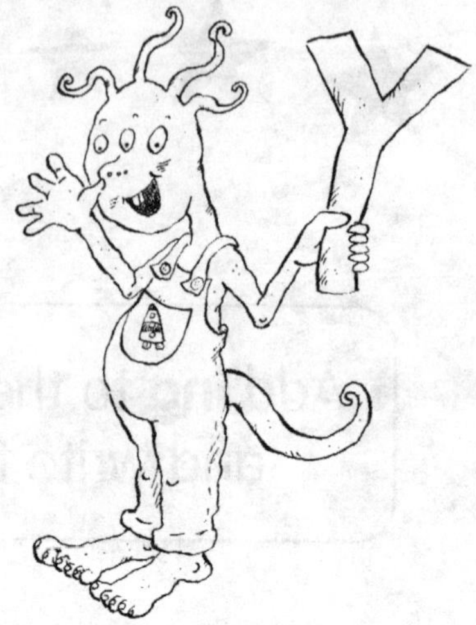

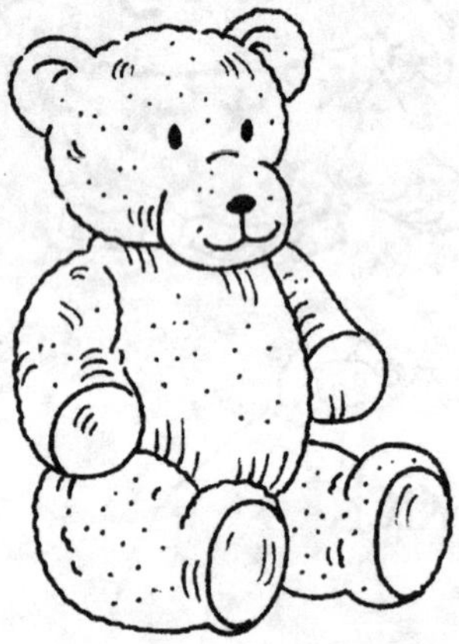

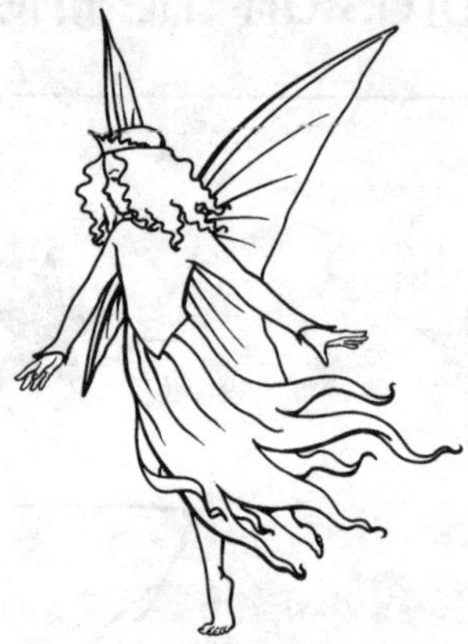

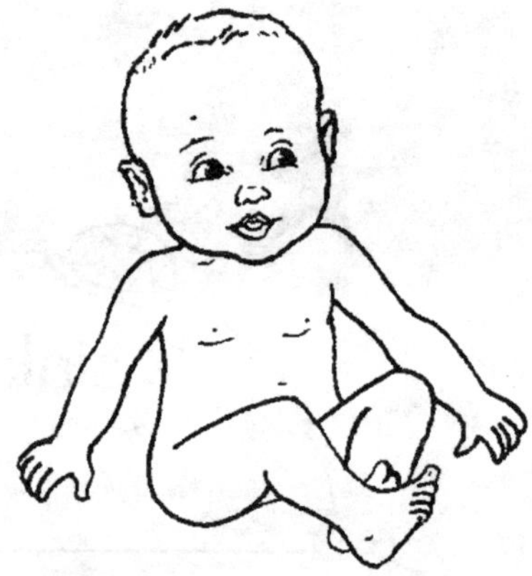

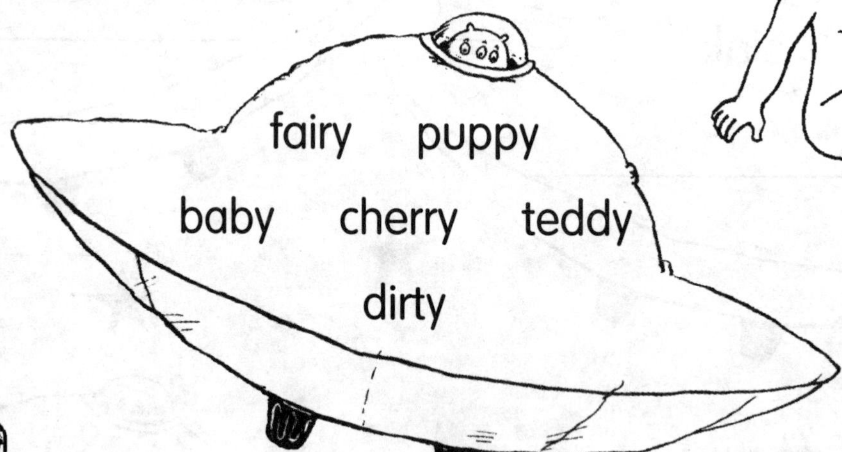

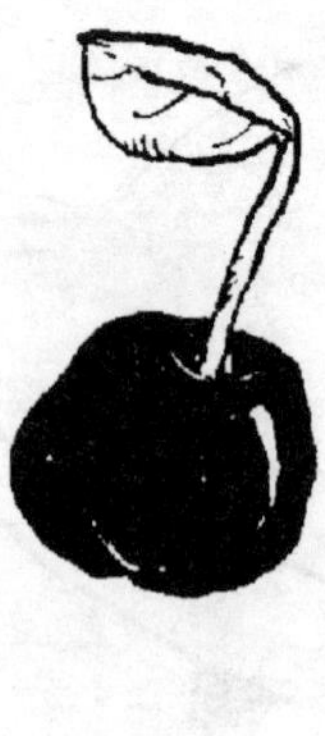

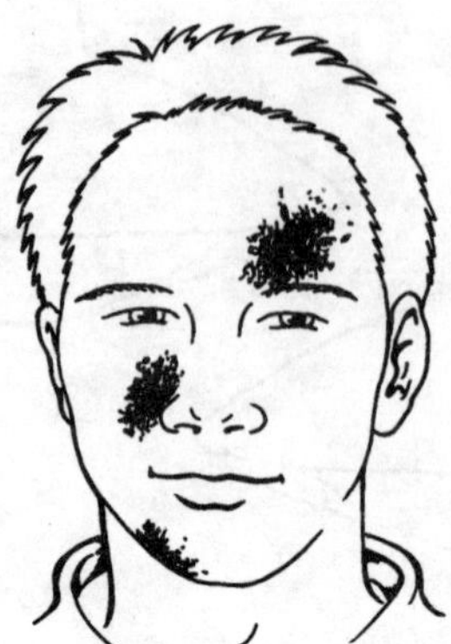

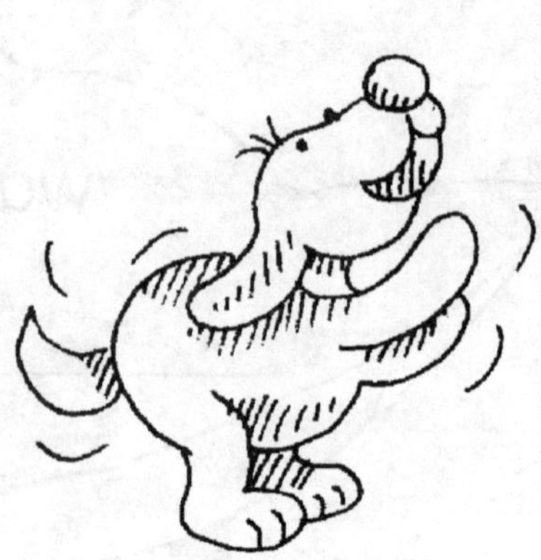

Words with double letters

Blend the phonemes to read these words: *letter, correct* and *running*. They have two letters in the middle which are the same.

Look at the pictures and say what they show. Write the double letters from the box below in the middle of each word. The last word has no picture clue to help you!

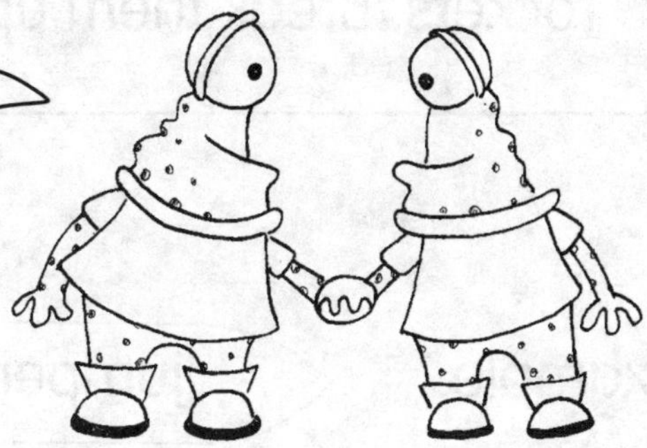

tt	pp	mm	nn	ff	bb

1. 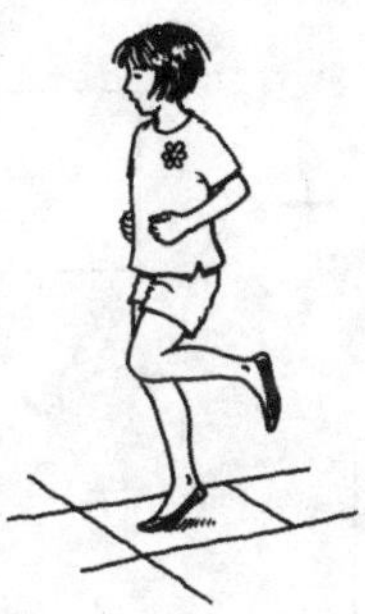 ho __ __ ing

4. 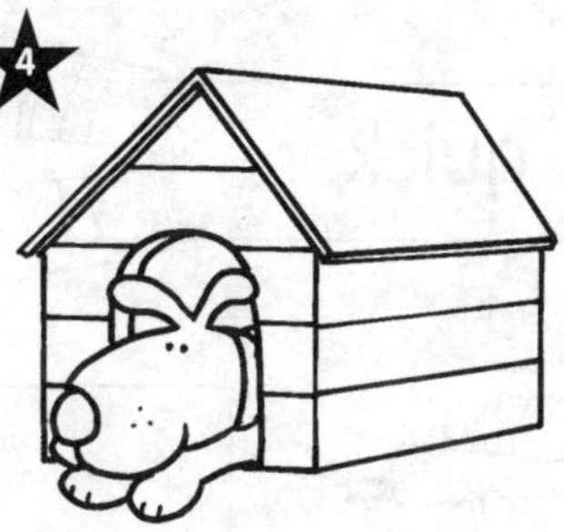 ke __ __ el

2. 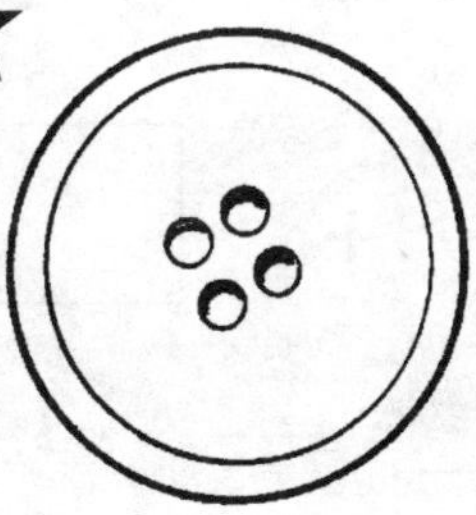 bu __ __ on

5. 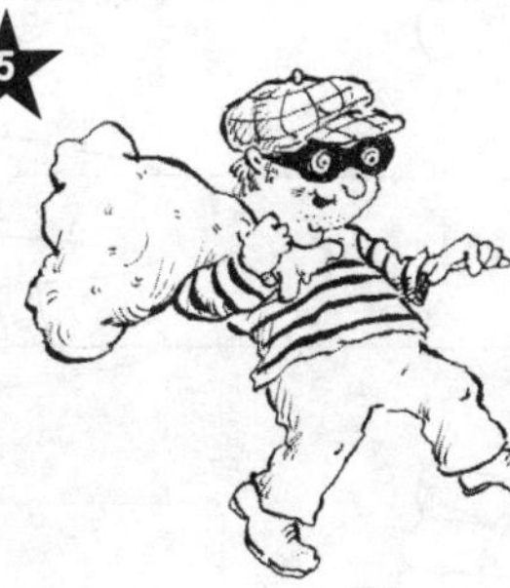 ro __ __ er

3. 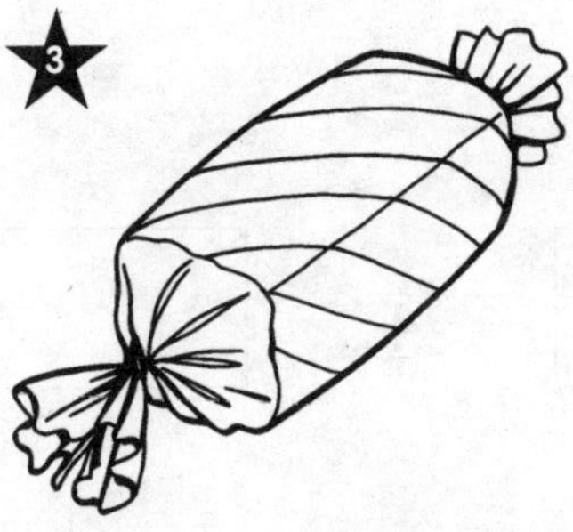 to __ __ ee

6. 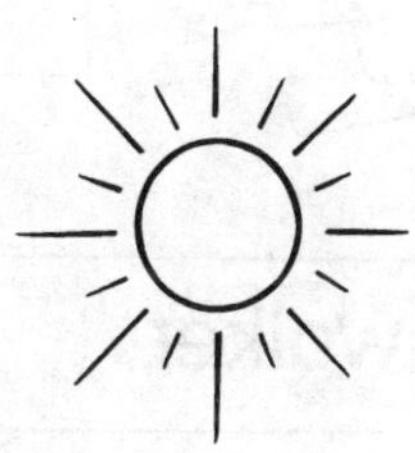 su __ __ er

Words with **er**

Blend the phonemes to read these words: *loud***er**, *sweet***er**, *teach***er** and *sing***er**. Can you hear **er** at the end of each word?

Blend the phonemes to read the words in the rockets. Break them up as in the example.

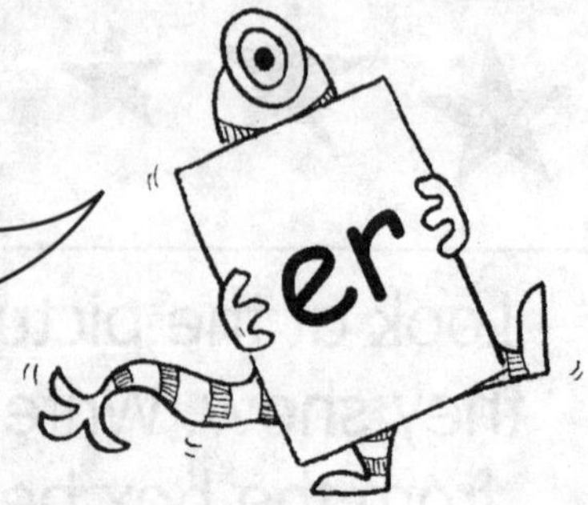

Example: jumper = jump + er

duster = ______ + ______

quicker = ______ + ______

cracker = ______ + ______

older = ______ + ______

taller = ______ + ______

walker = ______ + ______

recorder = ______ + ______

Words with ly

Blend the phonemes to read these words: *sweetly* and *loudly*. Can you hear **ly** at the end of each word?

Read the letters and letter strings below. Choose a letter or letter string from each rocket to spell words that end in **ly**. Write them on the lines. One has been done as an example.

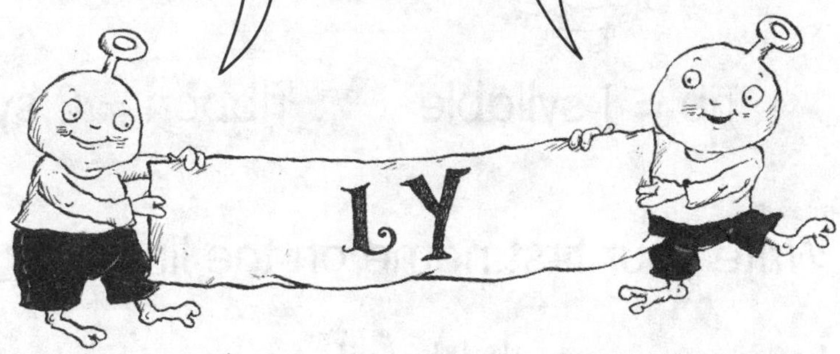

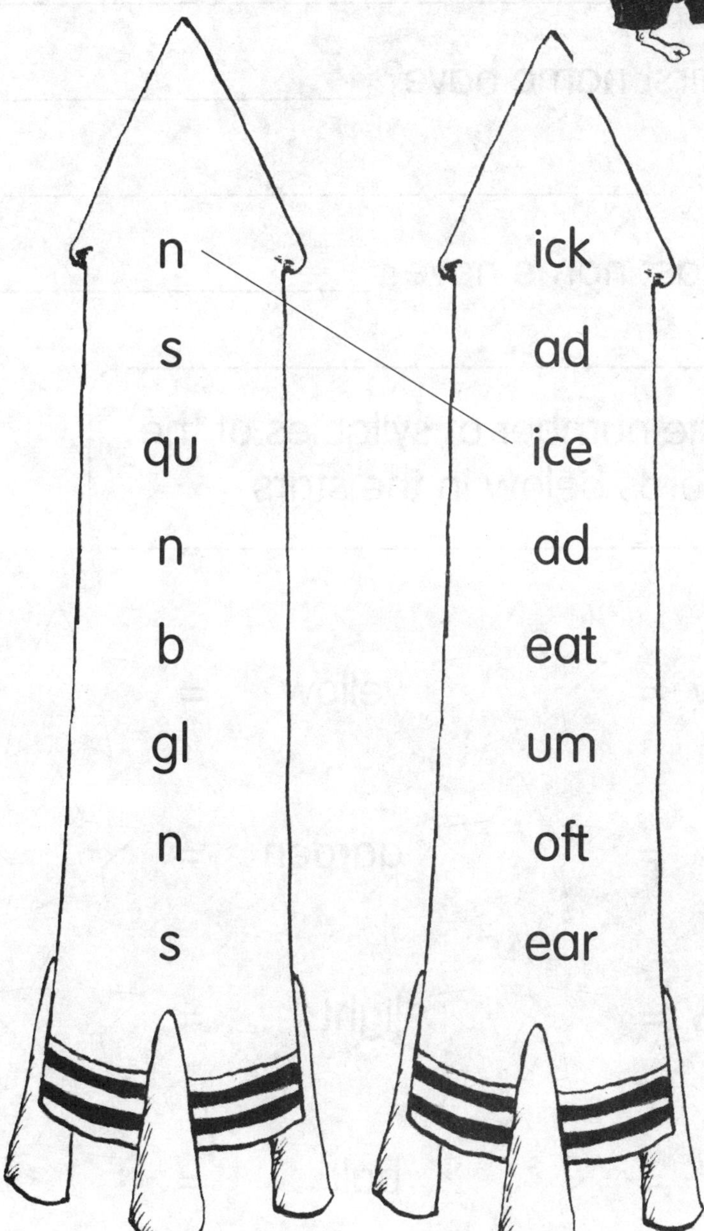

+ ly

nicely

Syllables

Blend the phonemes to read these words: *rib, ribbon* and *robbery*. Can you hear how many syllables each word has?

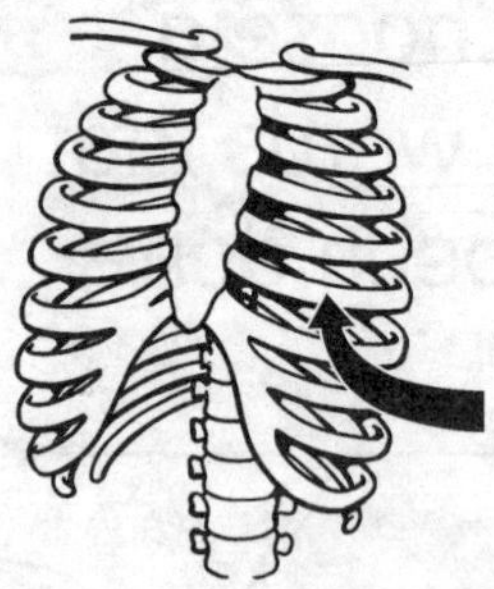

rib = 1 syllable

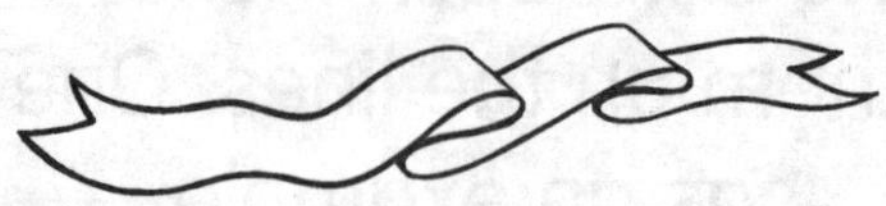

ribbon = 2 syllables

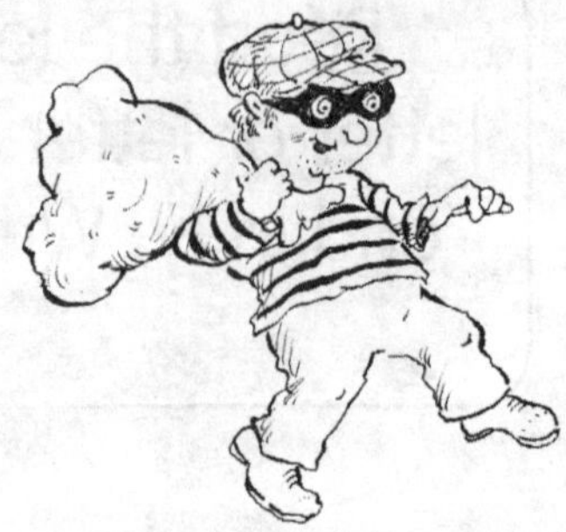

robbery = 3 syllables

Write your first name on the line. ______________________

How many syllables does your first name have? ____________

Write your last name on the line. ______________________

How many syllables does your last name have? ____________

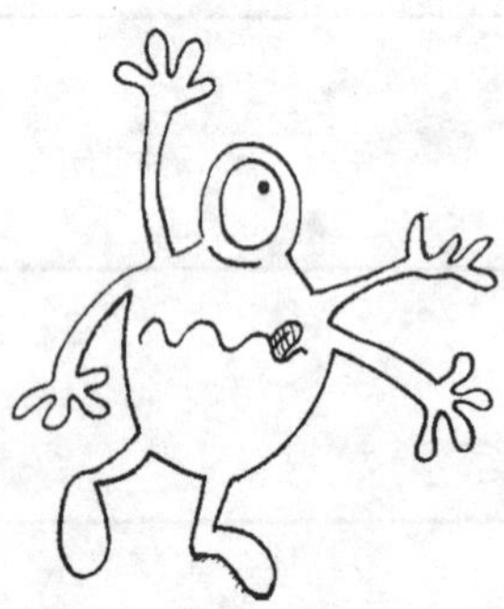

Write the number of syllables of the words below in the stars.

this = ☆ Saturday = ☆ yellow = ☆

mother = ☆ name = ☆ garden = ☆

door = ☆ suddenly = ☆ light = ☆

morning = ☆ window = ☆ ball = ☆

Compound words

Blend the phonemes to read these words:

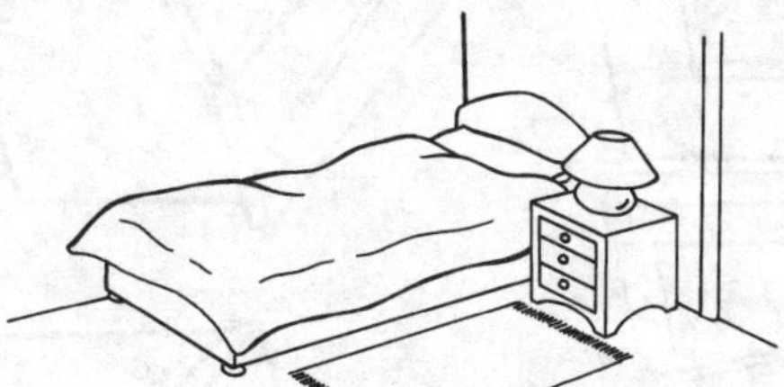

bedroom

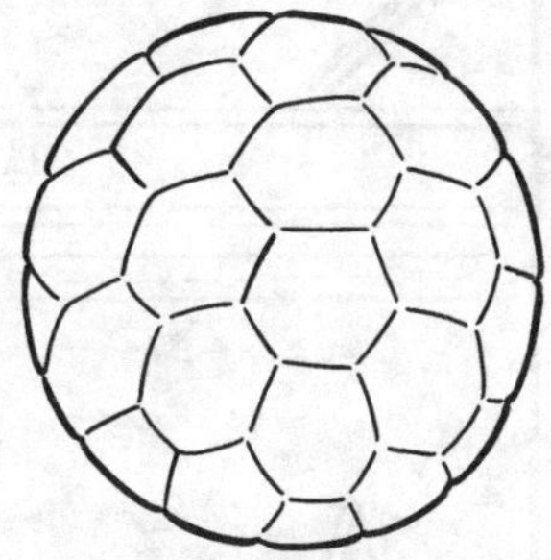

football

Can you hear the two small words that make the big word?

Blend the phonemes to read the small words in the table below. Join them together to write a big word. Draw the correct pictures next to the words.

Small words	**Big word**	**Picture**
butter + fly		
ear + ring		
toe + nail		
jelly + fish		
scare + crow		

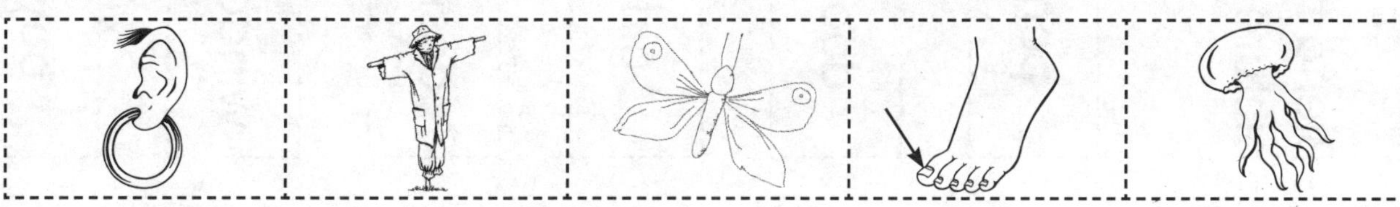

Things at school (nouns)

Blend the phonemes to read the words. Look at the picture. Write the words from the list on the picture in the correct places.

pen	chair
door	book
girl	ball
desk	table
window	light
boy	bat

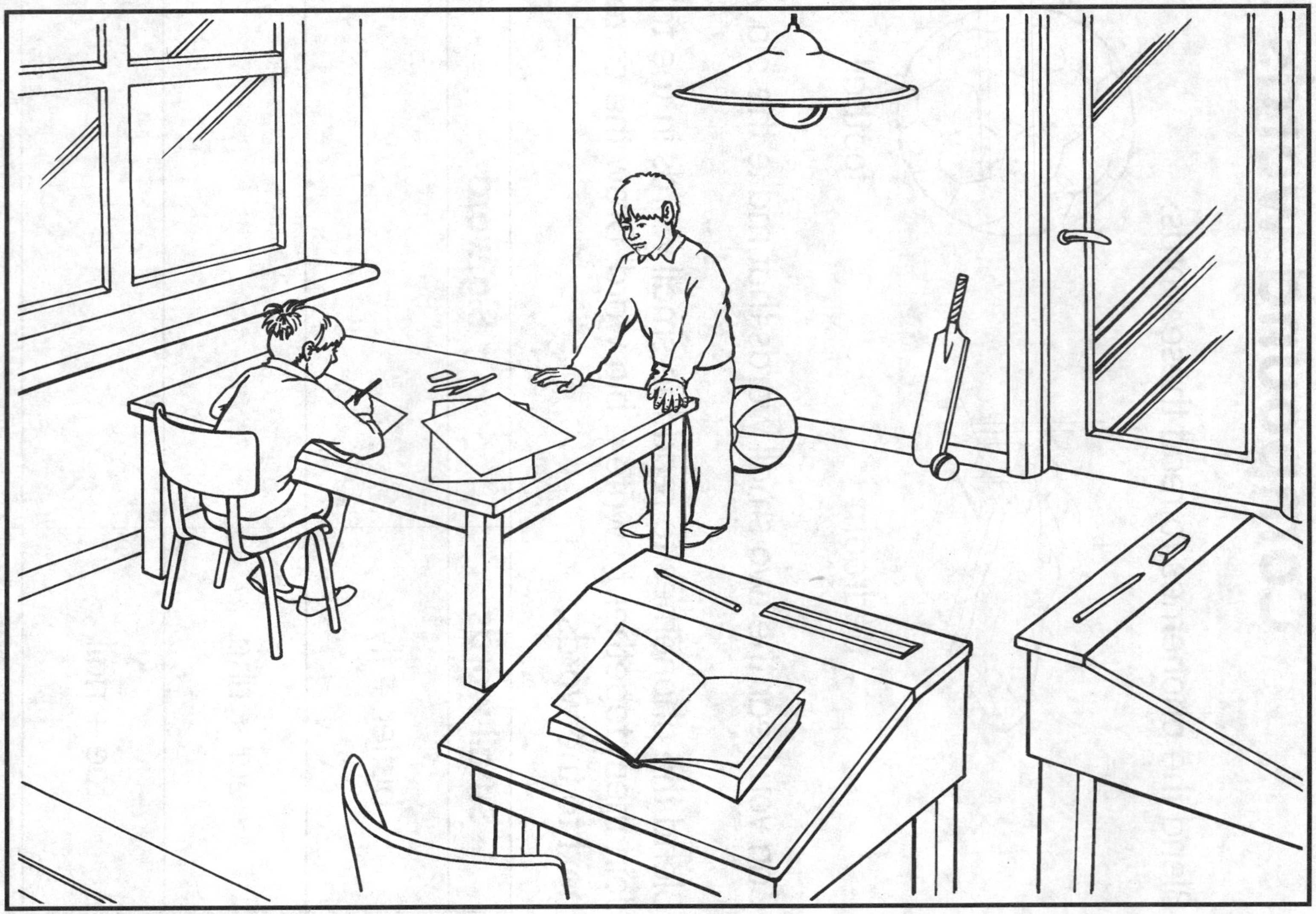

Things in the garden (nouns)

Blend the phonemes to read the words. Look at the picture. Write the words from the list on the picture in the correct places.

gate	dog
roof	peg
pond	bin
flower	cat
tree	slug
path	snail
grass	sun

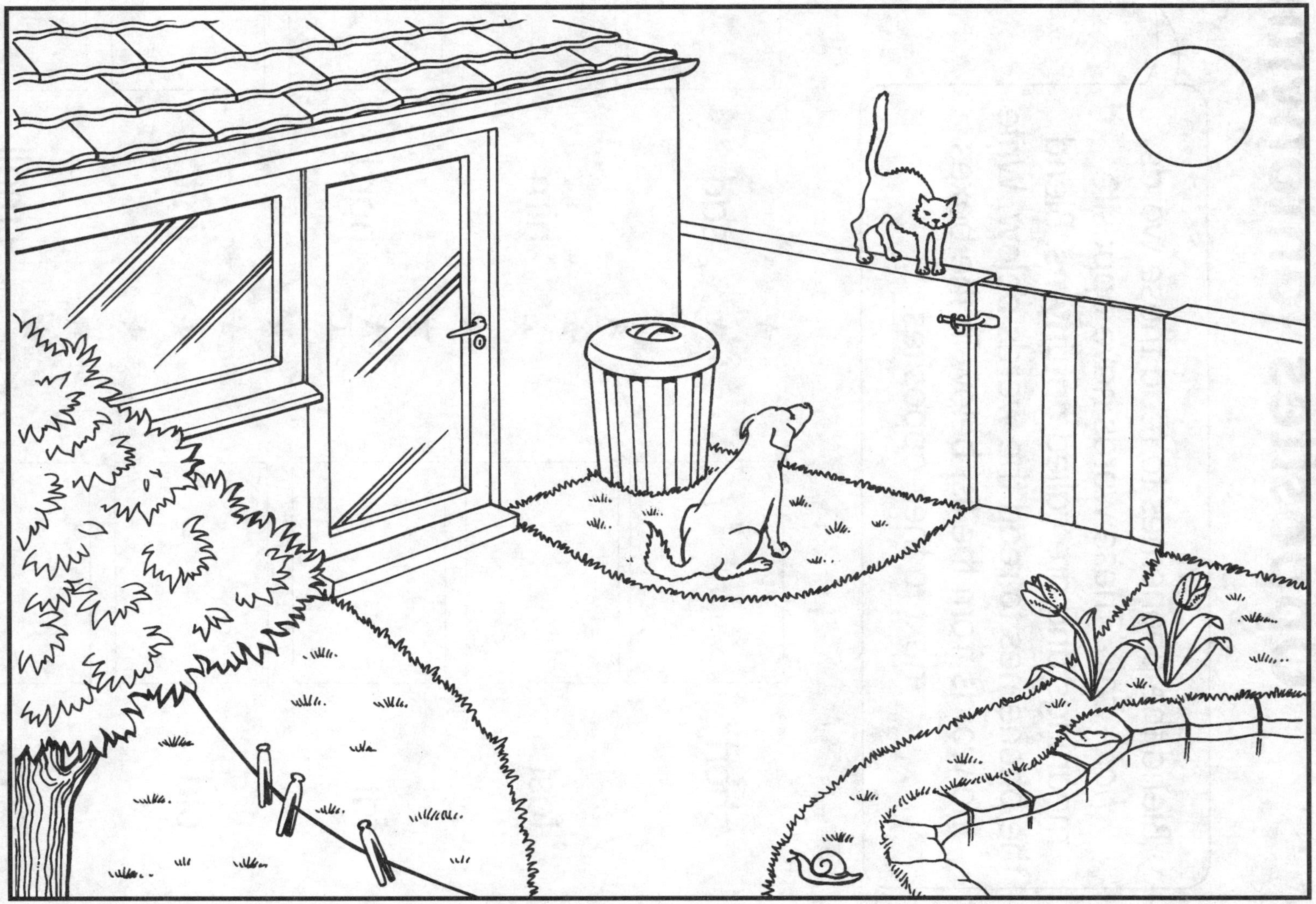

Opposites (antonyms)

Blend the phonemes to read these words: *hot – cold*. These words have opposite meanings and are called **antonyms**. Blend the phonemes to read the words below. Write the words from the list below in the boxes next to their opposites.

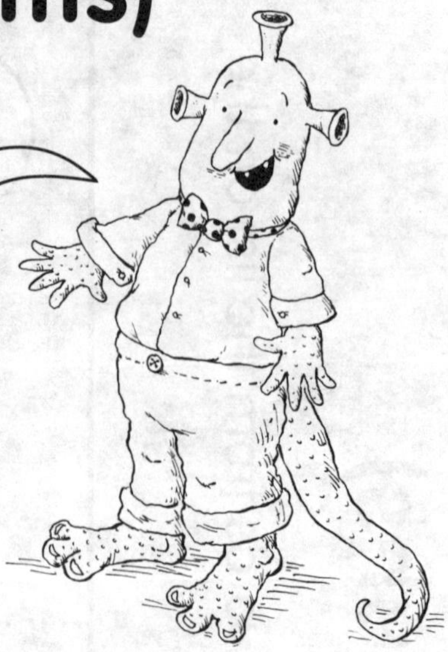

short		sad	
fast		him	
fat		hard	
old		first	
dry		small	

tall	thin	big	slow	her
happy	soft	wet	new	last

Words with un and dis

Blend the phonemes to read these sentences:

I am happy, but he is unhappy.

I like jam but I dislike butter.

Can you see that the words *happy* and *like* have **un** and **dis** in front of them? The letter strings **un** and **dis** make the words mean the opposite. Add **un** and **dis** to these words and write them on the lines.

un →

dress ________________

tie ________________

lock ________________

kind ________________

★ ★

dis →

cover ________________

agree ________________

appear ________________

Circle the correct words in these sentences.

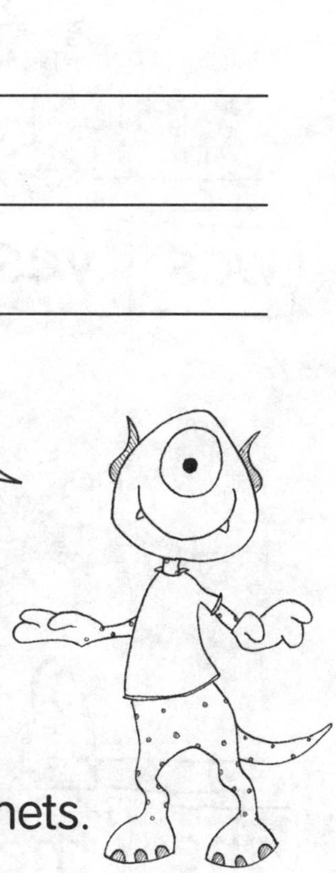

1. I **undress/unkind** when I have a bath.
2. To take off my shoes I **unlock/untie** the laces.
3. We **unhappy/unlock** the door to get in.
4. The ugly sisters were **unkind/untie** to Cinderella.
5. The aliens wanted to **disagree/discover** new planets.
6. My sister and I always **disagree/disappear**.

High frequency words

Blend the phonemes to read the words in the walls. Write the words in the word grids. Look at the letters in the words carefully to see where they will fit. Some letters have been written in the grids to help you. Find the hidden word shaded in each grid and write it in on the line.

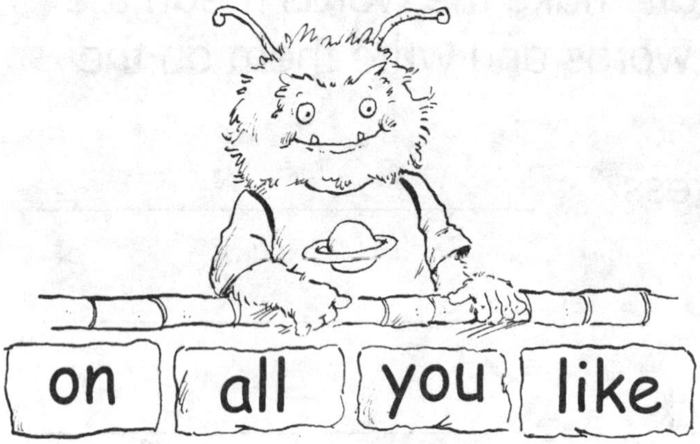

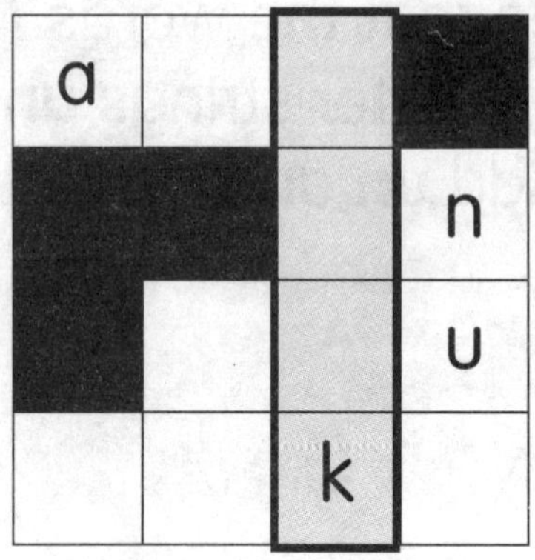

Hidden word: ______________

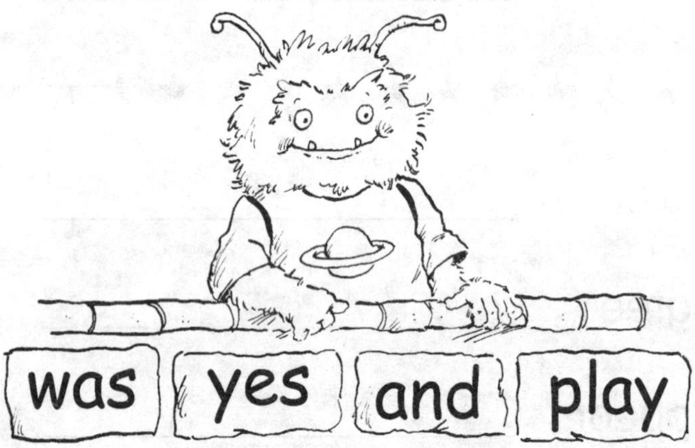

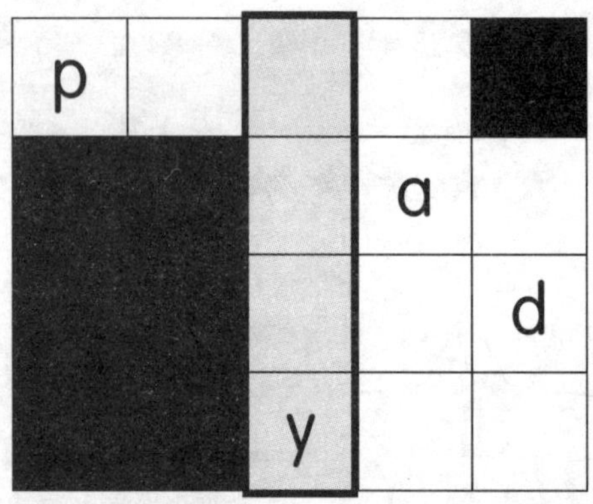

Hidden word: ______________

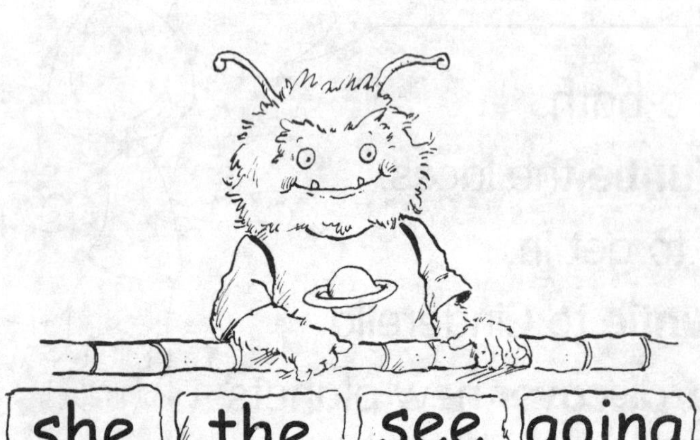

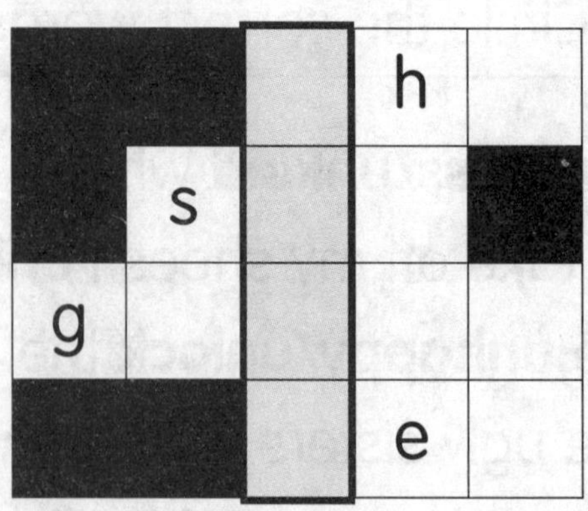

Hidden word: ______________

High frequency words in sentences

Read the sentences. Write the missing words in the gaps. The words you need are in the rockets.

1. My mum ______ I are ______ to the shops. (going, and)
2. I ______ to go fishing with ______ dad. (like, my)
3. You must ______ left and right when ______ cross the road. (look, you)
4. My dad ______, 'Go and ______ in the park.' (said, play)
5. We ______ to the beach ______ a holiday. (for, went)
6. I ______ see the ______ dog. (big, can)
7. Can you ______ the cat ______ the tree? (up, see)
8. We ______ going to ______ wet in the rain. (get, are)
9. She ______ sad and so were ______. (they, was)
10. My dad said, '______ and look at ______.' (this, come)

High frequency words – how many letters?

Read the words in the word bank. Find and circle them in the word search. The words can only be read across, not up or down.

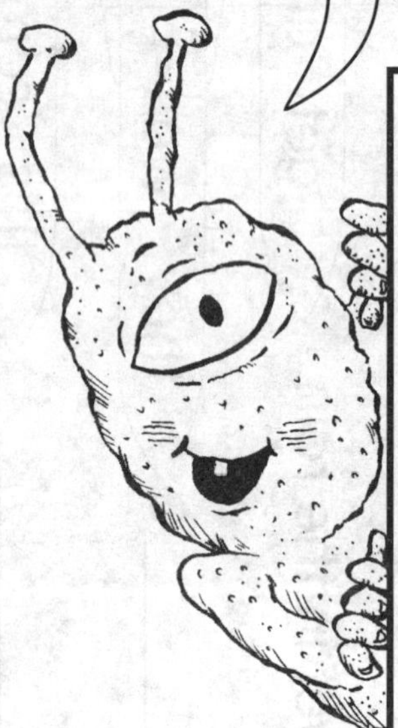

f	l	i	k	e	p	h
o	n	h	q	r	i	t
t	o	f	l	i	s	v
b	g	e	t	a	n	d
k	c	o	m	e	r	g
l	o	o	k	j	u	p
f	f	o	r	y	o	u

Word bank

come
get
on
up
look
of
it
for
is
you
like
and

Count the numbers of letters in each word in the word bank and sort them into the rockets below. One of each has been done for you.

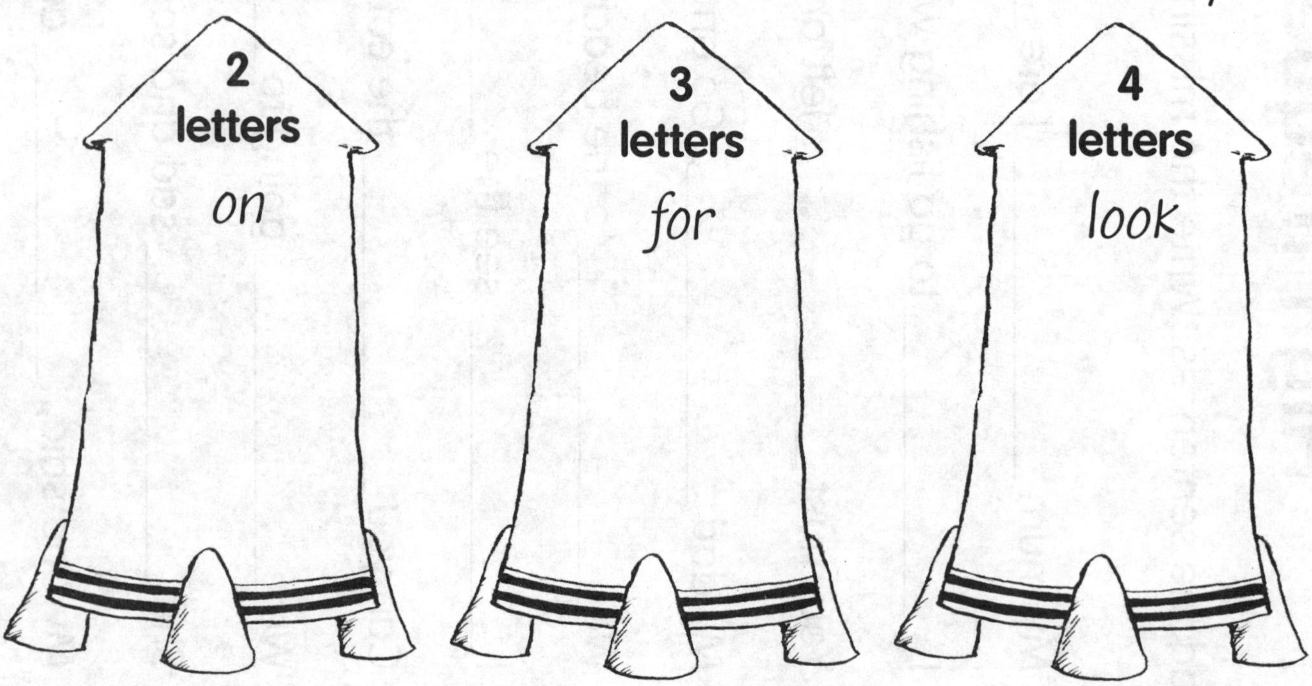

Sorting high frequency words by first phoneme

Blend the phonemes to read the words in the word bank. Find and circle them in the word search. The words can only be read across and down.

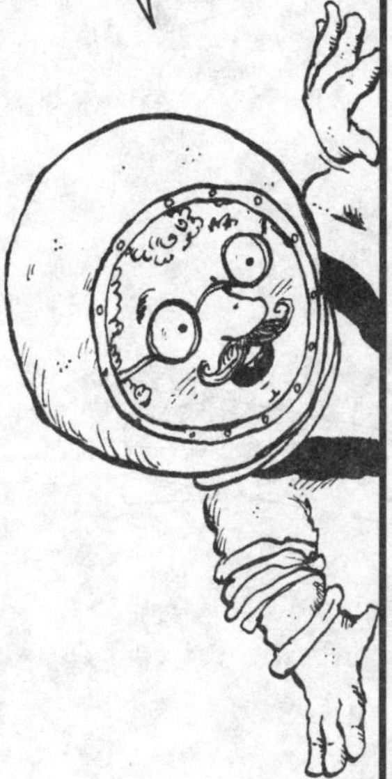

s	g	x	w	w	i	t	h
i	l	q	e	k	h	t	t
s	a	f	t	e	r	o	r
t	h	w	e	n	t	t	e
e	t	h	e	r	e	h	e
r	t	i	m	e	a	i	s
d	s	a	w	h	m	s	e
t	h	e	n	a	l	l	e

Word bank

am	with
after	this
all	then
see	there
saw	to
sister	tree
went	time
we	

Look at the first phoneme of each word in the word bank and write them in the correct boxes below. The first one has been done for you.

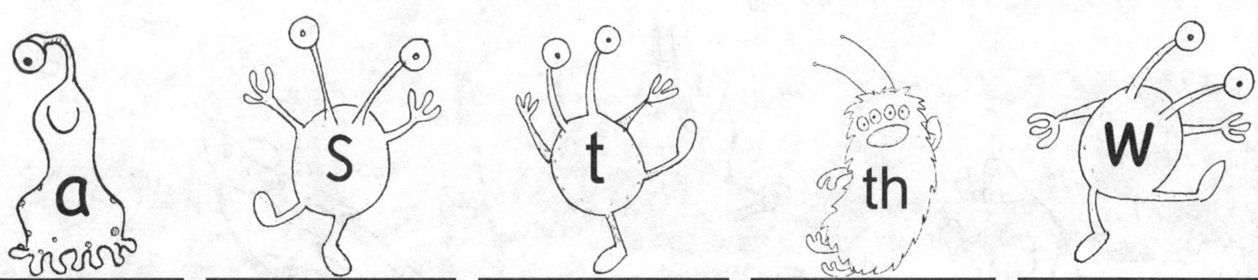

a	s	t	th	w
am				

What can aliens do? (verbs)

We can do lots of things. What can aliens do? Blend the phonemes to read the words in the rockets. They are 'doing' words which are called **verbs**. Join each word to the alien who is doing what it says.

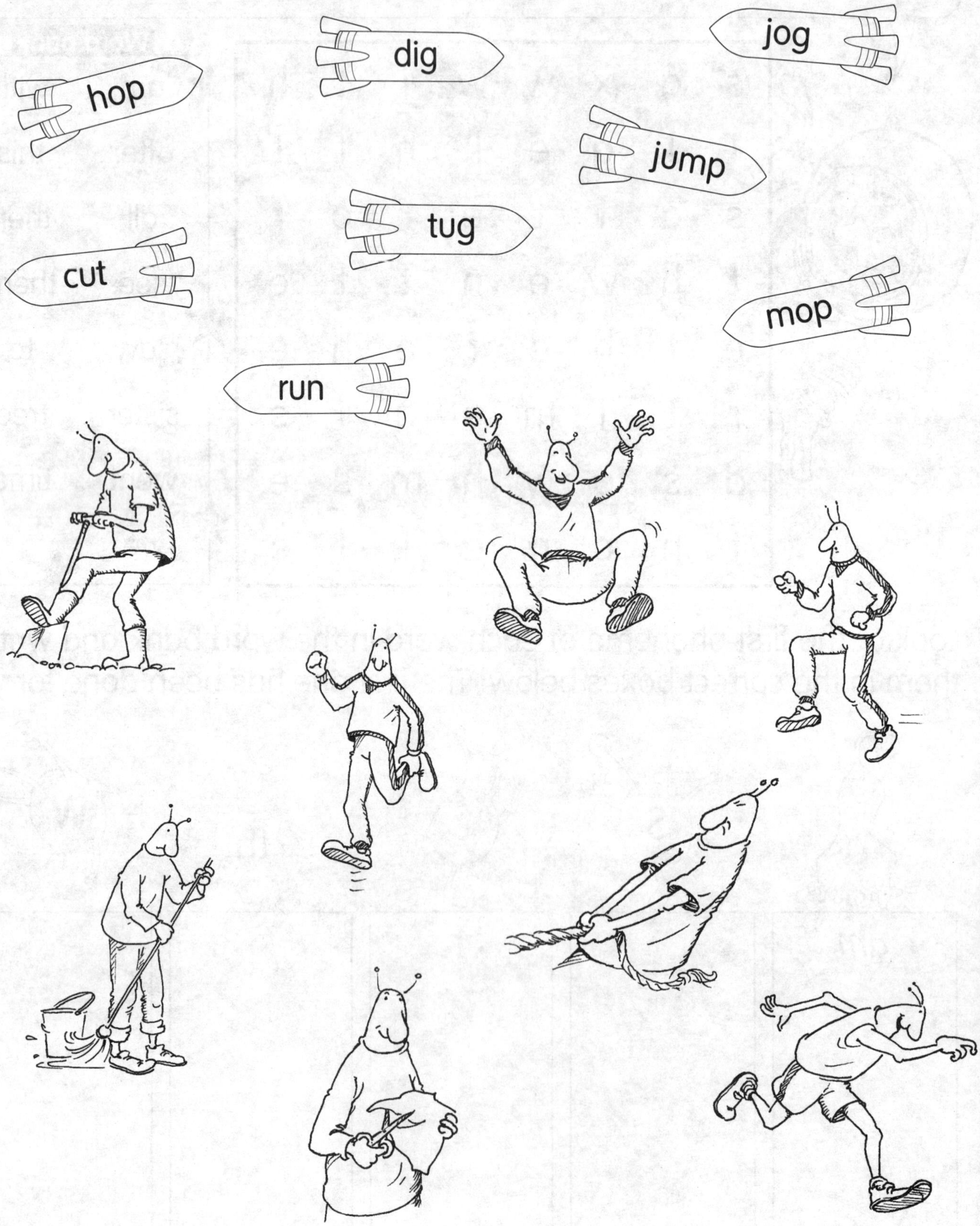

How do aliens feel? (adjectives)

Blend the phonemes to read the words in the word bank. How do aliens feel? Look at the pictures and the words in the word bank. Write the words in the boxes beside the pictures. The first one has been done for you.

Word bank

hot sad sleepy mad happy cold

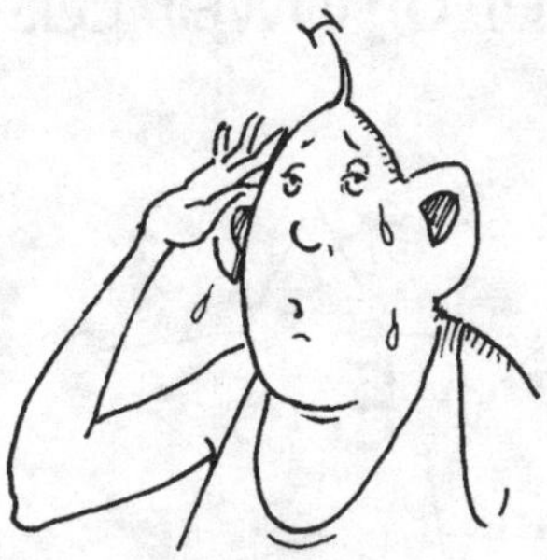

hot

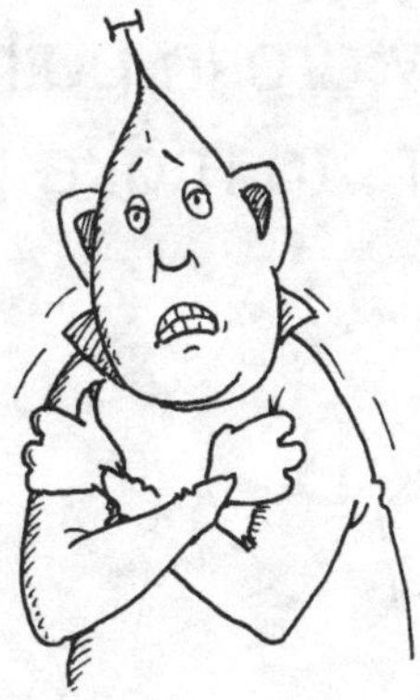

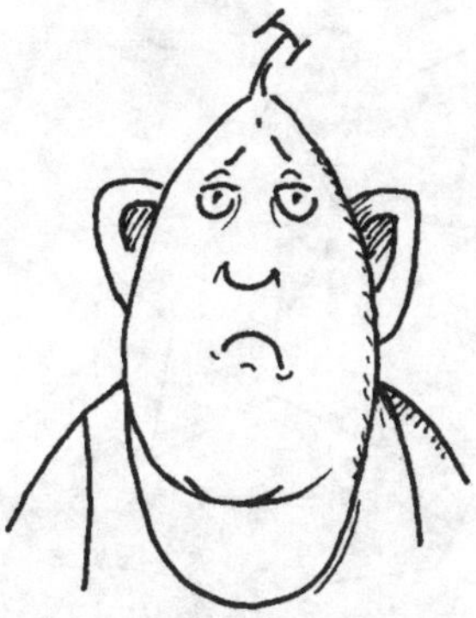

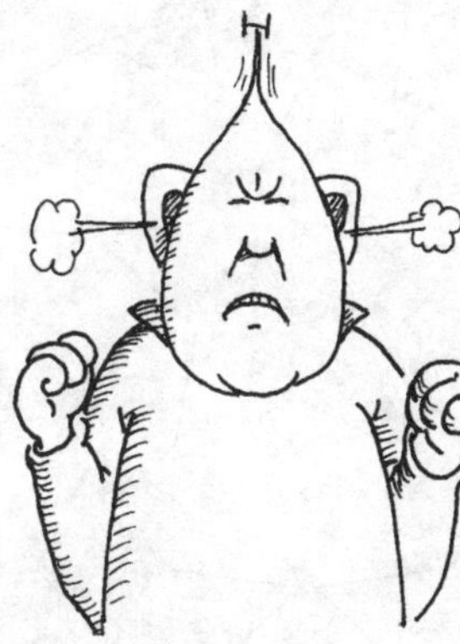

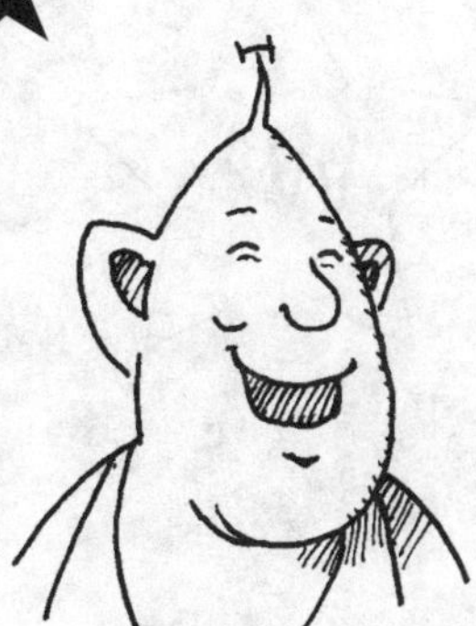

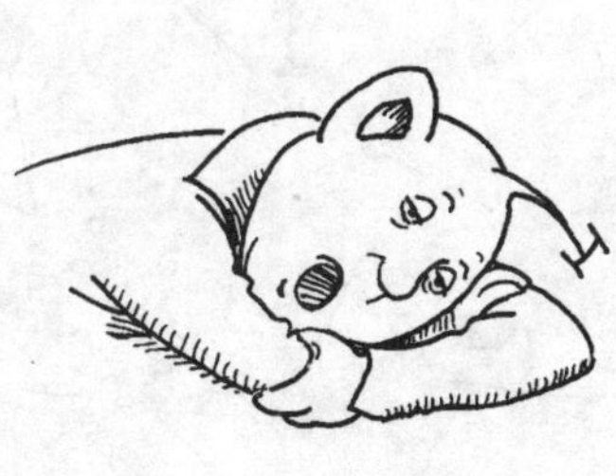

Upper and lower case letters

These are the upper case letters of the alphabet. They are also called capital letters.

A B C D E F G H I J K L M N O P Q R S T U V W X Y

These are the lower case letters of the alphabet

a b c d e f g h i j k l m n o p q r s t u v w x y

The letters below are in pairs. Write the missing upper or lower case letters in the stars to make pairs of letters.

Aa B C d E

f G h i

j k l M N

O p Q r

S t U v W

X Y Z

Upper case letters

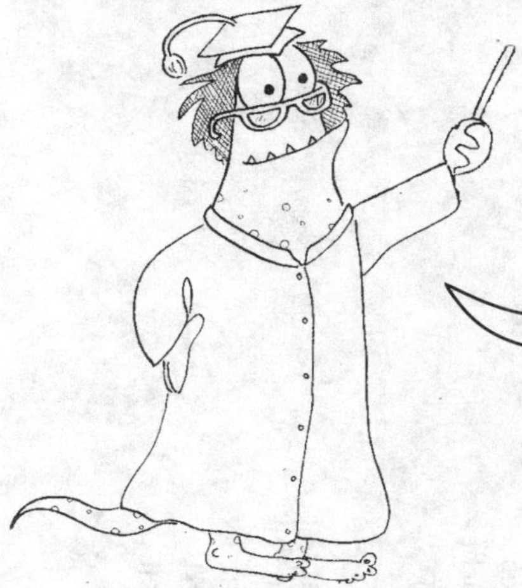

Capital letters are used for names of people, places, days of the week and months of the year. Circle the capital letters for the seven days of the week and write the missing phoneme for each day of the week next to it. Make sure that you use capital letters. Then do the same for the months of the year.

Days of the week

Monday	☐	onday
Tuesday	☐	uesday
Wednesday	☐	ednesday
Thursday	☐	hursday
Friday	☐	riday
Saturday	☐	aturday
Sunday	☐	unday

Months of the year

January	☐	anuary	July	☐	uly
February	☐	ebruary	August	☐	ugust
March	☐	arch	September	☐	eptember
April	☐	pril	October	☐	ctober
May	☐	ay	November	☐	ovember
June	☐	une	December	☐	ecember

Solutions

■ **PAGE 5**

bed ru**b** **b**lack
cat **c**ut **c**ub
dog be**d** **d**rum
fox **f**at **f**lag
go bu**g** **g**reen
hen **h**at **h**op
jam **j**og **j**et
leg ba**ll** c**l**ap
mop ja**m** plu**m**
nut he**n** ru**n**

■ **PAGE 6**

peg cu**p** **p**it
queen **qu**ick **qu**ack
rat **r**ain t**r**ee
sun ye**s** **s**ail
tap pe**t** **t**rip
vet **v**est ha**v**e
wet **w**e **w**ent
bo**x** fi**x** fo**x**
yes **y**elp **y**ou
zip **z**oo **z**ebra

■ **PAGE 7**

ant b**a**g r**a**n m**a**t
r**e**d b**e**d m**e**t n**e**t
in s**i**t d**i**g w**i**n
on p**o**t h**o**t st**o**p
up b**u**g dr**u**m l**u**mp

■ **PAGE 8**

a b c d e f g h i j k l m n o p q r s t u v w x y z

■ **PAGE 9**

a b c d e f g
h i j k l m n o
p q r s t
u v w x y z

a b c d e f g h i j k l m n o p q r s t u v w x y z

■ **PAGE 10**

def
ghi
jkl
mno

■ **PAGE 11**

pqr
stu
vwx
yz

■ **PAGE 12**

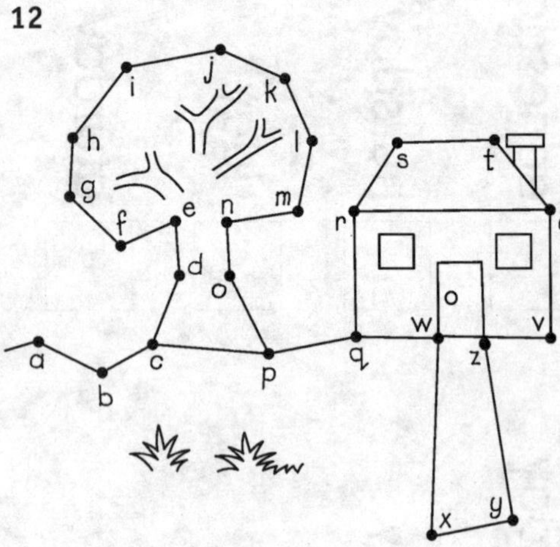

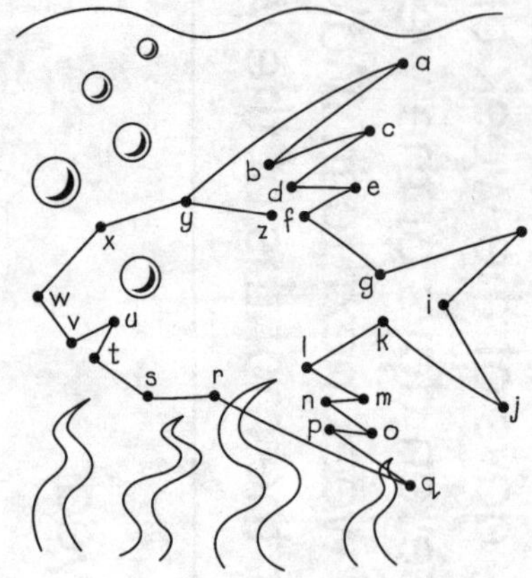

■ **PAGE 13**

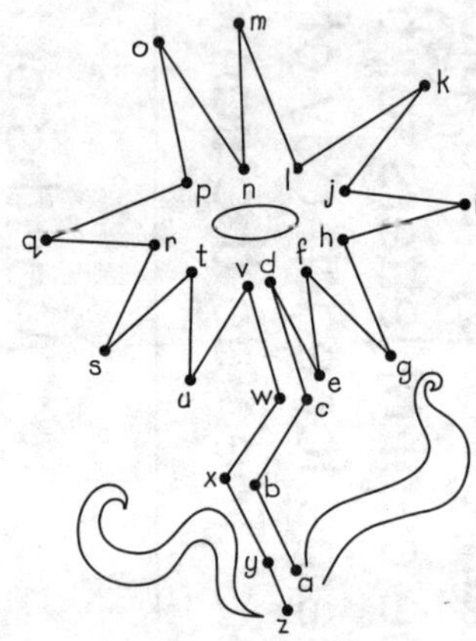

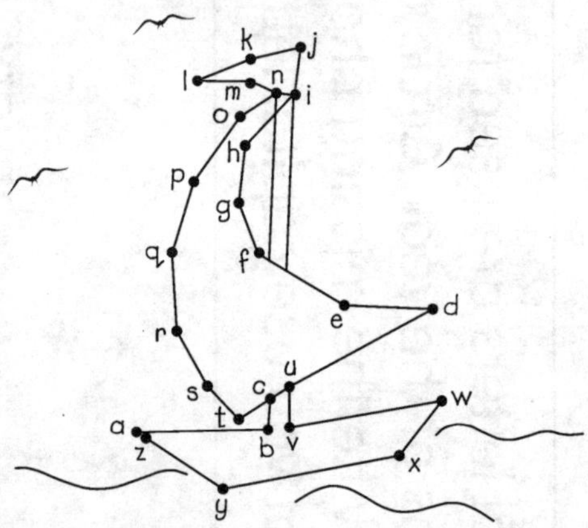

■ **PAGE 14**

bed
cat
fox
hen
jug
leg
map
pin
six
ten
umbrella
web
yacht
zip

■ **PAGE 15**

bat
cup
fan
hat
mop
net
rat
sun
vest
wall

■ PAGE 16

blow 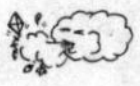
claw 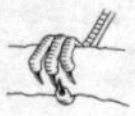
flag 
glue 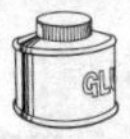
plug 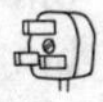
slug 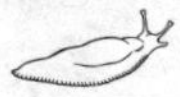

■ PAGE 17

crab 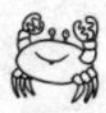
drum 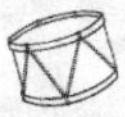
grin 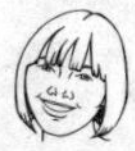
pram 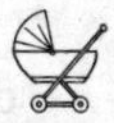
train 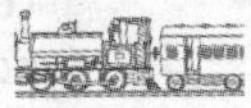
frog 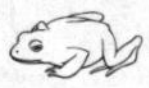

■ PAGE 18

twins swan swing dwarf swim twelve

twins 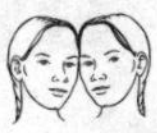
swan 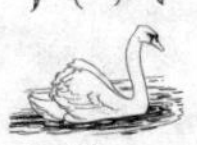
swing 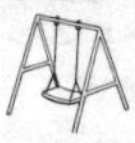
dwarf 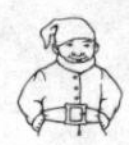
swim 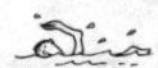
twelve 12

■ PAGE 19

1. The cut on my leg left a bad scar.
2. I like to skip to keep fit.
3. Some flowers smell nice.
4. Snap is a good card game.
5. It is very rude to spit.
6. The bus stop is next to the shop.

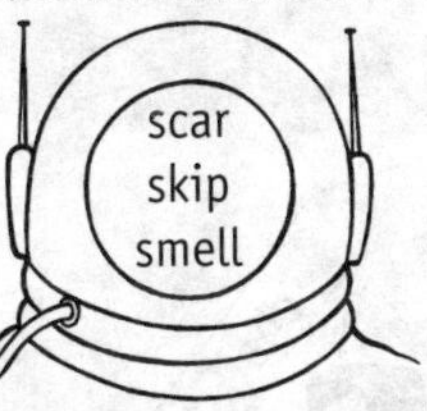

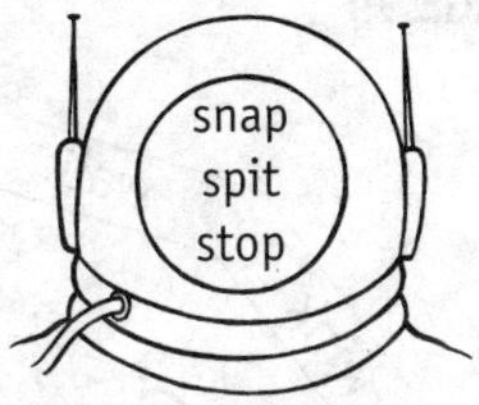

■ PAGE 20

1. My cut began to **bleed.**
2. Mud is **brown.**
3. The cake had **cream** on it.
4. He was a funny **clown.**
5. Catch the ball, don't **drop** it.
6. Birds can **fly.**
7. My painting had a red **frame.**
8. The fire began to **glow.**
9. My plant **grew** tall.
10. The princess was **pretty.**

■ PAGE 21

t	s	n	i	f	f	m	l
w	z	s	t	e	e	p	l
i	l	s	m	p	t	l	s
n	s	p	v	j	m	d	k
s	m	a	s	l	o	w	y
k	a	d	q	t	r	y	x
h	l	e	s	w	e	e	p
r	l	n	s	c	a	r	c

■ PAGE 22

1. I **chew** food with my teeth.
   My dog likes to **chase** cats.
2. I put the tins on the **shelf.**
   The **shop** sells ice creams.
3. You must **thank** her for the gift.
   The old dog was very **thin.**
4. After my swim, I had a hot **shower.**
   The sun made a big **shadow** under the tree.
5. My doll has bright red **cheeks.**
   Our teacher writes with **chalk.**

■ PAGE 23

screen
scratch
scream
scrub
splash
split

■ PAGE 24

spray spring square squirt

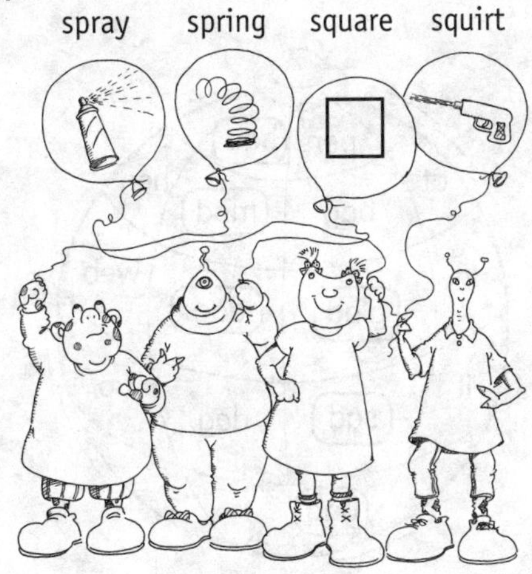

■ PAGE 25

straw
street
string
strong
strawberry
stretch

■ PAGE 26

1. screw
2. splash
3. scrub
4. string
5. splint
6. spring

■ PAGE 27

three 3
throne 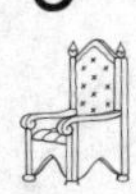
thrush 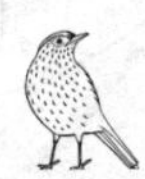
throw 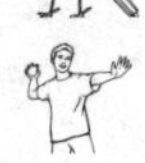

■ PAGE 28

th | r | i | l | l
th | r | u | sh
th | r | ow
th | r | ee
sh | r | u | b
sh | r | i | e | k
sh | r | u | g
sh | r | i | n | k

■ PAGE 29

1. I had a small **scrap** of paper to write my name on.
2. The **stray** dog had no home.
3. We had to **squash** the clothes into the small case.
4. The fish were in the **stream**.
5. I had to **thread** the needle to sew.
6. I **threw** the ball into the net.
7. He had a **splinter** of wood in his finger.
8. She jumps up and down as if she is on **springs**.
9. I **spread** the jam on my toast.
10. The mouse made my mum **scream**.

■ PAGE 30

white	ele**ph**ant	**wh**en
chorus	**wh**ip	**wh**eel
whale	**ph**oto	tele**ph**one

■ PAGE 31

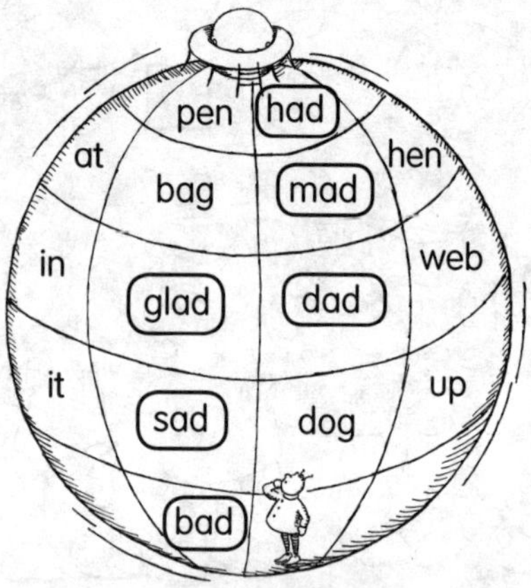

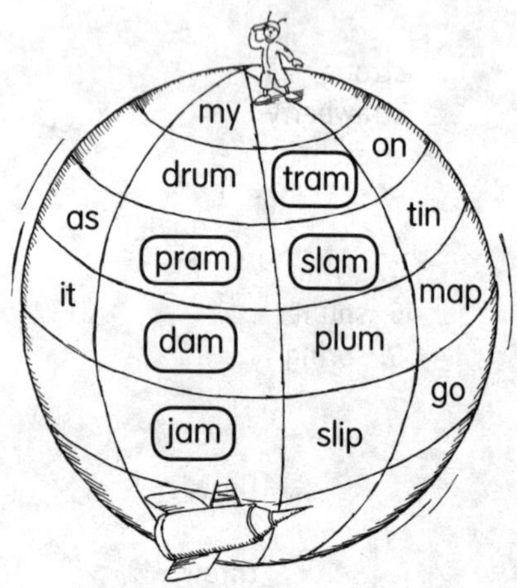

■ PAGE 32

can	clap	hat
plan	cap	cat
fan	trap	bat

■ PAGE 33

red	ten	shed	fed
hen	bed	men	peg
leg	beg	keg	pen

■ PAGE 34

ip	**in**	**it**
pip	pin	pit
sip	bin	sit
nip	sin	bit
hip		hit
		nit

■ PAGE 35

dog	**dot**
log	cot
jog	pot
fog	hot

■ PAGE 36

shop	**plug**
top	bug
mop	jug
chop	mug

■ PAGE 37

drum	**sun**
plum	gun
gum	bun
mum	run
sum	fun

■ PAGE 38

1. bald
2. hand
3. card
4. gold
5. sand
6. bird

■ PAGE 39

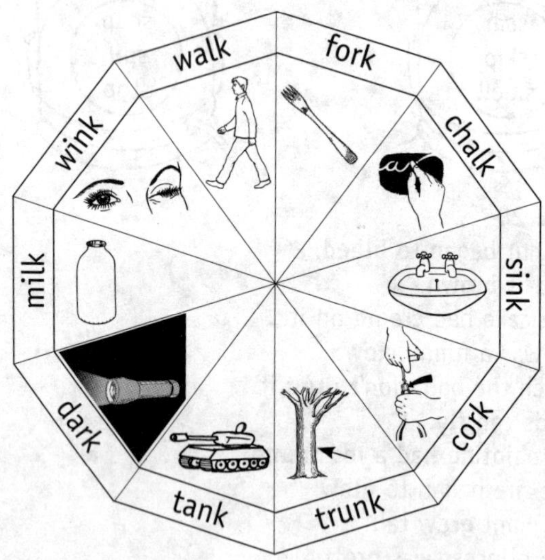

■ PAGE 40

1. There was no wind and the sea was **calm**.
2. On the island there were lots of **palm** trees.
3. Cows and sheep are **farm** animals.
4. There was a fire **alarm** at the hospital last week.
5. The boat sank in the **storm**.
6. A movie is the same as a **film**.

■ PAGE 41

elp	**ump**	**amp**	**isp**	**arp**
help	stump	camp	wisp	sharp
yelp	thump	lamp	crisp	harp

■ PAGE 42

insect – act
left – raft
smart – cart
belt – melt
tent – ant
fist – last

■ PAGE 43

church 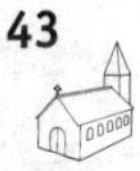
match 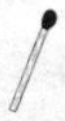
witch 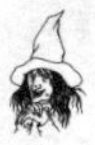
torch 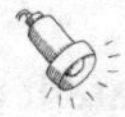
bench 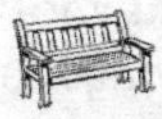
lunch 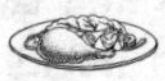

■ PAGE 44

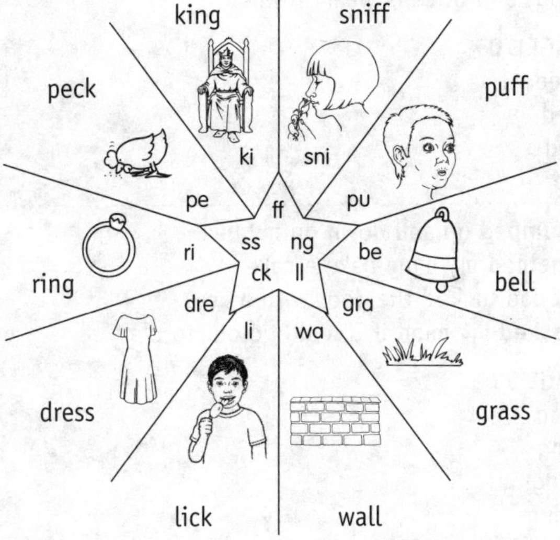

■ PAGE 45

sack	**truck**	**wreck**	**sock**	**brick**
black	suck	neck	rock	lick
pack	duck	check	block	pick
snack	luck	deck	shock	quick

■ PAGE 46

king – ring
fang – hang
wing – spring
rung – lung
ping pong – ding dong
swing – sling

■ PAGE 47

Hard g phoneme
go
girl
dog
garage
bag

Soft g phoneme
page
gara**g**e
cage
germ

■ PAGE 48

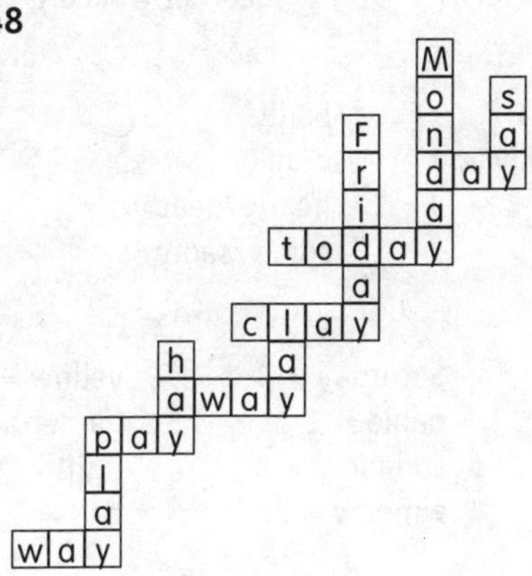

■ PAGE 49

safe
rain
pray
sail
tray
spade

■ PAGE 50

snail – tail
chain – lane
shake – make
tray – day

■ PAGE 51

green she me sea week eat bee

■ PAGE 52

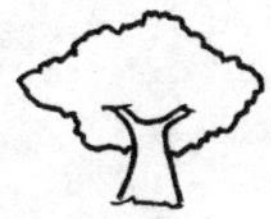
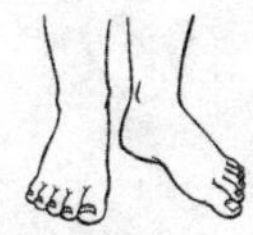

bee
sea
me
pea
tea
see
three

meat
seat
sweet
treat
heat

■ PAGE 53

fry 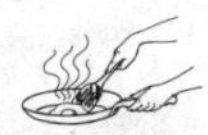
tie 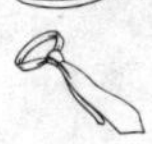
night 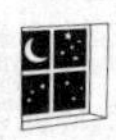
smile 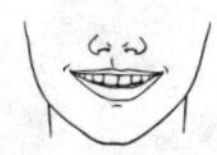
dive 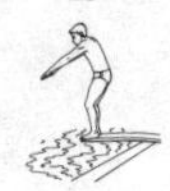

■ PAGE 54

high 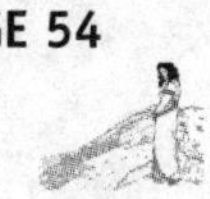
night 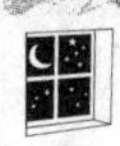
light 
knight 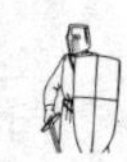
right 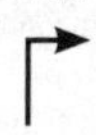
fight 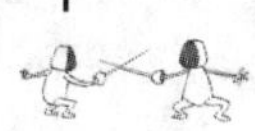

■ PAGE 55

dry – pie | cry | tie | high
kite – night | bite | white | fight
ride – wide | side | tide | hide
mine – line | fine | nine | shine

■ PAGE 56

boat 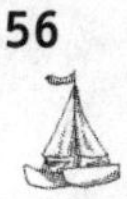
rope 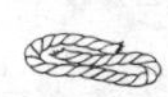
mow 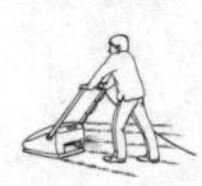
toast 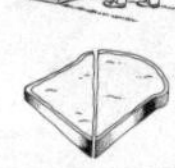
tow 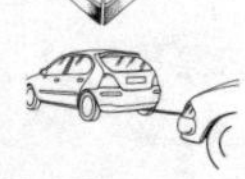
bone 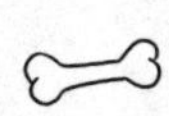
go 

soap 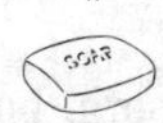
nose 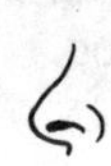

■ PAGE 57

boat	**bone**	**blow**	**oak**
goat	cone	bow	smoke
note	throne	toe	cloak

PAGE 58

screw 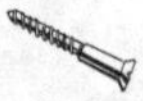
moon 
glue 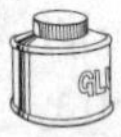
shampoo 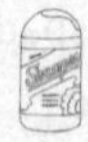

PAGE 59

blue – too
pool – rule
broom – room
spoon – moon
rude – food
boot – flute

PAGE 60

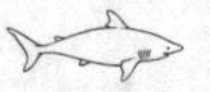 shark
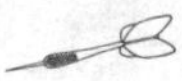 dart
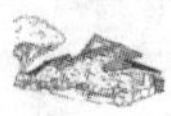 farm
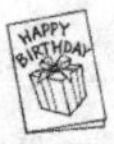

card
 warn

PAGE 61

claw 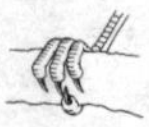
jaw 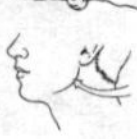
paw 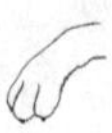
see-saw 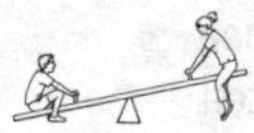
straw 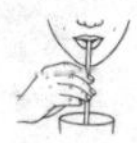
draw 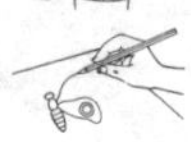

PAGE 62

bird
turn
fern
burn
skirt

PAGE 63

beads
meat
ice cream
leaf
beak
beach

PAGE 64

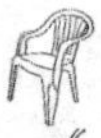 chair
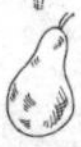 pear
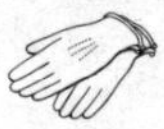 pair
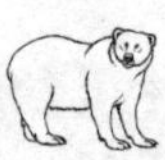 bear
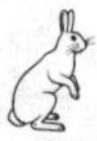 hare
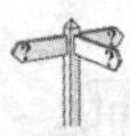 where
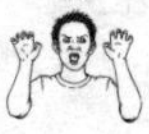 scare
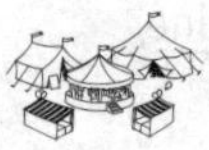 fair

PAGE 65

town: frown, crown, bow.
slow: row, elbow, snow.

PAGE 66

pool: moon, tooth, boot, broom.
book: wood, hood.

PAGE 67

oy: toy, boy.
oi: coin, point, toilet, soil.

PAGE 68

door
sore
fork
short
horse
horn
storm
fort
before

PAGE 69

1. In my class there are lots of **desks**.
2. We need ten **sacks** for the sack race.
3. A bird flaps its **wings** to fly.
4. I have two **hands** and two feet.
5. Giraffes have long **necks.**
6. I like to throw and catch **balls.**
7. Our **tents** got wet in the rain.
8. Kings and **queens** wear crowns.

PAGE 70

jumped
helped
locked
asked

---

1. I **jumped** up and down on my bed.
2. I **helped** my mum bake a cake.
3. My dad **locked** the door with a key.
4. I **asked** my mum if I could go out to play.

PAGE 71

sinking
kicking
walking
jumping

PAGE 72

fairy 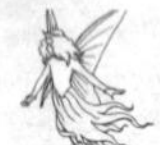
baby 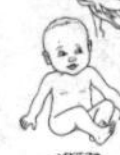
dirty 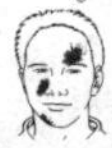
cherry 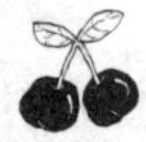
puppy 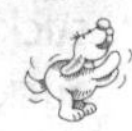
teddy 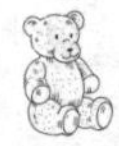

PAGE 73

1. hopping
2. button
3. toffee
4. kennel
5. robber
6. summer

PAGE 74

jumper = jump + er
duster = dust + er
quicker = quick + er
cracker = crack + er
older = old + er
taller = tall + er
walker = walk + er
recorder = record + er

PAGE 75

nicely
sadly/softly/sickly
quickly
neatly/nearly
badly
glumly
nearly/neatly
softly/sadly

PAGE 76

this = 1	Saturday = 3	yellow = 2
mother = 2	name = 1	garden = 2
door = 1	suddenly = 3	light = 1
morning = 2	window = 2	ball = 1

PAGE 77

butterfly 

jellyfish 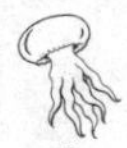

earring 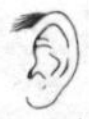

scarecrow 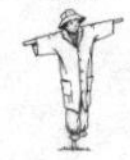

toenail 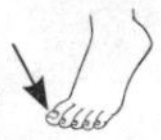

PAGE 78

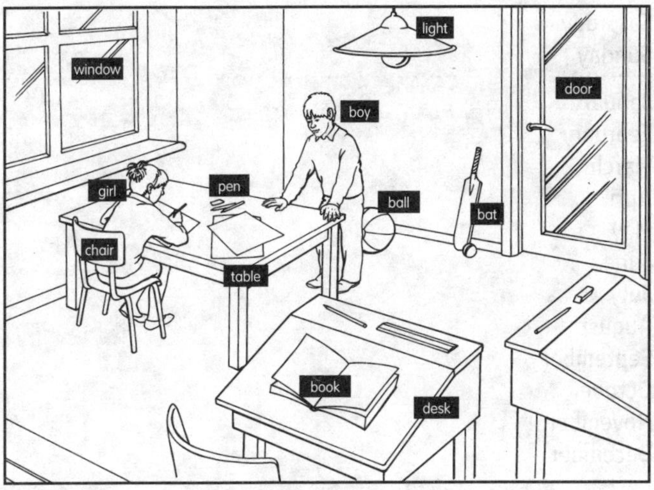

PAGE 79

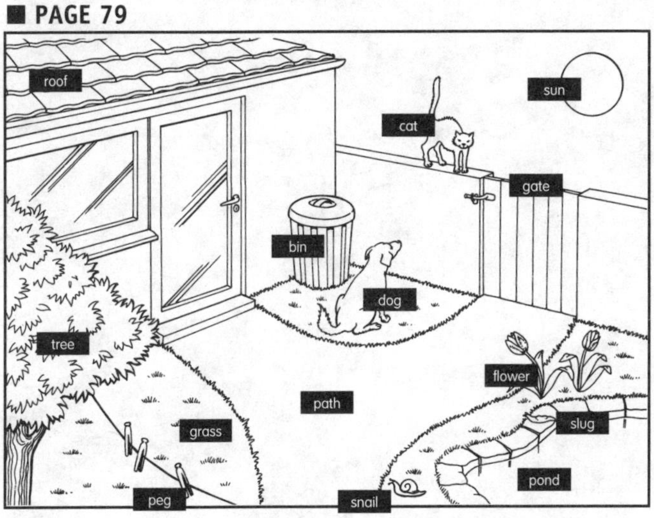

PAGE 80

short – tall
fast – slow
fat – thin
old – new
dry – wet

sad – happy
him – her
hard – soft
first – last
small – big

PAGE 81

undress
untie
unlock
unkind

discover
disagree
disappear

1. I **undress** when I have a bath.
2. To take off my shoes I **untie** the laces.
3. We **unlock** the door to get in.
4. The ugly sisters were **unkind** to Cinderella.
5. The aliens wanted to **discover** new planets.
6. My sister and I always **disagree.**

PAGE 82

a	l	l	■
■	■	o	n
■	y	o	u
l	i	k	e

p	l	a	y	■
■	■	w	a	s
■	■	a	n	d
■	■	y	e	s

■	■	t	h	e
■	s	h	e	■
g	o	i	n	g
■	■	s	e	e

PAGE 83

1. My mum **and** I are **going** to the shops.
2. I **like** to go fishing with **my** dad.
3. You must **look** left and right when **you** cross the road.
4. My dad **said**, 'Go and **play** in the park.'
5. We **went** to the beach **for** a holiday.
6. I **can** see the **big** dog.
7. Can you **see** the cat **up** the tree?
8. We **are** going to **get** wet in the rain.
9. She **was** sad and so were **they.**
10. My dad said, '**Come** and look at **this.**'

PAGE 84

f	l	i	k	e	p	h
o	n	h	q	r	i	t
t	o	f	l	i	s	v
b	g	e	t	a	n	d
k	c	o	m	e	r	g
l	o	o	k	j	u	p
f	f	o	r	y	o	u

2 letters	3 letters	4 letters
on	for	look
is	get	like
up	you	come
of	and	
it		

PAGE 85

s	g	x	w	w	i	t	h
i	l	q	e	k	h	t	t
s	a	f	t	e	r	o	r
t	h	w	e	n	t	t	e
e	t	h	e	r	e	h	e
r	t	i	m	e	a	i	s
d	s	a	w	h	m	s	e
t	h	e	n	a	l	l	e

a	s	t	th	w
am	see	to	this	went
all	saw	tree	then	we
after	sister	time	there	with

■ PAGE 86

hop – 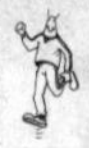

dig – 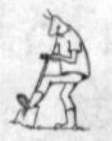

jog – 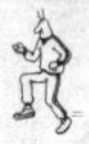

jump – 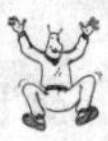

tug – 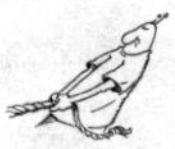

cut – 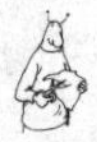

run – 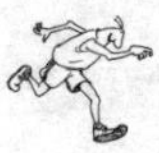

mop – 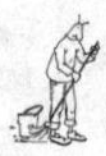

■ PAGE 87

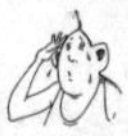 – hot

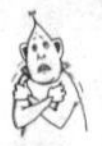 – cold

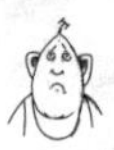 – sad

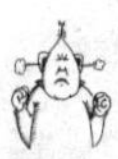 – mad

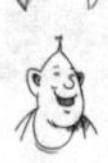 – happy

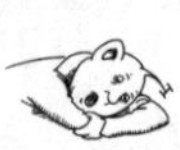 – sleepy

■ PAGE 88

Aa
Bb
Cc
Dd
Ee
Ff
Gg
Hh
Ii
Jj
Kk
Ll
Mm
Nn
Oo
Pp
Qq
Rr
Ss
Tt
Uu
Vv
Ww
Xx
Yy
Zz

■ PAGE 89

Monday
Tuesday
Wednesday
Thursday
Friday
Saturday
Sunday

January
February
March
April
May
June
July
August
September
October
November
December

Notes

Notes

Bridge Chapter

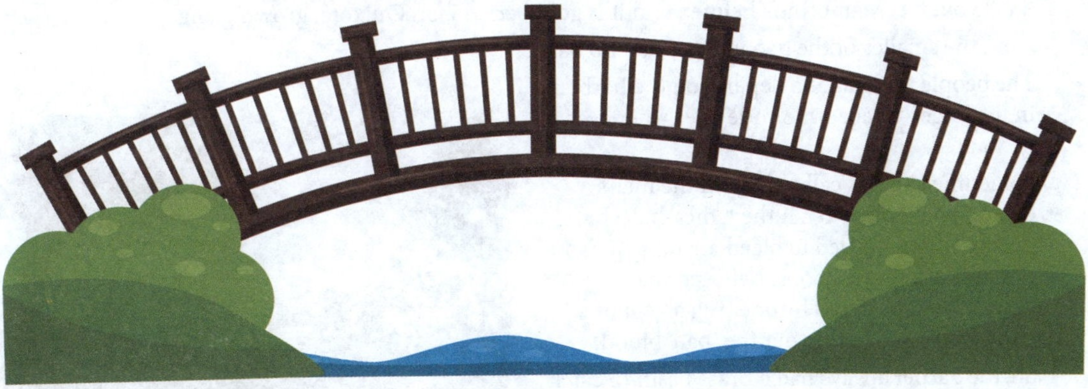

for Coursebook 6

A. Read the passage and answer the questions that follow.

Days passed and still Don Quixote rode bare headed, for as yet he had found no way to win a new helmet.

One morning, as the knight and his squire were riding along a highway from a small village to a larger one, they saw a horseman coming slowly towards them.

'See there!' cried Don Quixote. 'Now I shall have an adventure that will bring me glory.'

'I pray to God, master, that it isn't like our last adventure, when you chased windmills, thinking them to be giants!' exclaimed Sancho.

'Silence! Or I shall have you thrashed soundly. Don't you see that horseman?' said Don Quixote. 'He is wearing something on his head that glitters like gold. If I am not wrong, he is a knight, and it is Mambrino's helmet that he is wearing.'

Don Quixote had read in his books of chivalry about the Moorish king Mambrino, who owned an enchanted golden helmet. Anyone who wore it could never be attacked.

'Are you sure you are not mistaken, master?' Sancho asked nervously.

'Not a chance, Sancho,' Don Quixote said. 'For that knight who is riding towards us on his horse has a helmet of gold on his head.'

'I don't see any knight,' said Sancho. 'I see only a common man riding a grey donkey, much like mine. There is something bright on the top of his head; but all that glitters is not gold.'

'I tell you; it is Mambrino's helmet, and it is gold!' cried Don Quixote, growing angry.

Now, the smaller of the two villages had no barber.

The people there had to depend on the barber in the larger village, who rode over whenever he wanted.

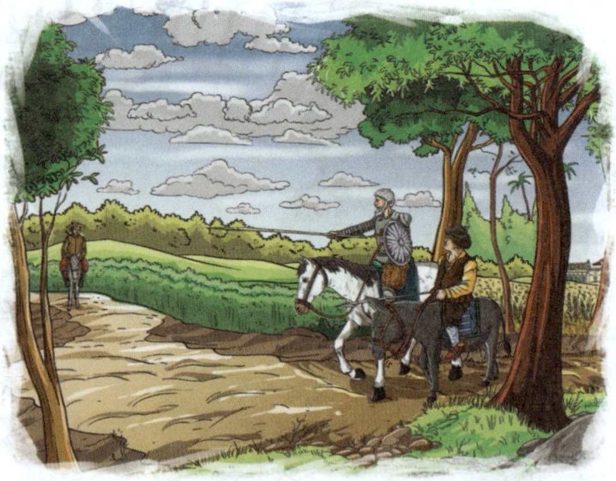

Sometimes he was called to trim the men's beards, sometimes to cut the ladies' hair; but he most often needed to bleed an ailing person. For in those times, people believed that any illness could be cured by opening a vein of a sick person and letting out the 'bad' blood.

So, the barber always had a brass basin to catch the blood as it flowed from the patient's arm. This basin was always kept very clean. The knight on the galloping horse was none other than the barber riding his grey donkey to visit his patients in the smaller village.

The morning was cloudy, and it was about to rain at any minute. The barber had a new hat which he did not want to spoil in the rain. So, he had worn the brass basin upside down upon his head. It covered his hat, and being clean, glittered at more than a mile's distance.

But Don Quixote had read so much about Mambrino's helmet that he could think of nothing else. If he wanted to find a golden helmet, his mind could turn anything he wished into one.

1. Why was Don Quixote riding bare headed?
2. What did Don Quixote see when he was passing through the forest with Sancho?

3. Why was Sancho nervous about Don Quixote's new adventure?
4. According to Don Quixote, who was riding on horseback and what was he wearing?
5. What had Don Quixote read about Mambrino?
6. What did Sancho see in place of a knight on horseback?
7. Why was the barber carrying a brass vessel with him?
8. Why did the barber have the brass basin on his head?

word meanings, making sentences

B. Write the meanings of the following words and make sentences with them.

1. **helmet:** ______________________________
   ____
2. **enchanted:** ______________________________
   ____
3. **mistaken:** ______________________________
   ____
4. **flowed:** ______________________________
   ____
5. **galloping:** ______________________________
   ____

contextual usage: crossword

C. Solve the crossword with the help of the given clues.

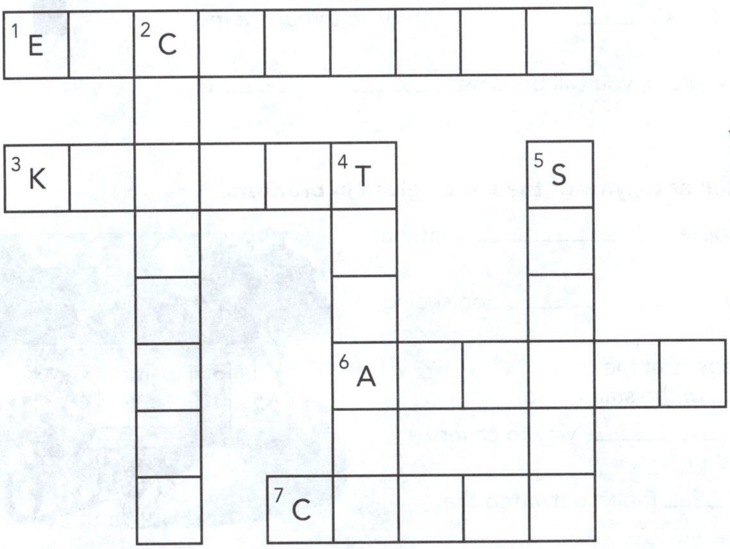

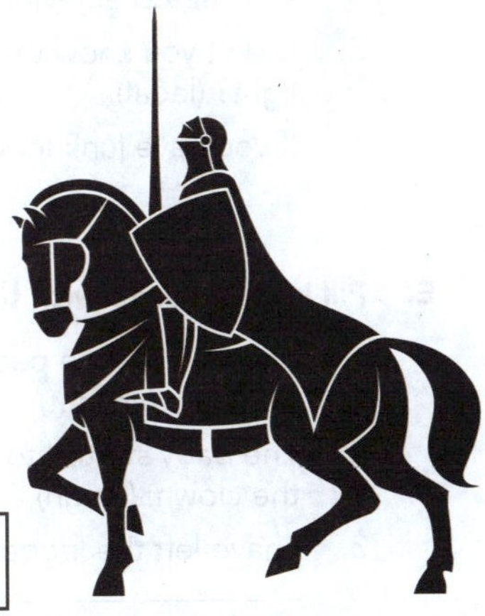

ACROSS

1. under a magical spell
3. a soldier in armour
6. in poor health
7. run after someone to catch them

DOWN

2. very polite and kind behaviour of men towards women
4. beat violently with a stick
5. (in olden times) a young man who was an assistant to a knight

prefixes

D. Fill in the blanks by adding a suitable prefix to the words given in brackets. Choose the prefixes from the box.

il-	mis-	un-	im-	dis-	in-

1. Sethu ________________ wasting time on the Internet. (like)
2. It will be ________________ to reach the museum on time because of the heavy traffic. (possible)
3. Safiya was upset because she felt that Sheila had ________________ her. (understood)
4. Samantha used to be ________________ during maths classes until she started enjoying algebra. (attentive)
5. Didn't you know that it is ________________ to drive through a red light? (legal)
6. If you have junk food often, you will become ________________. (fit)

antonyms

E. Fill in the blanks with the antonyms of the words given in brackets.

1. There were nine people ________________ at the meeting. (absent)
2. The baby started to ________________ on seeing the clown. (laugh)
3. I have left the luggage is at the ________________ of the stairs. (top)
4. Cycling is a ________________ way to cover short distances. (costly)
5. The ________________ rabbit outwitted the lion easily.
6. Can I ________________ your pencil for the exam? (lend)

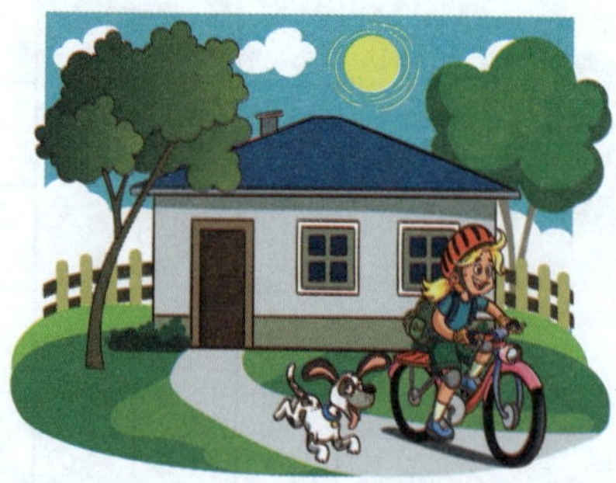

spelling

F. Underline the incorrectly spelt words in these sentences. Write the correct spellings in the blanks.

1. I completly forgot that it is Raghu's birthday tomorrow. ____________
2. Simmy is working very hard to acheive her goals. ____________
3. Despite their diffrences, Rishi and Rajat are great friends. ____________
4. I missed the begining of the movie. ____________
5. Alice followed the White Rabbit out of curiousity. ____________
6. The shopkeeper gifted us a new calender. ____________
7. The hotel can take in fourty guests. ____________

analyzing a dictionary entry

G. Look at the entry for the word *knight* in the Collins online dictionary at https://www.collinsdictionary.com/dictionary/english/ and answer the following questions.

1. Is the word *knight* an adjective?
2. What is the meaning of the word *knight*?
3. Write another meaning of the word *knight*.
4. Can the word 'knight' be used as a verb?
5. Complete the idiom: knight in ____________ armour

conjunctions

H. Fill in the blanks with the correct conjunctions.

1. Please hurry ____________ (and/or/but) you will miss the flight.
2. Harish is hardworking ____________ (and/or/but) he is also dishonest.
3. I went out for a walk ____________ (so/because/or) the sun was shining brightly.
4. She is naughty, ____________ (if/yet/and) she always does well in school.
5. The little girl came ____________ (and/or/but) sat beside her parents.
6. I ran to the door ____________ (still/but/and) the postman had left.
7. The tiger ____________ (if/yet/and) the lion are both wild animals.

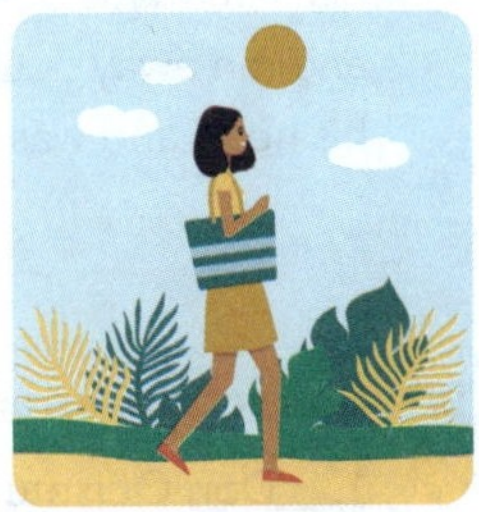

punctuation

I. Rewrite the paragraph using correct punctuation marks.

when don quixote saw the poor 'knight' come nearer he raised his lance which was only the branch of a tree without any warning whatsoever he charged on his mare towards the startled man as he galloped close he pointed the lance at him determined to run him through

____

____

____

____

____

____

tenses

J. Fill in the blanks with the forms of verbs given in brackets.

1. Meetu and I ________________ in a baking competition next week. (*participate*, simple future tense)
2. Sebastian ________________ a hot chocolate and a cupcake for his sister. (*buy*, simple past tense)
3. My sister ________________ me to clean my room, but I forgot. (*ask*, past perfect)
4. Farzana ________________ her grandmother in Mumbai. (*visit*, past continuous tense)
5. Rumi ________________ Japanese. (*learn*, present continuous tense)
6. Our teacher ________________ a play for us to perform on Independence Day. (*write*, present perfect tense)

prepositions

K. Fill in the blanks with the given prepositions.

across over at off on of in

The barber, seeing a wild-eyed old man charging __________ him __________ a horse, threw himself on his donkey. He leapt __________ the thorny hedge on the side __________ the road and ran away __________ the fields as swiftly as a deer. But the brass basin slipped __________ his head and was left lying __________ the dust.

error correction

L. Correct the error in each of the following sentences and rewrite them.

1. Don Quixote couldn't find a way to winning a new helmet.

   Don Quixote couldn't find a way to win a new helmet.
2. They noticed horseman approaching them.
3. The head for which it was made must have being big.
4. Half of the helmet were missing.
5. I'm going to have a adventure.
6. 'What are you laughing with now?' cried his master.
7. There were no barber in one of the villages.
8. It was about to start rain.

M. Look at the picture and write a story based on the picture in about 80–100 words using the given clues. Also, give a suitable title to the story.

Sancho pointed out his mistake – Don Quixote would not listen – angry with Sancho, called him a coward – believed that a magic spell had changed the giants to windmills

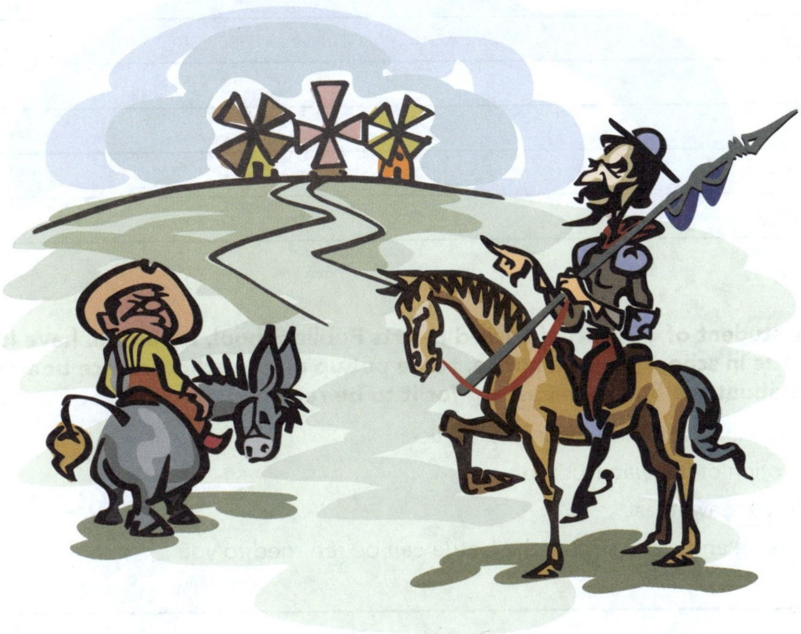

Don Quixote pointed towards the windmills. He was sure that they were giants standing over the fields.

informal letter

N. Write a letter to a friend describing a funny experience you recently had. It can be related to a person or an object.

notice

O. You are a student of class 6B of Sacred Hearts Public School, Delhi. You have lost your water bottle in school. Write a notice, to be put up on the school notice board, informing everyone about the bottle and asking for it to be returned, if found.

You should include the following in your notice:

- description of the water bottle
- where you saw it last
- your name and class, so that the bottle can be returned to you

NOTICE

Lost Water Bottle